THE
ORIGINS
OF HISTORY

THE
ORIGINS
OF HISTORY

Herbert Butterfield

Edited with an Introduction
by Adam Watson

EYRE METHUEN · LONDON

First published 1981
© 1981 Pamela Butterfield
Introduction © 1981 J. H. Adam Watson
Printed in Great Britain for
Eyre Methuen Ltd
11 New Fetter Lane, London EC4P 4EE
by Willmer Brothers Limited, Rock Ferry, Merseyside

British Library Cataloguing in Publication Data
Butterfield, *Sir*, Herbert
The origins of history
1. Historiography
I. Title
907'.2   D13

ISBN 0-413-48370-3

Contents

Introduction

by Adam Watson

This book contains Sir Herbert Butterfield's distilled conclusions about how history came to be written, which he reached after research and meditation on this subject during the last quarter-century of his life.

Butterfield approached this vast and largely uncharted subject in a characteristic way, with no preconceptions, not knowing in what direction his researches would lead him. He was always particularly interested in the general conclusions that could be drawn from a detailed historical narrative, what he called the story itself. The Whig interpretation of history bothered him, as he explained in his book under that title, as well as the popular Marxist interpretation, and such personal simplifications and diagrams of the historical process as Spengler's and Toynbee's. The trouble was that in all of them the theory or interpretation or diagram came first. They were *a priori* intuitions. Sometimes, as he once said to me, it was a grandiose and imaginative one, but derived only very partially from the facts and owing more to other beliefs and other purposes in this world. Once you had such a theory, the selection of facts to fit it and demonstrate it became all too easy; the more so as selectivity is usually unconscious, and the aspects of the story that you underline and emphasise are the ones that seem to you genuinely important because they bear out your view of the world. Butterfield was concerned to start with the facts, the representative facts seen in their context; and where the facts were inadequate or seemed unrepresentative the answer was more detailed research. Then you needed to brood over the facts, and see what generalisations distilled themselves from them. He developed an extraordinary flair for this kind of open-minded deduction.

This approach to the understanding of history Butterfield liked to compare to the methods of Sherlock Holmes. After Lestrade had fitted many but not all of the facts into a plausible reconstruction of the events, Holmes would engage in minuter, more detailed microscopic research, and would then meditate over all the facts for long hours until a solution emerged from them which he recognised as right. This refusal to force the facts, to suspend judgement until they offered you their own answer, the ability not to pre-judge anything, Butterfield called elasticity of mind.

This openness of mind about historical evidence was made possible for him by his belief in a Christ whose Kingdom is not of this world. In this way could be avoided the seductive 'worship of abstract nouns' which he considered much more dangerous than any worship of graven images. Christianity as he saw it did not merely permit you to be absolutely neutral about mundane events, so that you were no more committed about current affairs than (as he liked to say) about 'the blues and greens in the hippo-drome in Constantinople': it positively required this detachment. To render unto Caesar the things that are Caesar's was an explicit command. The concluding sentences of Butterfield's *Christianity and History* express this concept with great feeling:

> We can never meet the future with sufficient elasticity of mind, especially if we are locked in the contemporary systems of thought. We can do worse than remember a principle which both gives us a firm Rock and leaves us the maximum elasticity for our minds; the principle Hold to Christ, and for the rest be totally uncommitted.

In a note to me he once said, in his oblique and undogmatic way, that he was sometimes inclined to wonder whether any lesser degree of detachment from mundane causes (in the formative centuries of European civilisation) would have left the way clear for the development of the scientific and historical thinking that was a unique characteristic of the West. The same thought appears in several contexts in the present book.

If the history that really mattered to Butterfield was the generalisations that emerged from the facts, the most interesting questions of all concerned history itself. What was the relationship of men, at different times and in different civilisations, to their history, to their own past, to the past in general? Much of his earlier work points in this direction. *The Whig Interpretation* deals with the Whig and liberal Lestrades. *The Englishman and his History* traces what has changed and what is constant in our national attitudes to our past – for the Irish, the Scots and the Welsh have very different relationships with their very different histories. *Man on his Past* deals with Western historiography from the eighteenth century to the present. But that was only the end of the story. The great question of how it all began remained unanswered, and by most people almost unasked.

The fundamental questions of the origins of historiography came to occupy a central place in Butterfield's thinking. How did men first begin to be aware of the past beyond living human memory, as something to take account of in their lives? By what stages, in which civilisations, did men's ideas about their past move towards history as a fully self-explanatory system of cause and effect? Why was this concept of the past, which excluded chance and divine intervention, something that has been finally achieved only in the West? And why, since it is so analagous to the western concept of 'science', did it not develop until some hundreds of years after the objective study of the natural sciences? The first questions were the hardest. The evidence available for the later stages of a panoramic view of historiography is abundant, and in places almost overwhelming; but in earlier periods, and especially the beginning, the clues have largely been lost, and it is difficult to detect what happened, difficult to recapture the spirit of such high and far off times.

What emerged in Butterfield's mind as the key question of all, the one which would do most to help our understanding of history if only we could answer it correctly, was the part attributed to God in the narration of human events. God in his many forms, including the local gods of each city, the rival gods of the pagan pantheons, Fate and Chance, El and Jahweh, the Holy Trinity, Allah and Providence, Progress and the Dialectic, and all the other supernatural forces whose hands men have seen in history. He puts the problem musingly towards the beginning of the last chapter of this book: 'After all,' (my dear Watson, he might have added) 'the thing that the outward eyes of men actually see is the succession of mundane events. Sometimes one might feel that the introduction of God, or the hand of God, or Providence, is the thing which is really the afterthought, the result of an attempt to find an explanation of what happened. The introduction of God into the story is then the thing that needs to be explained.' How did God get into history? And how, once in, was he finally got out again? This is what Butterfield felt it necessary to discover.

Butterfield spoke to me several times during the early 'sixties about his growing interest in man's earliest perceptions of his past. When I was about to return to England in 1966 from the comparative isolation of being ambassador to Cuba, I wrote to ask him how this interest was shaping in his mind. He answered me on 25 May 1966 from the Villa Serbelloni on Lake Como (which is maintained by the Rockefeller Foundation for the benefit of scholars who need to write free from distractions, and of which he was a member of the advisory council) as follows:

After feverish attempts to do some writing amid the turmoils and dis-tractions of a Master's Lodge in Cambridge, I have secured a three months' leave of absence (dating from the middle of March) and have thoroughly buried myself in the writing of what I hope will be fit to be a considerable book. . . .

I am engaged in what I regard as something very interesting in any case, though I am not sure that it is not the most impracticable adventure of my life. About ten or a dozen years ago an incidental assignment compelled me to turn my attention to the question why in one region after another men originally became interested in history, and how (with practically no ground to stand on at first) they came to have any concept of the past and came to give this past a certain amount of shape. It seemed to me that the people who had the material for answering these questions had failed to put the questions and didn't know what the 'history of historiography' requires. Also I found that the character of the historical writing that was produced here and there bore a peculiar relationship to the way in which the thing had been initiated in one region and another – a traceable relationship with large-scale historical experiences. When asked to give the Gifford Lectures recently I found this to be the only thing left in the bag that could be adapted to such a purpose and, taking a terrible gamble, I said I would try to work the thing up. Now I am busy working up one set of the lectures for publication and preparing another set for delivery. I wish I could be sure that the excitement they give me had any relationship with the interest that they might arouse in other people.

Butterfield only explored the theme of the origins of history in his celebrated Gifford Lectures at the University of Glasgow. But he decided against publication at that stage, because it became clear to him that this vast and largely uncharted subject required a much fuller and more rounded treatment, based on further research and reflection. He continued to work on it for the next twelve years.

More than once during the 'seventies he said that the book which he was developing on this theme was the most important task remaining to him. On one occasion, on the banks of Lake Maggiore, he described to me the plan of the work, explaining that it was necessary to deal with the different cultures separately – there was no straight line. But he became increasingly concerned that he did not concentrate systematically enough on this book, but let himself be distracted by other writing. Towards the end, his health also made long periods of concentrated work almost impossible. In January 1979 he told me in Cambridge that the first half of the book was substantially written, but there was still a good deal to do on the last chapters. I had arranged with the Rockefeller Foundation to provide a dictaphone or a shorthand typist to transcribe what he still wanted to record; but he assented dubiously, and said that 'someone like you would probably have to take a look at it'. He also mentioned his unfinished work on Charles James Fox and on the history of diplomacy. In the event I left for Virginia a few days later, and when I returned to Europe he was too ill for serious discussion.

After his death, Pamela, his widow and literary executrix, turned over to me his manuscripts and notes on the history of historiography and the history of diplomacy, to edit and publish as best I could, since on these two subjects I had probably had more contact and discussion with him than others had done. I found indeed that the first five chapters or sections of the book on historiography, which dealt with the origins of historical consciousness, the pre-classical Middle East, the Old Testament, the Greeks and the Chinese, were substantially rewritten and required only minor editing. The last three chapters, following the plan he outlined to me in Italy, deal first with the emergence of a Christian attitude to history, which, as I have indicated, Butterfield considered the climax of the matter; secondly with historical criticism – a subject so broad that he thought of dealing with it in a separate book; and finally with the great secularisation of modern times. These sections consisted largely of heavily hand-corrected typescript, extensive manuscript amplification, and notes, sometimes in French, German or Italian. These I have pieced together to form what I hope is a coherent statement. The writing is all his. The bibliography is compiled from his card indexes. The original papers have been deposited with his other documents in the Cambridge University Library, where the Librarian has kindly agreed to make them available for consultation.

There are some deficiencies. Had Butterfield had more time, he would certainly have written more fully about the sense of history under Islam. There were many books on this subject in his library. He discussed it with several Islamic scholars at various times. He seized on what I said in my book, *The War of the Goldsmith's Daughter*, about the nature of the Islamic written records of the conquest of southern India and the lack of a corresponding historiography on the Hindu side. He had the idea of a separate chapter, like that on Chinese history. But what little I found in his manuscripts was intended, according to his indication, to be included in the account of the secularisation process, where it now stands.

Butterfield did not carry the rewriting of the subject matter of his Gifford Lectures beyond his account of the great secularisation, which therefore forms the last chapter of this book. More recent developments were already covered in *Man on his Past*, published in 1955, and he only touches on them in order to complete the earlier story.

I should like to thank some of those who have helped me with the preparation of this manuscript, by advice, financial assistance, and work on the papers. In the first instance Pamela Butterfield, who was familiar with the manuscript and who has made herself available for consultation throughout. Hedley Bull set me an example by his own work on the unpublished papers of our mutual friend Martin Wight, and encouraged me to do the same for

Herbert Butterfield. Desmond Williams, who has known Butterfield and me for a long time, has been particularly insistent about my making this book available to the public. Michael Carroll, a teaching assistant at the University of Virginia, did much preliminary work on the manuscript and compiled the bibliography. My daughter Polly typed out the most illegible passages and made many helpful suggestions about ordering them. The British Academy made an exceptional grant towards the costs of preparing the manuscript for publication. I am also very grateful to the Center for Advanced Studies of the University of Virginia, who readily agreed to my working on the Butterfield manuscripts and provided secretarial assistance for doing so.

Center for Advanced Studies   Adam Watson
Charlottesville, Virginia
1981

Preface

We are often reminded that the civilisation of the West is scientific in character; and we do not always remember that it is equally remarkable for being so historically-minded. In both respects the only known parallel to it is to be found in the China of comparatively early days, which, besides its amazing feats of science and technology, produced an historical literature of almost incredible vastness. Even in China, however, there did not develop those modern techniques which, in our section of the globe, led to the scientific revolution of the seventeenth century and the somewhat parallel historiographical revolution in the nineteenth. In both fields the development that took place in Europe was unique; and in both fields the Chinese themselves have had to become the pupils of the West.

Some civilisations, like that of ancient India, remained curiously un-historical – failing to develop their writing or their scholarship in this field in the way that China and the West developed theirs. In fact, it seems that men can have basic views of life which deny the significance of history – their outlook formed by religions and philosophies which operate to dis-courage any great interest in the facts of history as such, or the sequence of events in time. Hinduism, Buddhism and Neoplatonism have tended to induce men to deny the significance of that network of chance and change in which human souls seem to be caught for an earthly lifetime. Yet between a culture that is soaked in historical memories and one for which the events of the past are no more than the froth and foam of last winter's ocean there must develop great differences in general mentality and in intellectual habits – differences calculated to affect very radically, for example, the degree of control that can be acquired over the course of events. And the differences must extend to deeper things that must alter in still more subtle ways the very nature of the human consciousness. In any case, the interest that we Westerners take in the past – our very sense for the past – (like our prowess in the natural sciences) is a thing which requires to be explained.

The case that we today might make for the study of history would have no meaning for those earlier generations of mankind that gave the start to the whole endeavour. We of the twentieth century might say that a society is going to be very constricted in its development unless it looks behind itself, organises its memory, reflects on its larger and longer experiences, learns to measure the direction in which it is moving, and gets some notion of long-term tendencies that have been observed. But this kind of diagnosis – this way of seeing where we stand in the processes of time – is a thing that comes only late in the day, when civilisation and scholarship itself have progressed very far. Nobody could have known in advance that by the study of the past we should be able to examine the processes of things in time. Indeed, until the world was fairly mature, nobody could have guessed that there existed such things as historical processes which might call for analysis. In general we have perhaps too little idea of the hurdles which the human mind had to surmount before it could arrive at any conception of the possibility of history or secure any serious notion of the past, any effective grip on bygone things.

What concerns us, therefore, is not just 'the History of Historiography', the mere story of the development of a branch of literature, but the un-folding of a whole great aspect of human experience. We need to know how man came to acquire a concept of 'the past', and gradually to clarify that concept and endow it with a structure. We have to ask ourselves how it occurred to some men – but apparently not to others – to keep records of the things that happened in the world, and to meditate upon the possible connections between events. How was it that the knowledge of what had happened in the limbo of former times ever became a matter of concern to a later generation? What factors induced human beings to feel that, apart from any mere desire to learn what had happened, they were in any sense committed to a past which somehow or other had a sort of claim upon them? It might be true to say that, for the carrying on of life itself, men had to make terms with history as they understood it. They had to have views about the way in which things happen, notions about the causes of disasters, ideas about the character of human destiny, theories about the ups-and-downs of states. The story of the development of man's consciousness of history involves a large-scale aspect of the whole evolution of his experience. It is a major part of his attempt to adjust himself to the world in which his life is set.

In the early stages of this development, and indeed for thousands of years, thought on these matters had not become specialised. Concepts were dim; and great lengths of time would be needed to achieve any considerable degree of clarification. But nature seems to have been prodigal in faiths and superstitions, and the real progress would take place, not in the realm of historical ideas as such, but over the whole area of man's undifferentiated beliefs. Human beings would be aware of the cycle of the seasons, but also of the way in which the years accumulated, the way they themselves grew older and palaces or temples would fall into ruins. They would be sensible of time's terrible insecurities, of the cataclysm that so often lurked at every fresh turn of the road. They would know the inexorability of death. Their dim reflections on all these things would show themselves, not in specifically historical ideas at first – not in any realm of specialised or technical thought – but in the beliefs and practices of their religion. The emergence of a feeling for history and a sense of the past could come only as part of the development of the whole human outlook. We who today attempt to compare our civilisation with another and try in a sense to get behind the history of civilisations, are continually learning the degree to which it was religion that shaped the mentality of our distant ancestors, deciding the 'set' of their minds and governing the way in which they conceived the world of human happenings. Their way of formulating to themselves their whole notion of the human drama that takes place under their sun is the clue to their historical ideas, but it emerges as the product of their religious outlook as a whole. If we today trace early science back to an undifferentiated endeavour which included what we should describe as magic, we must trace early history – early notions of human vicissitude and of temporal succession, for example – to the religious outlook in its entirety. For thousands of years, indeed until a remarkably recent period, it remained true that the influence of religion on man's general outlook was supremely important in the formative stages of societies and cultures. It would be important to learn how far man's ideas of history and his picture of the course of ages has been now governed by established religious beliefs, now affected by the development of what might be called a healthy worldly-mindedness.

Both our science and our historiography are to be traced for the most part to the lands lying near and beyond the eastern coast of the Mediterranean Sea. It is perhaps Mesopotamia that we ought to regard as the cradle of our civilisation; and in a sense it is also the cradle of our religion, for it provided the essential context out of which the religion of Israel emerged. One of the remarkable features of this whole region throughout such antiquity as has left its memory amongst us was the peculiarly intimate character of the relationships that existed between history and religion. This also remained (at least until a very recent period) a remarkable feature of the culture of Europe. The concern with both the history and the religion was connected with the tremendous anxiety which our primitive forefathers appear to have had about the problem of their destiny. It is interesting to see that the rise of history as well as the development of religion reflects this concern of man.

CHAPTER ONE

The Origins of Historical Writing

1 STORY TELLING

It is comparatively easy for an individual to keep some remembrance of his own personal past; but the difficulties are great if the human race or the body politic wants to achieve and organise and refine its collective memory. So far as mankind in general is concerned, the difficulties are *real* if even for a moment there is question of recovering the memory of anything that has once been lost. Some hurdles in fact need to be surmounted before one can acquire the notion that the past is something to be recovered at all. In the civilisation of ancient Mesopotamia the arts had reached a remarkable level and technology had wonderful achievements to its credit before there existed any serious historical writing or anything more than the dimmest notion of the existence of past times. Until a very recent period the past was simply a world to which one could not return. Bygone events were like the pattern of last year's wind on the surface of a lake – not things which one could feel were really capable of recapture. Even in the modern centuries the development of historical scholarship has proceeded at a slower pace than that of the natural sciences. The intellectual revolution which established the modern fertile techniques of discovery occurred amongst the scientists in the seventeenth century, but amongst the historians only in the late eighteenth and nineteenth centuries. In the middle of the nineteenth century, when the archives of the European capitals were being opened, one saw a tremendous development in the technique of using them. As a result, great stimulus was then given to the whole subject. Men felt that now, at last, they could really get down to the study of history. Clearly there had existed for thousands of years serious hurdles obstructing not merely the recovery of the past but the very notion that the story was in any authentic sense recoverable. And the project of reconstructing the past for oneself – putting it together by means of detective work exercised on primary materials – is for the most part a much more recent undertaking than most students of the subject will have imagined. Those who set out to examine the physical universe were free of the most serious of the hurdles, free of the obstructions most calculated to kill hope at the very start. The hills, the ocean, the flowers, the plants, the sun and the stars were at any rate patently there before their eyes, inviting speculation and enquiry day after day, year after year, century after century. But where was the past before men had discovered it or had recaptured forgotten events – how could one even think of the questions that were to be asked about it? We must picture our predecessors at first in the position of not even knowing what there was to look for.

It is necessary, therefore, that at the first stages of the story we should use our imagination not for the purpose of diagnosing what existed but for the purpose of realising the tremendous difficulties under which men laboured when they lacked so many of the clues that we possess. Some things may safely be regarded as universal – we can be sure of their existence even in those areas of the globe which took no part in the development of an historical interest in the past. Men are always likely to remember something of their own former years, of friends of theirs who have died, and of events that have impinged on their own experience. Also the young would always have sat at the feet of their elders – until the twentieth century at any rate (and in the time of Thomas Hardy in particular) some of the most vivid of the things that they knew about the past would have come to them through the tales of a grandfather. There is ample reason for saying that some things would linger in the memory, at any rate for a time, for the simple reason that the world so loves a good story. Something of the recent past of at any rate one's own locality would pass at least from one generation to another in what one might describe as just broken glimpses of narrative. But though from a certain point of view this might be the source of every-thing else that was to come, it was never in itself a sufficient basis for the development of a more sophisticated interest in the past. It hardly provided the ground on which a course of serious enquiry could develop; for the mere love of telling tales is too much its own end, too much its own source of satisfaction. It never seems to have been sufficient in itself to drive the mind to serious research or scholarly endeavour or a passionate quest for truth. Legends are still born every day amongst us; doubtful scandal will be blithely repeated at Oxford high tables; even journalists today will transmit stories that they have taken no great trouble to check. The *raconteur* knows too well that, if he investigates the truth of the matter, he is only too likely to lose his good story. Even in the temper of the modern world one has to become quite sophisticated before it occurs to one to check the tales of a grandfather. We might wonder what would happen in the remoter child-hood of the world if a story were so remarkable that it endured beyond the times of the grandchildren and spread over a wider area than a merely local one. What happens when a story is handed down in an age of oral trans-mission, but under conditions that make it impossible to go back to the past to check its authenticity? In the case of a famous old king in Mesopotamia called Sargon, and in the case of Solon of Athens, scholars have expressed surprise at the speed with which the story of a hero would acquire legendary accretions.

It looks as though the first histories ever concocted may have been the stories about the gods, and these achieved literary elaboration earlier than anything else, acquiring considerable form and elaboration while still in the state of oral transmission. They seem to have built themselves up into a world of myth which provided an explanation of everything and accom-panied the ritual ceremonies of the people as a whole. Here was something which men recognised as the past – though perhaps not their own past – at any rate a past so dim that one wonders what they could have done about it except believe and carefully preserve the stories handed down to them. But there was something of a past also which came nearer home; for the arts had flourished greatly and magnificent buildings had been erected before anybody had learned to write. Some concrete evidence of more ancient times would lie around men in their cities; and, once writing had developed, there would be monuments that preserved the name of a monarch, dedicatory inscriptions referring to recent events. In the various cities of Mesopotamia lists of the local kings would gradually be accumulated, and would be avail-able to somebody. It has been noted that in the very earliest kinds of literary production there are liable to be just slight references to one and another of the famous dynasties of the past, showing that at least a vague memory of them had been handed down. Possibly the nearest thing to history would be the traditions handed down in courts and governing circles, at any rate in royal and noble families.

For any history that has connection and meaning, however, one has to turn to the epic which seems to make its appearance in the earliest literature of the region to which it belongs. It is itself the most elaborate of the results of the process of oral tradition, and can be used to mark the stage at which the oral tradition is transformed into a written one. It appears amongst many peoples in widely differing sections of the globe; and it appears at a fairly identifiable stage in the development of these peoples, though a stage which is reached by different nations at widely differing times. Sometimes it seems to contain a high proportion of what we should call mythological matter, but there are occasions when it comes much closer to a human narrative, the story being placed in something like the work-a-day world.

Whatever we may think about the producers of the epic there can be no doubt that those who heard it recited or read the text regarded it as an account of the history that lay behind them. One might almost say that for most of them, it would be the only history they knew.

We ought to be able to understand what happened, for our own generation has had its flying saucers and its Loch Ness monster; and possibly a saga of Winston Churchill has been developing before our eyes. The technique of oral transmission had clearly become a specialised affair, developed here for a count and there for a noble family – elsewhere perhaps for the community as a whole. The narrative came to be handed down through travelling minstrels and professional reciters; and there are certain regions, in the Balkans for example, where the tradition has continued as a living thing down to very recent times. And the study of what has been happening in these cases comparatively near at hand has helped to confirm one's impression of the kind of thing that tended to take place in more ancient days. In the case of the epics that come closest to being straight human stories, the heroes often turn out to have been authentic people – a point that can sometimes be confirmed by independent evidence. Some of the stories will also be the product of an authentic tradition; for, though the narrators would be capable of altering their narratives in one way and another, they would be limited by factors that tended to the preservation of the tradition. The audience would be the chief arbiter, the ultimate guardian of the tradition; and it would not easily tolerate the loss or the alteration of a story about one of its favourite heroes. The audience might be happy enough, however, if an extemporising minstrel transferred to a famous personage some deed or prowess originally associated with a minor character. If the slaying of Goliath was originally attributed to somebody who was otherwise unknown, and was then transferred to the young man David, everybody might well be happy – the story fitted beautifully into its new context. Many of the stories might well be true, therefore, but not necessarily true of the people to whose names they had become connected.

The separate stories, therefore, are to be regarded as the essential units of the tradition, and any single one of them would possibly possess some original core of historical truth. Whether we deal with the oldest narratives in the Old Testament or the epic of Homer or the sagas of Scandinavia, we resolve the written narrative into its tiny units – these are the things that are handed down from the past. Sometimes the separate units still remain almost unattached stories, and some of the oldest bits of history that have been handed down to us are simply thrilling battle-songs or anecdotes of individual prowess. But the minstrels and reciters would assemble such units into groups, producing for example a cycle of narratives clustered around the name of a single hero. Then the organisation would be carried still higher; the stories would be fused into a more or less continuous epic;

they would be brought within the framework of a comprehensive theme. But the very thing which gave the epic its continuity would be the matter that was added later; it would be the product of the author's artistry; the coherence would be just the thing that was the product of invention. The total result would be a mixture of history and fiction which even the modern scholar cannot disentangle except in a few cases where there happens to exist some independent evidence.

This, for the people or the nation concerned, would be its history: it would be history *par excellence*. It was the story that was handed down and there would be no means of checking it – there would be nothing to suggest that here were assertions which ought to be submitted to some sort of control. The general historical background of the whole poem might well have reference to something which had really existed, something that remained vivid in the folk-memory. There was a hero-king of Akkad called Sargon; very probably there was a siege of Troy; it is likely that there was something corresponding to an 'exodus' from Egypt; and certainly an expedition under Charlemagne lies behind the medieval *Chanson de Roland*. Yet the main narrative of the epic itself might have only a remote and tenuous connection with the larger background theme that gives it its historical identity. The main narrative of the actual epic might be just the thing that resulted from the inventiveness or the combinatory and constructive endeavours of the actual narrator. Alternatively, the poet might seize upon what was really a minor episode – a thing quite peripheral and even unconnected with the actual history – and might work this up as though it were the main line of story. An episode that was purely local might be taken into the epic, and might be brought from the periphery to the centre purely because it received this advertisement. Owing to the literary success of the epic, a purely local episode might be turned into the main story, the presiding tradition of the nation as a whole. In general the epic was often calculated to awaken a kind of romantic interest in the past; and its popularity, its widespread occurrence, suggest that there was some nostalgia for ancient times – a nostalgia that had to be catered for somehow. Sometimes the epic would become important to a people because it inspired a feeling of national pride or a martial spirit or a sense of honour. But, precisely because of the emotional satisfaction that it gave, it might operate to postpone the need or the desire for anything more authentic. We can see that people were capable of being stirred by ancient, unhappy, far-off things and battles long ago. But the epic still leaves the world without any powerful reason for developing something that could be more authentically described as history.

For this reason, the rôle of the epic in the general development of historiography might well give rise to discussion and controversy. Even the vaguest survey of the whole scene brings to light some glaringly anomalous features of the case. The epic in ancient Mesopotamia does seem to have encouraged an interest in the past and assisted the development of history as a literary genre. But in ancient Egypt no epic has survived and the rich annalistic literature of the Pharaohs seems to have developed without its help. At a comparatively late date we find Egyptian battles submitted to what we might call epic treatment, but the effect of these experiments on the actual writing of history would seem to have been unfortunate. In the case of India something in the nature of the epic existed but it neither produced an interest in the past as such nor assisted the rise of a genuinely historical literature. China, on the other hand, seems to have had no epic, yet developed one of the richest of historiographical traditions. So far as the Greeks are concerned, one would like to be sure that the possession of Homer was not too satisfying for the mind – in some ways an obstruction to the quest for anything better.

2 LISTS AND RECORDS

It seems clear that, even with the help of their mythologies and their epics, men in ancient civilisations must have seen the past as a vague, undifferentiated thing, which struggled vainly perhaps to achieve some shape in their minds. Apart from what they remembered of their own early life, and what they learned from their immediate predecessors, they would have only a vague notion of 'long age', with still no real impression of the length of time involved, but rather perhaps a feeling that the days when the gods walked in the world were not very far behind them. If one of the experts has not been loose in his translation and wrong in his appended comment, the words 'once upon a time' were familiar in the most ancient civilisation of Mesopotamia. Perhaps each of us has passed in this respect through something of the whole experience of the whole human race, so that we ourselves can half-remember the time when 'the past' was almost a no-man's-land – almost an ocean without direction, without landmarks, without light. If we take the measure of things at the time when writing began, there would only be certain ways in which the past had any shape at all or was more than a rag-bag of old stories. There would already be a consciousness of the distinction between ante-diluvian and post-diluvian; for the Flood had appeared in the epic, and the archaeologists have shown that, since something of the sort undoubtedly occurred in Mesopotamia, it might well have imprinted itself on the folk-memory of that region. There existed also, probably even then, the belief that the ante-diluvian world had differed in character from that of later times, with men living to fabulous ages, for example. It almost seems as if the Flood was the pivotal thing, on which the notion of time itself depended. Here at any rate there was a recognisable landmark and the limbo of bygone things acquired a contour.

All this will enable us to realise the tremendous progress that was made when the mind learned to project itself into the remoter past with some sense of the distances involved, something more precise than 'long ago'. It was a case of turning time into something like a long tape-measure, with markings that roughly indicated either succession or duration or degrees of remoteness. This was a thing not so easy to achieve as we may often have assumed, for we cannot really imagine the hurdle that required to be surmounted by men who had not learned to serialise the years, or to particularise amongst them, by the very simple device of numbering them in the way that we are accustomed to doing. Fortunately, however, our distant ancestors seem soon to have acquired what can only be described as a mania for making lists. The Chadwicks in their study of the Heroic Age have noticed how this craze would appear at a certain stage in the development of society in widely differing parts of the globe. The phenomenon is apparent in ancient Egypt and Mesopotamia at what in some respects was the equivalent point in the story. When the lists are concerned with objects in the natural world we regard them as in a sense the beginning of natural science, because they seem to represent the earliest gropings towards a classification of data. When they concern the succession of things in time they can be taken as representing in a certain sense the beginning of historical science. Mere lists might seem dull things to discuss, and very casual, very trifling documents to stand as a turning-point in man's evolution. It would be a mistake to overlook the real interest which they have for the student of the history of historiography.

Perhaps the earliest surviving list that possesses an imposing character is the one which is embodied partly in the famous Palermo Stone and partly in other fragments that were once attached to it. It belongs to the period some centuries before the year 2000 B.C.; and it is a long string of dynasties and kings which, when it was complete, would appear to have gone back to something like a thousand years before its own compilation – back perhaps to a time when actual gods were supposed to have reigned in Egypt. It also records events, and though these occur only rarely at first, they become more numerous as time proceeds, until, as the list approaches the time of its own production, there will be eight or even fifteen events for a given year. One might expect it therefore to provide almost a complete conspectus of Egyptian history, if it were not for the fact that the events recorded are generally of a curious nature – they would seem to justify our describing the whole document as a list rather than a set of annals.

It does not seem that the real object was to record the unique event, and a great many of the facts enumerated would seem to be things that could have occurred every year. From a remarkably early date, the monument provides for each year a certain measurement – so many cubits, palms and fingers – which seems to record the height of the annual inundation of the Nile. From a date almost equally early, it reports at times the numbering of the population or the cattle or the lands – a kind of census, taken presumably for taxation purposes. When it reaches more recent times, so that the items become thicker, the list of events for each year is largely concerned with religious festivals, the building of temples and the delivery of ceremonial offerings. Very rarely there is something more like what we today would regard as an historical event – a laconic reference to 'the hacking of the negro' for example. But equally often the event recorded is of a miscellaneous character that is calculated to puzzle the historian – in a reference, for example, to 'the shooting of the hippopotamus'.

For one of the years of King Snefru of the Third Dynasty, therefore, we read:

> Building of 100-cubit dervatowe-ships of mera wood and of 60 sixteen barges.
> Hacking the land of the negro.
> Bringing of 7,000 living prisoners and 200,000 large and small cattle.
> Building of the wall of the southland and the northland [called] 'Houses of Snefru'.
> Bringing of 40 ships filled [with] cedar wood 2 cubits 2 fingers.

For one of the years of King Userkaf of the Third Dynasty we read:

> The Spirits of Heliopolis: 20 offerings of bread and beer at every [–] and every [–] feast; 36 stat of land [– –] in the domain of Userkaf.
> The gods of the sun-temple [called] Sepre.
> State of land in the domain of Userkaf.
> 2 oxen 2 geese every day.
> Re: 44 stat of land in the nomes of the Northland.
> Hathor: 44 stat of land in the nomes of the Northland.
> The gods of the House of [–] of Horis: 54 stats of land; erection of the shrine of his temple [in] Bute of the nome of Xois;
> Sepa: 2 stat of land; building of his temple.
> Nekhhet in the sanctuary of the South: 10 offerings of bread and beer every day.
> Bute in Pernu: 10 offerings of bread and beer every day.
> The gods of the sanctuary of the South: 48 offerings of bread and beer every day.
> Year of the third occurrence of the numbering of large cattle. 4 cubits 2'/2 fingers.

It stands to reason that the entire list which we associate with the Palermo Stone was compiled out of previously existing lists. Its importance lies in the fact that it strings the earlier ones together and so produces a comprehensive survey. In the later parts of the document the reference to the pre-existing sources is often quite explicit. The above details concerning a year in the reign of King Userkaf, for example, are preceded by the note that the King had 'made this as his monument', in other words he had had these items placed on record for the year. Clearly these earlier lists (which were of a kind that had been produced annually before the time of King Userkaf) had not been historical in their intention at all. They were scribal records drawn up for some utilitarian purpose. They certified that the King had given so many lands, so many oxen, so many geese and so many offerings of bread and beer to one god and another. It is as though these things and 'the worship of Horus' and the temple-building were being ticked off as so many duties actually carried out. And in some years there would be other things that were royal functions or governmental chores – 'the circuit of the Wall', the worship of 'the gods who united the Two Lands of Upper and Lower Egypt', or the numbering of the people or the cattle. Always, in any case, there would be the measurement, presumably the record of the inundation of the Nile. When it occurs to somebody to string together a number of inventories of this kind, the result is a curious and anomalous beginning for what was to develop into historical writing. It has been argued that the object of the compiler was to serve some dynastic purpose; but the nature of the purpose and the way in which it would be effectuated are not clear. We must be careful about imputing to men of such ancient times a modern kind of political motivation. It has been said that the list, as finally assembled, was in any case only a selective one, those items being chosen which would suggest that the monarchy or the dynasty was pious and had taken care to secure the favour of the gods. But it is not clear why we should not accept the fact that the monarch, like everybody else, really did take his religion seriously – did seek to please the gods and show that he had carried out his duties to them. When we are dealing with these ancient times it may be wise to be prepared to believe that those who copied the records of the past chose superstitiously to put down everything they could find – however anomalous to the final result – because they could not bear the thought of losing anything that might have survived from the past. Men who were so interested in making lists might even need no special motive for producing one which was so imposing in itself – especially one which might give the impression of providing a conspectus of the whole of time.

There is a similar colossal list in the oldest civilisation of Mesopotamia: the almost equally famous Sumerian King-List, which, too, may go back well behind the year 2000 B.C. Once again it was formed by the assembly of a number of shorter lists enumerating the successive monarchs in the various city-states that existed in that region. In this case, the construction of the final comprehensive list went wrong; for the intention of the compiler had been to designate only those rulers who had enjoyed a kind of overlordship throughout the area. This overlordship would pass on occasion from one city to another, and the King-List would report the fact. One reads, for example, 'Ur was smitten with weapons; its kingship was carried to Awan'. Then somewhat later one will read: 'Awan was smitten with weapons; its kingship was carried to Kish'. The compiler would list the kings first of Ur, then of Awan and then of Kish; and it is clear that, sometimes at least, he learned the names from lists already existing in the cities concerned. But he would not always know which city held the predominance; and sometimes he would produce in succession two dynasties which in fact had been contemporaneous, only one of them holding the real supremacy. For this reason the Sumerian King-List was calculated to create some problems for the modern student of chronology. It purports to go back in fact to a legendary period when some of the kings were gods and some bore the names of animals. It tells us how long each monarch reigned, and sometimes it describes his relationship with his predecessor. The names of some of the kings would seem to have been obtained from royal inscriptions and this would suggest that a certain historical interest lay behind it. But, in any case, men who had the passion for compiling lists might want their lists to be complete, especially if they nursed the hope of possibly covering the whole of time. At a later date a further set of names was prefixed to the main body – a score of ante-diluvian kings whose combined reigns were supposed to have lasted 400,000 years. This was taken from legendary material which is described as coming from Eridu in the extreme south. Once again, one has the impression that there is a desire to achieve completeness, to span the whole of time.

The curious feature of this list, however, is the fact that on rare occasions the compiler has identified a particular monarch by a short-hand note. When he reaches Gilgamesh he lets us know that this is the king who was the son of a *lillu* demon. When he mentions Sargon he reminds us that this is the king who was brought up by a gardener or date-grower. What is interesting is the fact that on all these occasions he is making reference to the epics or legends in which these rulers had become known to the world in general. He is virtually saying: 'This is the man about whom the well-known story is told'; 'Etana – he is the person everybody knows about, the shepherd who was carried to heaven – this is the place that he occupies in the series'. It is interesting to see that this epic-material is treated as the single outside source to which reference can be made. Perhaps this gives us an index to the kind of historical knowledge that was regarded as being 'in the air'.

A different kind of list is identified with the First Dynasty of Babylon, and though it is rather later in date it comes not many centuries after 2000 B.C. Its meaning will not easily be apparent unless we remember once again that men had not yet learned to number the years and to recognise them by their number; but they still needed to have a way of identifying them. I am reminded of the people of my own village who, when I was young, would locate an event by stating that it happened in 'the year of

Queen Victoria's Jubilee'. They would have been unable to give the number of the year, and it would not have occurred to them to imagine that the Jubilee was the thing which historians would regard as the most important event of the year. In ancient Babylon they would designate the year in a similar way, by reference to a particular event with which it came to be identified in their minds. Some time after the year had begun, its name would be officially announced, and until this had been ceremonially decreed, the year would be described as simply the one that came after the event used to designate its predecessor. In the case of Sumu-abu, the following Date-List shows the designation for each of the fourteen years of his reign.

1. [The year in which Sumu-abu became king . . .]
2. [The year in which . . .]
3. The year in which the wall of [. . .] was built.
4. The year in which the temple of Nin-sinna was built.
5. The year in which the great temple of Nannar was built.
6. The year after that in which the great temple of Nannar was built.
7. The second year after that in which the great temple of Nannar was built.
8. The year in which the great door of cedar was made for the temple of Nannar.
9. The year in which the wall of the city of Bilbat was built.
10. The year in which the crown of the god Ni of the city of Kis was made.
11. The year after that in which the crown of the god Ni of the city of Kis was made.
12. The year in which the plantation of the gods was made.
13. The year in which the city of Kasallu was laid waste.
14. The year after that in which the city of Kasallu was laid waste.

We can be fairly sure that this list is a correct one; business documents had to be dated somehow or other, and an official key would be necessary – a recognised way of describing the year. A German scholar has suggested that when the successive reigns had been enumerated year by year in this way, any person who ran his eye down the accumulated list would easily acquire the notion of a chronicle – here is the origin of the annalistic survey. For the time being the chronicle would be curious in character: for the events that were chosen to designate the year tended to be such things as religious ceremonies, the building of a temple or the digging of a canal.

It will be apparent that nothing can have been more conducive to the making of lists than the fact that the world had as yet developed no way of numbering the years. The Babylonian method was cumbrous and, at a later date, possibly as a result of foreign influence, the practice of numbering the regnal years was adopted. In Assyria they identified the year by attaching to it the names of the holders of a given office – a system more familiar to us because it appears again in ancient Greece and Rome. It necessitated the production of official lists, the *Limmu*-lists, giving the names of the men who played the leading part in the important New Year celebrations in the Assyrian capital. It appears that these lists were sometimes expanded by the addition of notes, briefly recording the events of the year. Once again the assembly of a list seems to mark a stage in the development of something like a chronicle. With the passage of time, the Assyrian lists became very long; and it required a considerable effort to go through them in order to discover that a given temple had been constructed over 600 years previously or that a given king had reigned 800 odd years ago. The counting seems not always to have been correct; and as the later estimates of the lapse of time since some past event tended to become smaller than the earlier estimates, it has been suggested that the tablets might have got broken, the missing pieces being left out of the count.

It is not clear that any of the lists that have been mentioned were the products of a genuine interest in the past, though the accumulated Egyptian list and, still more, the Sumerian King-List may have shown a sort of desire to have a conspectus of the whole of time. The long lists, however, are of considerable significance to those who are interested in the very beginnings of history, for they showed people the immensity of the period that lay behind them, while at the same time they suggested a way of sub-dividing or measuring the period. The ancient Greeks had inadequate lists, and they were ready to believe that the time when the gods had walked and sported on the earth was not very far behind them. When some of them saw the length of the Egyptian lists – the lists not only of rulers, but also of priests, father succeeded by son for a very long period – they left evidence of the way in which this surprised them. Now, at last, they came to the realisation that history had already been going on for thousands of years. Herodotus is one of the writers who explains at length how important this knowledge was; but he describes also how a predecessor of his, Hecataeus, had similarly been taken by surprise. When Josephus came into controversy with the Greeks over the question of history in the first century A.D., he mentioned the lists that his own people – the Jewish people – had similarly preserved. The comprehensive lists that have been described provided an outer framework for the assembly of historical knowledge, but our remote predecessors, starting from such meagre beginnings, were not likely to find it easy to recover anything very authentic to fill the time-spaces that had now become so glaringly apparent. Fortunately, the problem of history was open to an entirely different method of attack.

3 DISPUTES AND WARS

Though it is difficult for society or the body politic to recover the happenings of the distant past when the memory of them has once been lost, a short-term memory is a more practicable thing and it is this which in the first place turns out to be the serious objective. It is not easy in fact to avoid thinking about the things that happened only the other day; and we ourselves, partly perhaps because we have become so historically minded, and partly because we are so aware of the continuity of historical processes, constantly see the problems of the present in terms of the recent past, and even need the past to help us to give them their proper formulation. Whether we are discussing Vietnam or the state of the shipbuilding industry, we slip into a kind of historical retrospect almost before we know what we are doing. Talk about the present, therefore, tends to slide almost insensibly into talk about the past. Moreover, something of the same tendency is visible, in Mesopotamia for example, thousands of years ago, before anything like historical study really existed and before past and present were quite separated in men's minds. We could not say that it was a case of interest in the past for the sake of the past, but it must always have operated as a stimulus to historiography, a help to the cultivation of at least a short-term memory. Even if all this were not the case, it is often necessary in the actual conduct of business – the direction of commerce, for example, or of affairs of state – that decisions should be recorded in a formal manner and transactions carefully minuted. Some of the earliest examples of historical recapitulation and of the narrative art would appear to have been the result of this practical need – not historical in their real intention or purport, but becoming historical for a later age, that is to say, by the lapse of time. And such documents carry us back almost to the year 2500 B.C. – behind even the famous King-List of ancient Sumer.

Our attention is still focused upon ancient Sumer, but it fixes itself now upon the great days of the city of Lagash. This city is of special interest to those who are looking for the beginnings of historical writing, for it has handed down to us a group of literary pieces which seem to take us to the root of the problem. Yet Lagash may not have been unique and the fame that it has acquired in this field may be fortuitous. It may be due to the chances of archaeological investigation and documents of a similar nature might well be discovered at any time elsewhere. Particularly important to us is a series of inscriptions which describe a long-standing conflict over the frontier between Lagash and the neighbouring city of Umma. And one of the texts is again associated with a famous monument, the so-called Vulture stele, a work of some significance to the historian of both art and religion, especially in view of its actual pictorial account of one of the battles. It celebrated the victory of Lagash over Umma in a war that arose out of an infraction of a boundary settlement. Scholars have suggested that this may be the earliest historical document so far recovered in the Near or Middle East – the earliest surviving attempt to give an account of wars and battles. But later accounts of this territorial conflict have survived, since successive rulers of Lagash found themselves involved in successive phases of the conflict, and all would have the same motive for placing the facts on record. It seems to have been a natural thing that a boundary-stone, marking for the time being the settlement of this running controversy, should refer back to the dispositions that had been made at the very first, and then recapitulate the infraction of the original decree thereby rehearsing the rights and wrongs of the case, as well as announcing the latest settlement. Then, when a later ruler of Lagash suffered a repetition of the offences committed against his city, it was natural that he should produce his own monuments, covering the whole ground again. The latest of them gives, therefore, an historical *résumé* covering a period of something like 150 years.

These Lagash documents were remarkably religious in a sense, and it is interesting to see to what a degree the gods figure in the story, though what is in question is the record of a business transaction, not merely a piece of historical writing. In the first place it had been the chief of the gods who had adjudicated upon the boundary question, and the monarch who was the overlord of both the rival cities – both Lagash and Umma – had merely registered the results of the divine decree. It was Ninsurga, the local god of Lagash, who was regarded as the sufferer when the city's land was depleted, for the city was in a peculiar sense his property. Even the inhabitants of the rival city, the men of Umma, were not regarded as the ultimate culprits – the real blame was placed on their own local god who was regarded as having inspired their offensive action. And the ruler of Lagash, when his land was invaded, made no response until he had consulted his god, against whom the offence had been committed. Only after he had received direction and encouragement from Ninsurga did he make the actual resort to war. Nor did he for a moment claim to have secured the victory. He simply reported that his patron deity had prevailed. Yet in the Vulture stele the monarch has described the concrete events which enable us to understand the whole episode. In a sense there might have been no more miracle involved than when Englishmen used to say that God had given them the victory. An interesting feature of the document is the regard that it shows for the relevant points of historical detail.

The following is a fairly close paraphrase of one of the later records of this dispute:

Enlil, the king of all the lands, the father of all the gods, marked off the boundary for Ningirsu and Shara by his steadfast word.

Mesclin, the king of Kish [the overlord of Lagash and Umma], measured it off . . . [and] erected a stele there.

[But] Ush, the *ishakku* [or ruler] of Umma violated both the decree of the gods and the promises given by men. He ripped out the [boundary] stele, and entered the plain of Lagash.

Then did [the god] Ningirsu, Enlil's foremost warrior, engage in battle with [the men of Umma in order to fulfil Enlil's word]. By the command of Enlil he hurled the great Shush-net upon them, and heaped up their skeleton (?) piles in the plain . . .

Eannatum, the *ishakku* of Lagash, the uncle of Entemena, the [later] *ishakku* of Lagash, marked off the boundary with Enakalli, the *ishakku* of Umma. He led out its ditch from the Idnun [canal] to the Guedinna; inscribed stelae along that ditch; and restored Mesclin's stele to its [former] place. But he did not enter the plain of Umma. He built there the Imdubba of Ningirsu, the Namnunda-Kirgaria, the shrine of Ningirsu, [and] the shrine of Utu [the sun-god]. He allowed the Ummaites to eat the barley of [the goddess] Nanshe, and the barley of Ningirsu, to the amount of one *Karû* per person [in return for a charge]. He levied a tax on the Ummaites, and brought in for himself a revenue of 144,000 'large' *Karû*.

This barley remained unpaid. Ur-Lumma, the *ishakku* of Umma, took away the water from the boundary-ditch of Ningirsu and that of Nanshe. He ripped out the [boundary] stelae and put them to fire. He destroyed the dedicated(?) shrines of the gods which had been built in the Namnunda-Kigarra. He obtained [help] from foreign lands. Finally he crossed the boundary-ditch at Ningirsu.

Ennatum fought with him in the Gana-ugigga [where are] the fields and farms of Ningirsu, and Entemena, Eannatum's beloved son, defeated him. Ur-Lumma fled. [Entemena] slew [the Ummaite forces] till he came to the city of Umma. On the bank of the Lumma-girgumta canal he wiped out [Ur-Lumma's] elite force of 60 soldiers. As for the men [of Umma] he left their bodies in the plain and heaped up their skeleton (?) piles in five places.

At that time, Il, the *sanga* of Hallab (?) ravaged (?) [the land] from Girsu to Umma. Il took to himself the *ishakku*-ship of Umma; stole the water from the boundary-ditch of Ningirsu, the boundary-ditch of Nanshe, the Imdubba of Ningirsu, that Girsu tract of arable land which lies towards the Tigris, [and] the Namnunda-Kigarra of Nintrussag. When Entemma, the *ishakku* of Lagash, repeatedly sent [his] men to Il because of that ditch, the latter, the *ishakku* of Umma, the plunderer of fields and farms, the speaker of evil, said: 'The boundary-ditch of Ningirsu and the boundary-ditch of Nanshe are mine'. He said: 'I shall exercise control from the Antasurra to the Dimgal-abzu temple'.

Enlil and Ningirsu did not allow him this.

Entemena, the *ishakku* of Lagash, whose name was pronounced by Ningursu, made this ditch from the Tigris to the Idnun in accordance with the straightforward word of Enlil, in accordance with the straightforward word of Ningirsu [and] in accordance with the straightforward word of Nanshe [after] he had constructed with bricks the foundation of the Namnunda-Higarra. May Shulutula, the [personal] god of Entemena, the *ishakku* of Lagash, to whom Enlil gave the sceptre, and Enki gave wisdom while Nanshe fixed upon him in her heart, the great *ishakku* of Ningirsu, the man who had received the words of the gods, step forward [in prayer] for the life of Entemena before Ningirsu and Nanshe unto the far future.

The Ummaite [leader] who ever crosses the boundary ditch of Ningursu and that of Nanshe in order to take fields and farms by force – no matter whether he be a genuine man of Umma or a foreigner – may Enlil destroy him; may Ningirsu, after hurling his great Shush-net on him, bring him down, on his lofty hand, his lofty foot; may the people of his city rise in rebellion against him and strike him down in the midst of his city.

In the case of early historical narratives it is not always quite clear for whom the record is intended or to whom it is addressed. References to contemporary events may be found on statues, stelae, vases, cones, cylinders and tablets, where the text is clearly a votive inscription. There are times when the monarch, producing an historical *résumé*, seems to be giving an account of himself to a god, or performing an act of thanksgiving. Sometimes he seems to be explaining how he has carried out a divine commission; and this might be important, since wars were so often felt to be carried out as a duty imposed by the god. It is clear that the gods themselves were not regarded as all-knowing and omnicompetent; and at a comparatively late date, the rulers of Babylon, Nabopolassar and Nebuchadnezzar, for example, could instruct the temple to tell the god Marduk of their pious deeds when he came within its walls. The narrative of Entemena, quoted above, culminates in an address to the gods, and in a sense it is somewhat in the form of a treaty. For very many centuries we shall find that treaties in Western Asia will have a long historical preamble, and will culminate in the same kind of curse, the same ultimate address to the gods.

From Lagash we have the account of another recent event, the sacking of the city by the same enemy, the men of Umma, who were then under the rule of Lugal-Zaggasi. But here, as in some other similar pieces of writing, we must regard the text as simply a song of lamentation. It runs as follows:

The men of Umma have set fire to the Eki [Kala]; they have set fire to the Antasurra; they have carried away the silver and the precious stones.

They have shed blood in the palace of Tirash; they have shed blood in the Abzu-banda; they have shed blood in the shrine of Enlil and the shrine of the Sun-god.

A long enumeration follows – always the shedding of blood, the burning of temples, the theft of the silver and precious stones. Then the document ends:

The men of Umma, by the despoiling of Lagash have committed a sin against the god Ningirsu! The power that is come to them shall be taken away from them. Of sin on the part of Urukagina, King of Girsu, there is none. But, as for Lugal-Zaggisi, *patesi* of Umma, may his goddess bear this sin on her head.

Again from Lagash, and indeed from the very ruler Urukagina, who reigned at the time of the sacking of the city, there occurs a document which throws light on recent social troubles. It is a notice about a radical measure of governmental reform, and it is preceded by a description of the ills that were suffered by the people under the pre-existing system. In a concrete manner the sufferings of different classes at the hands of an exploiting bureaucracy – the oppression of the farmers, the robbing of the temples, the bleeding of anybody who had relatives to bury – are described. It is the earliest surviving example of what still surprises us when we find it amongst the Hittites a thousand years later – namely the production of a *résumé* of recent history for the purpose of explaining governmental policy. Again, however, the gods would seem to be involved, and we should need to know more before we could be sure that this exactly paralleled the propaganda addressed by a modern government to the public at large.

From the work of scholars like S. N. Kramer we can gather materials which give us some measure of the way in which the sense for the past was developing in the period down to about 2000 B.C. There had been some writing about the Creation which had shown how human beings had been formed in order that the gods should be more adequately served. There had been a story of the Flood in which the gods, terrified of the cataclysm they had produced, had fled from its horrors, climbing to 'the heaven of Anu', and then crouching there like frightened dogs. By their own wilful actions the temples had been destroyed and their food supplies cut off; so that when the Sumerian Noah emerged from the ark and offered up a sacrifice, they 'scented its sweet savour and gathered like flies' above it. And now they resolved that never again would they attempt the destruction of all man-kind. Stories of Gilgamesh had been put into writing – some of them quite mundane in character like the account of the way in which he failed to persuade the elders of Erech to make a firm stand against the demands of the dynasty of Nish; but then he appealed to the troops and the 'convened assembly' of the city's inhabitants and won their support for a bolder policy. Because Gilgamesh had become so popular a hero there were stories about other people which had been transferred to him. Also some of the tales about him were mythological in character, remote from real life, and even the story of the Flood came to be included in the cycle of narratives connected with his name. Only part of all this material was incorporated in the epic of Gilgamesh that has been handed down to us – itself a moving document because it shows the ultimate despair of men – the failure of even so great a hero to escape the relentless hand of death. Still another ruler of Erech had been the subject of something like epic poetry – Emmerkar, who, for example, unloosed a 'war of nerves' against the city of Arattu in Persia, and succeeded in breaking its ruler's resistance. Indeed, ancient Sumer seems to have been the original home of the epic, and many fragments of its literature that have survived seem to belong to a form of heroic poetry. From some of this writing there emerges the notion of a 'golden age' in the distant past—a time when 'there was no snake, there was no scorpion . . . there was no fear, no terror. Man had no rival' and 'the whole universe with one tongue gave praise to Entil'. The mind had even reflected on the problem presented by the existence of civilisation. There had emerged the view that one of the gods had been responsible for establishing arts and industries, and the invention of the pick-axe had been celebrated. The famous ruler of Erech, Emmerkar, had been described in his epic as having been the first to produce writing on clay tablets. Already, therefore, men had been wondering about the origin of things and cherishing myths of origins.

Much of this was so legendary and remote that the interest in bygone times can be regarded as having been a matter of religion rather than of history – a fact which would not lessen the power of such material over the mind. Closer to genuine history were the victory stelae, the boundary-stones, the songs of lamentation and the dedicatory inscriptions which have been found in Lagash but may well have existed also elsewhere. These had references to a much more recent past, and touched the vicissitudes of life as they were bound to be known in actual experience. The things most relevant to the development of the historical outlook were no doubt the stories of the famous ruler, Sargon of Akkad (or Agade) who, not long before 2300 B.C., had come from the north to establish his ascendancy over the whole of Mesopotamia. He became the first imperial conqueror in world history and it was important that he was a man of such stature that he never went out of the public memory. Stories of him were told and retold – stories of his advance into Anatolia, for example, and then to the coast of the Mediterranean. Some of the narratives became twisted in the transmission, and a reference to his crossing of the Eastern Sea (the Persian Gulf, near at hand) became changed to a story of his crossing the Western Sea – the Mediterranean – a much more portentous affair. At least one section of his travels became transmuted and highly coloured in an exercise of what we must call historical fiction. The unhappy fate of his dynasty after a comparatively short interval, and especially the misfortunes of one of his successors, Naram-Sin, helped to give to a period of over a century something of the unity and the quality of an organic theme. Here was just the thing that was calculated to assist the transition from mere dry King-Lists to the notion of continuous narrative, and to produce a more genuine interest in a past that had been real, as well as a desire to give to history a certain literary form. The fall of a dynasty after its sensational rise under Sargon led to solemn reflections on the connection that might exist between the misdeeds of a monarch and the misfortunes of the body politic. The student of omens found interesting materials in this chapter of history, and, in this connection, the exercise of moral judgement became significant.

It would seem to have been towards the end of the Sumerian period and in the region of the year 2000 B.C. that much of the writing of this ancient culture achieved its developed literary form. We are told, however, that the earliest catalogues of Sumerian literary productions – catalogues which belong to the same period – though they include the epic, make no reference to history as a form of writing. King-Lists and Date-Lists might not have been regarded as literature; and the kind of writings that have come down to us from Lagash might not have been regarded as primarily historical, or historical in intent, even where they might have been held to rank as literature. It is possible that what we call history was as yet no more a recognised *genre* than science-fiction would have been in literary text-books of a century ago.

4 FIRST INTERPRETATIONS

At an early stage in the history of ancient Mesopotamia there emerged an outlook on life which was to be of some significance for the development of historiography. It helps to explain why the historical writing of Western Asia became so much more profound than that of ancient Egypt, in spite of the superiority possessed by Egypt in the purely literary sphere. Therefore, though its main idea looks simple, this is a thing that cannot be dismissed as a colourless and characterless commonplace. It led to the appearance of the first hitherto known example of what might be called an interpretation of human history. And this interpretation itself was to be of such long-standing importance in the history of civilisation, and was to affect so profoundly the mentality of men, that its origin is bound to be a matter of some interest to us.

We have come today to be highly conscious of the way in which geography and material conditions affected not only the general development but also perhaps the mentality of ancient Sumer. Whereas the annual flooding of the Nile was a thing that could be counted upon, being so regular and so calculable that it was comparatively easy to bring conditions under control, the behaviour of the Euphrates was flighty and capricious, and its flooding was a much more chancy affair. The causes of the flooding were beyond the range of observation; everything depended on the melting of the snows in the farthest of the upper reaches of the river, and the secret lay in another country altogether – in the mountains of Anatolia. Perhaps it was partly because of this that the Sumerians were haunted so constantly by the sense of the insecurity of human existence, a feeling that the inhabitants of the Nile valley seem to have been very far from sharing. Even the divinity that was responsible for the flooding in Egypt would seem to have been regarded as a beneficent power. The corresponding deity in Meso-potamia was felt to be a malignant agency.

Whether it was partly the result or partly the cause of the prevailing mood in ancient Sumer, the religious outlook of the people of the region answered to their general impression of the cataclysmic character of life on the earth. It is held by some scholars that the belief in what we call anthro-pomorphic deities was not very old in Mesopotamia in the period with which we have been dealing, though quite an elaborate pantheon existed when the epic of Gilgamesh was taking shape not very long before 2500 B.C. These anthropomorphic gods were woefully inadequate creatures, however. They were not uncreated and evidently not endowed with immor-tality, not at all omnipresent or omnicompetent or all-knowing, in spite of the impressive connection that they might have had with one or another part of the cosmos. Though the hymns and the liturgies might have very moving things to say about the virtues, the beneficence and the good feel-ings of some of their number, the kindness of these deities was apparently not a thing on which men could rely, and we ourselves have noted one or two cases where it was the god who incited the city to commit an offence. Their divinity might not prevent their being overcome by fear – there were stories about their fleeing from the battlefield – and there appears to have been a sense in which they, like human beings, were the prisoners of a sort of destiny. They were remarkably dependent on their human servants, as they discovered when they released the Flood and found that it resulted in the stoppage of their food supplies. The defeat of a human ruler in battle could involve also the discomfiture of the god himself, the patron and the owner of the defeated city, where he would have his abode. But it was the wilfulness and the levity of the gods that was most surprising. According to the Babylonian myth of creation, their own begetter could decree the destruction of the whole tribe of them because they were making too much noise. It appears to have been upon a doubtful pretext that the gods decreed the Flood which was to destroy the whole of mankind. The insecurity that human beings felt in the face of geographical conditions had at least its counterpart in the insecurity which they felt *vis-à-vis* their gods, who in any case lacked the power to save them. The destinies of men hung precariously on the whims of an assembly. They were fixed annually at what has sometimes been called a Parliament of the Gods.

But Mesopotamia, though initially so intractable a landscape, was a country that provided a tremendous return for a highly-organised endeavour. If the flooding of the Euphrates were properly utilised, the harvest gave magnificent results for the minimum of effort, and the silt brought down by the river added to the richness of the earth. The chief necessity was the development of irrigation and drainage, and this was achieved on a considerable scale with canals twenty-five yards wide running from the Euphrates to the Tigris and innumerable smaller channels to spread the water over the land. The work required what for those days must have been high organisation and fine technical accomplishment. A strong governmental control was needed to secure the forced labour, to see that everything was kept in repair and to prevent single individuals from acting to the detriment of their neighbours. The mere voluntary cooperation of men living in villages would never have been sufficient to secure the organisation and the direction required. It was necessary that the state should be developed on a more imposing scale, and Mesopotamia became a congeries of city-states, some of which would have thirty or forty thousand inhabitants. Each city would be the domain of its local god, and its chief temple would serve as a residence for him; there appear to have been times when the whole economy would be centred upon the temple. But the cities would struggle with one another, and part of the conflict would be for the supremacy over the whole country. Each would be fighting at the same time for the honour and advantage of its own god – it would take to arms after receiving the divine command or the divine encouragement. When armies went out to battle in those days the contest was apt to be more subject to chance than in the warfare of a more modern period. The issue would often be more incalculable. There seems to have been an extraordinary genuineness in the belief that victory, when it came, was really the work of the patron-deity.

Some scholars have expressed surprise at the fact that the early writers of history showed no sense of the continuity between past and present, no feeling for the existence of what we call process. It is important that we should eliminate all such considerations from our mind, for notions of this kind were achieved only after men had been studying and reflecting upon history for thousands of years. The ancient Sumerians found themselves in a world in which things happened; and if they stole a march on chance by the development of agriculture, the creation of an irrigation system and the establishment of government, they still felt caught in a frightening realm of booby-traps and accidents. History to them would be the range of what we might regard as mere happening. It involved discontinuity; it meant the alternation of good times and bad; too often it confronted men with events that came as bolts from the blue. The one thing that the ancient Sumerians really knew about life was the fact that their destiny was beyond their control. The simplest initial explanation that was open to them was the theory that the caprice of the gods decided the various turns of fortune. There was an arbitrary fixing of destinies in heaven, and this itself was an exposure of the discontinuity of history. A new decree of destiny was issued by the gods every year.

Even the Sumerian King-List had shown how, in this congeries of city-states, one particular locality or dynasty would have its period of power and then would come to its fall. The city of Kish would hold the real kingship, the over-all predominance, but then it would be 'smitten with weapons', and another city would rise to the top. It seems to have been the ups-and-downs in this group of cities that led to serious reflection upon the whole problem of the rise and fall of the body politic. The glories of King Sargon of Akkad and the subsequent disaster to his dynasty seem to have been one of the chapters of history which gave rise to solemn reflections about human destiny. It came to be held that the alternation of times of blessings and times of curse had their *rationale* after all. They were to be interpreted as a judgement on human conduct. Misfortune came as the result of sin, though the sin might be simply that of the ruler himself, and indeed it might be no more than a ceremonial transgression. The essential point was perhaps not what we today would regard as an 'ethical' issue, but the offence committed against the god, or the mere neglect of some duty to him. Nor was it always even the case that the culprit would be aware of the way in which he had provoked the divine anger.

One of the most remarkable of the Sumerian writings is a highly poetic piece of narrative which describes how 'Enlil had given to Sargon, King of Agada, the lordship and kingship from the lands above to the lands below'. The enormous good fortune and prosperity of the whole empire are described, but less than a century after its rise it had come to tragedy, and clearly men had been troubled by the change of fortune, anxious to learn why it should have come about. The explanation now produced is that Naram-Sin, the successor of Sargon, had conquered and destroyed the ancient city of Nippur, and in the course of this he had flouted the god Enlil, committing all kinds of sacrilege against Ekur, the particular sanctuary of this god. From this moment, 'counsel left Agade' and 'the good sense of Agade turned to folly'. Foreign invaders had broken into Mesopotamia, covering the earth 'like locusts', and famine had supervened. Eight of the Sumerian gods had then decided that the offended Enlil must be soothed, before the whole of mankind had been brought to destruction. They decide that if Agade, the original culprit, suffers due punishment for its sin, the anger of

Enlil will be satisfied and he will cease indulging his rage against the rest of the world. The eight of them, including Inanna, the patron goddess of Agade itself, utter against the offending city a tremendous curse: 'May your place . . . be turned into a depressing ruin. . . . Over the places where your rites and rituals were conducted, may the fox (who haunts) the ruined mounds glide his tail. . . . May your canal-boat tow-paths grow nothing but weeds.' Inanna herself attacks the city and betrays it to its enemies, and within a matter of days Agade itself is desolate, its ruler Naram-Sin in misery. The curse itself proves to be effective. And, while the narrator is telling the story, the canal-boat tow-paths are in fact still growing nothing but weeds.

In this kind of reflection there lies the origin of the basis of a view of history which was to become important to the world, partly because it spread through all the countries of Western Asia and forms the lowest stratum of all in the ancient Hebrew scriptures. It was in the development of this idea that Mesopotamia, and the whole of Western Asia, came to closer grips with the problem of human destiny than the inhabitants of the Nile valley were ever to do. They came to grips with it first of all in their confrontation with the problems of contemporary life, rather than in their meditations upon history, though the notion itself must have been the result of their reflections on things past. It led them to deeper questions – to earnest wrestlings with the gods who, even on the new terms that had been established, would be felt to have been unfair at times. Already in the Sumerian period the situation produced serious self-searchings, serious attempts also to understand the *rationale* of the divine politics. Professor Kramer has called attention to something like a precursor to the book of Job at this early date. The complainant cries:

You have doled out to me suffering ever anew . . .
The man of deceit has conspired against me
And you, my god, do not thwart him . . .
On the day [that] shares were allotted to all, my allotted share was
    suffering . . .
Suffering overwhelms me [and I am] like one chosen for nothing but
    tears . . .
My god, you who are my father, who begot me, lift up my face . . .
How long will you neglect me [and] leave me unprotected?

It is perhaps in order to meet the reproach of having sinned that he says:

Never has a sinless child been born to its mother,
. . . a sinless youth has not existed as of old.

The problem is ultimately circumvented, for, before the story ends, the god is pouring out blessings on this innocent sufferer. But the whole piece is based on the assumption that the righteous man can claim favour and prosperity as his reward.

During the First Dynasty of Babylon – that is to say, in a period well on this side of the year 2000 B.C. – there appears the first unmistakable use (and some might say the first glaring abuse) of an interpretation of history for polemical purposes.

Babylon had existed for some centuries, but it had long been unimportant, and its local god Marduk had been a comparatively insignificant member of the Mesopotamian pantheon. The city had advanced to the supremacy, however, and had come to have the direction of a great empire; and its priests determined to secure a corresponding elevation for their local deity. In this particular case, therefore, we meet again an example of the way in which the ups-and-downs of cities might affect the fortunes of their patron-deities. The later, Babylonian version of the epic of Creation was an attempt to show how, in heaven as well as on earth, the supreme honours really belonged to Marduk, and how in fact they had been his due ever since mankind had existed. The work describes how he had seemed the primary and the really effective power in heaven through the part that he was prepared to play in a famous battle of the gods. On the theory now presented, the creation of man was the result of his victory in the conflict – it was a by-product of the whole episode. Now that their city had acquired the political ascendancy, in fact, the priests of Babylon were not only asserting the supremacy of their local deity, but were antedating it or making it retrospective, imputing to Marduk at a time when he had been only a minor deity at least the right to the highest position of all. They reinforced their propaganda in further literary productions which turned their view into an interpretation of all history, though this again meant the reading of the present back into the past. In what is known as the Weidner Chronicle, for example, they touched on the fall of various cities and rulers of Mesopotamia; but always they imputed the catastrophe to some neglect of Marduk, though the men concerned could not have known of any duty to Marduk at the time, and he must have appeared as an upstart god both to them and to their successors. It became the burden of myths and chronicles and songs of lamentation that, from the beginning of time, the misfortunes of men and cities were a punishment not for the neglect of one's local deity but for the failure to recognise the rights of Marduk.

The question was calculated to engage human beings more closely than ever with the problem of their history and their destiny, especially as the issue was bound to be a controversial one from the very start. It is clear that the population of even an empire that was under the sway of Babylon did not find it easy to transfer its affections to Marduk in the way that was demanded; nor did the project ever quite succeed. All the same it has often been pointed out, and appears to have been true over a very long period, that historiography was seriously affected by the rise of Babylon, and the cause of history owes a great debt to the endeavours of the priests of Marduk. Any serious recording of the past that we have so far noticed has been the work of the monarch or his appointed scribes – a thing associated with the actual conduct of a government. It was important that now the priests were engaged upon the task, and they were not acting as mere agents of the monarch – they were exerting upon historiography what we might call ecclesiastical influence. The intervention of priests changes the character of historical writing, which no longer – whether consciously or unconsciously – reflects the interests of government. Even at a much later date it has been noted that the monarchs of Babylon, when they promoted historical writing, seemed to put into the building of their temples the pride that the Assyrian rulers had in their military achievement. The priests, when they come to history, are not as imprisoned in a national-political outlook as the representatives of kings and governments. Precisely because they are preoccupied with religion, they tend to engage themselves with the larger problems of human destiny. Because they were so intent on their religious object, the priests of Marduk tended to emphasise what was then the religious but was soon to be recognised as the ethical factor in history.

One aspect of the ancient attitude to historical events is likely to defeat the modern imagination more than any other; and, though in some respects it continued in existence until recent centuries, it seems clear that we of the twentieth century never clearly visualise the important part that it played in life and thought. Even the readers of Herodotus, however, must be struck by the place occupied in statesmanship and government by various forms of divination such as the oracle, the omen and the dream, and by the attention which that historian so consistently pays to this matter. In the civilisations that were older still, the preoccupation with these practices greatly affected conceptions of history and of politics.

History developed for a very long period in Europe as a separate realm of discourse – as essentially a human drama and a study of human relations, with nature providing the background, simply the stage on which the performance took place. In other regions and other times, nature and history have not been so radically separated, and for a long period in ancient China the official historian at court had the express duty of recording unusual natural phenomena as well as happenings in the world of human affairs. Scholars have even suggested that, though the two functions came to be divided from one another, the character of Chinese historiography remained still affected by the prevailing assumption that nature and history operated in somewhat the same way. In the earliest myths elsewhere, what happened in nature would be explained by telling a story, narrating a piece of history. In the earliest reflections about the past it would be moments in the history of the natural world – the Creation and the Flood – which provided the dramatic events, the first famous landmarks. For the understanding of the mentality of ancient Mesopotamia, it is serviceable sometimes to eliminate the boundary between nature and history.

From very early times it was the practice in that region to gather omens in various ways, and particularly to examine the livers of sacrificial sheep. This remained a most important practice, though there were other ways of divining the future, and in some of the narratives with which we have been dealing the god would communicate with the ruler or his representative through a dream. We have already noted that in those days the student would have his eye on the discrete event, and would see each event as a separate thing, instead of making those connections between them which for us today really give meaning to history. But that men in those ancient days were not without the ability to make connections, the instinct to hunt for correlations – and thereby to move somewhat in the direction of science – is illustrated by their treatment of the problem of omens. We might say that they were almost hankering after a kind of science of human events, and they failed because they looked for it in the wrong direction.

They rose to the notion that if the presence of some anomaly in the liver of a sacrificial sheep was accompanied by a certain event, there might be reason to expect the recurrence of something like the same event if a similar anomaly were ever discovered again in a similar sheep. This gave them a powerful motive for recording both the omen and the event together, and it led to the production of yet another kind of list: one which would have the description of the omen in one column while in an accompanying column there was a note of the event with which it was associated. It was as though they were developing a primitive form of filing-system, and somebody has compared this with the recording of finger-prints at Scotland Yard. The lists in question have not been without their importance for the twentieth-century historian, since they had at least the effect of putting certain facts on record. There was one event in the life of King Sargon of Akkad which, until discoveries of a comparatively recent date, had been known only from one of these omen-lists. It is not clear that the practice did not lead to an early kind of historical research, for in the case of one of the lists the events seem to have been taken from a certain chronicle and the omens must have been recovered from a different source.

We even meet the suggestion that the examination of animals for the purpose of divination must have represented the very beginning of the science of anatomy. That it led to the adoption of certain quasi-scientific procedures is shown by the attempt to establish principles – to achieve generalisations and then to work by inference from these. The conclusion was reached that if a deformed foetus had a defect on the right-hand side, this must be regarded as unfavourable to the party that was taking the omen. A defect on the left side, on the other hand, meant misfortune for the enemy. There was one occasion on which it was said of a given omen that it was held to carry a certain interpretation but that the king's diviners were proposing to look into the matter. The evidence does not suggest for a moment that the resort to divination was a hypocrisy or a hoax but that the matter was taken very seriously, and that kings, before they took action, had to consult the omen just as they had to consult their local assembly.

There was even a disposition to allow a certain kind of semi-scientific speculation to run ahead of the facts, for interpretations were provided for certain types of omen that could not have been met with in actual experience. One note tells us that, if a ewe gives birth to three lambs at once, this means a threat to prosperity. Four lambs at once means the approach of a usurper. Nine must then be a very serious matter indeed – it foretells the end of the reigning dynasty. At a late period in the history of Babylon there were produced a series of astronomical reports intended to record particularly certain lunar observations. But along with these, they reported the weather at the given date, the height of the Euphrates, the price of current crops and certain events, such as military expeditions and revolts. It appears that, at this period, runners would be regularly employed to bring the latest observations and reports from separate cities of the empire to the capital. The mind was evidently greatly occupying itself with events in the natural world and in the human realm, though the results were not showing themselves in what we should call 'historical thought'.

In the year 2000 B.C. some of these developments were still reserved for the future. But by that date the omen-lists had begun to appear.

CHAPTER TWO

The Annals of the Pre-classical Empires

1 NARRATIVES OF EVENTS

Between the year 2000 B.C. and the earliest date to be assigned to the historiography of the Old Testament there lies a period of over a thousand years. The understanding of the historical writing of this period is necessary for any assessment of the contribution made by the ancient Hebrew Scriptures; but, though the millennium in question was not by any means unproductive, the slowness of the development that took place is one of the amazing features of the story. Here, once again, we become vividly conscious of the obstructions that checked any effective grappling with the problem of the past.

The essential feature of this second millennium B.C. was the development of the narrative treatment of events and the emergence of history as a literary *genre*. Attention is confined, however, to the recording of what were virtually contemporary happenings; and there is little sign of anything like an enquiry into bygone times. The great characteristic of the period was the production of the annals that were to become so famous; and as the first appearance of history had been connected with royal government and matters of state, these annals are a peculiar feature of widespread imperial systems – they are associated chiefly with Egypt and the Hittites, and with the Assyrian and Babylonian Empires. They would be engraved on the walls of palaces or temples, or on self-standing monuments or cylinders – we even find them carved on great faces of rock. They achieved considerable proportions, and the world-shaking rulers clearly liked to achieve the monumental manner, liked to do things with great style. At the beginning the texts seem to have consisted of almost disconnected notes, and nobody would feel tempted to see any beauty in them, or feel that they offered a path to glory. They made very slow progress but, with the passage of time, they acquired something of the continuity of narrative, they grew to a surprising length and they came to be handled with conscious artistry. For a thousand years they represent the thing that we call 'history' – now a self-conscious affair, strutting pretentiously before the world.

For the most part, it is official history, produced on behalf of the monarch, and serving his interests or those of the state. It may have had much to say about the ruler's relations with the gods, as well as with human beings, but here the interplay had its reference to public affairs. The annals were produced by the king himself, or were written for him – presenting him as speaking in the first person; and their purpose was to celebrate his building achievements (always a matter of special pride) or his prowess in the hunt (then a matter of greater moment than we might expect today) or his bravery in battle and his success in war. At the time when this literary artifice was brought to its climax they were just about the most boastful pieces of writing ever produced by anybody. The monarch may have sponsored them because it was important to him to impress his subjects, or because he wished to overawe other princes, or because he was anxious about his future fame. He might even produce such things as an expression of thanksgiving to heaven, or by way of report to the gods on the carrying out of a mission they had entrusted to him. One thing is clear: they are not to be taken as evidence of the interest men showed in bygone things and in the recovery of the past. All we might say is that if a ruler was concerned about his future fame he had no doubt learned by the reputation of predecessors, and acquired a certain sense of time.

Much more remarkable were the uneasiness and the concern that were shown about the future. The monarch revealed a desperate anxiety about the way in which he would be commemorated – a dreadful fear that his monument, his own record of his achievements, would not be properly preserved. His text would always instruct his successors not to erase his name, not to interpolate their own instead, not to deface the inscription and not to leave it in a neglected state. However, there would still be an ineradicable distrust of the future, and at the end of the narrative there was invariably appended a solemn curse against whatever person might do violence to the memorial. The curse itself grew to inordinate length, and might become as long as a chapter of the Old Testament. It was evidently important to cover specifically every possible case of insult or injury – to leave no loophole for some unusual way of maltreating the monument. The man who defaced the inscription or threw the tablet into the river or destroyed the article by fire or broke the stone in pieces or altered the text; the man who stole the glory by inserting his own name instead of the one that belonged there – all were threatened with a terrible doom. It is remarkable that there should have been such a determination to make the monument endure. And equally remarkable was the dark distrust of the generations to come.

The annals represented history in a sense, therefore, but history of the type of what one would call the commemorative tablet. And this no doubt is the reason why, in spite of the extraordinary literary development of the *genre*, it changed so little in essentials in the course of a thousand years. It was bound to come to a dead end.

The early historical writing of the Near and Middle East differs from that of ancient Greece and modern Europe in that it seeks to achieve authenticity by preserving the first statement of anything that happened – it claims therefore to present history as coming straight from the horse's mouth. The Jewish Josephus had this in mind when in the first century A.D. he criticised the historical writing of the Greeks and formulated the issue between East and West, claiming that the Greeks had no absolute history, no fixed story, but only speculative reconstructions that might vary from one author to another. On this view the strength of ancient Hebrew historiography lay in the fact that for so many centuries it had presented to the world a settled and unchanging story. It has sometimes been held that here lies the essential distinction between the Orient and the Western world, the former preserving a hard narrative which might be regarded as the impersonal voice of the past itself, while the latter regards history as subject to revision (better indeed for having been revised) though this opens the door for speculation and the conflict of opinion, different versions coming to be identified with different authors. Possibly, however, it is simply in the very earliest stages of historical writing that men cling superstitiously to what has been handed down from the past itself, following it to the letter because it represents an actual survival from a previous age – holding to it as a piece of absolute history, and not yet realising that there is a work of reconstruction that one might do for oneself. In the case of the history that bears the character of the commemorative tablet, the reader has the advantage of being able to hear what a former age had to say for itself, but the story tends to acquire a peculiar fixity. It is almost true to say that it is as rigid as the stone on which it is engraved; though there are occasions when a monarch produces successive versions of a narrative, and modern scholars have sometimes made the mistake of assuming that the latest one might be the most accurate. In general, history was a settled affair, inexorably engraved on stone, and there was no question of getting behind this record – only rarely any hint of the possibility of getting behind it. Any later piece of historical writing would authenticate itself merely by showing that it had accurately copied the basic text. There was no question, therefore, of one author saying one thing while another author said another thing – no feeling that history in fact had an author who needed to be identified. History was just the hard unchanging record, to be accepted in the way that, passing through a strange village, one would accept the names engraved on a memorial to those who had lost their lives in the First World War.

2 ANCIENT EGYPT

The ancient Egyptians were not so earnest and persistent as the inhabitants of Mesopotamia in their wrestlings with the gods on the issue of their earthly destiny. They brooded early on questions of right and wrong but the vicissitudes of life in the ordinary mundane sphere were not their main preoccupation. Writings of theirs which belong to the fourth millennium B.C., and which were once described as presenting 'the oldest thoughts of men that have anywhere come down to us in written form', not only showed a consciousness of the moral defects of human beings but suggested that, once upon a time, all the sin and strife had been unknown. Even in those early days, however, the Egyptians had been chiefly preoccupied with the problem of the after-life; and, possibly because the world was more kind to them than to the inhabitants of Sumer, death presented itself as the one appalling problem that they had to face. The protest against human mortality was the most remarkable feature of the entire Egyptian attitude and outlook; and there can hardly have been any other region where the notion of life beyond the grave so affected religion and so dominated the activities of men, so directed the operations of the state itself. Because Egypt early became a united empire, it was more possible for its religion to achieve a certain universality than in Mesopotamia where the disorders of the pantheon seemed to match the diversity of city-states. Religious thought, therefore, advanced in many ways more quickly in the Nile Valley; but from early times it was held back by the profundity of the conviction that the catastrophe of death could be countered by human devices, by quasi-magical practices and by highly materialistic engineering projects. It was believed from an early date that kings at least – and then the distinguished people who were near to kings – could escape the sordidities of life in the netherworld and acquire something of the happiness that was enjoyed by the gods. In some of the very ancient Pyramid Texts, the man who attains this state is even better than the gods, for they 'are afraid of him', 'his superfluity of food is greater than theirs'. When he arrives, they throw down their white sandals and cast off their garments, saying, 'Our heart was not at ease till thou camest'. Virtue in itself was not sufficient to enable a man to achieve this objective, however, and monarchs engaged in colossal enterprises which would guarantee their future – guarding their bodies from the malignity of either man or nature, for example. Masses of human beings would be enslaved for the purpose, and there were times when it seemed that the whole organisation of the state was directed to the building operations that would secure the future felicity of the monarch. But, particularly if one were not a monarch, all the precautions that one took might still be insufficient. One depended upon the sympathy and cooperation of those who went on living in the world. This, too, gave rise to considerable anxiety; and the obsession with this problem affected the development of historical writing.

Monument after monument would show this pathetic dependence of the dead upon the living. Mere commemoration was not the objective; the point was to implore the passer-by to prepare the necessary libations or to make an offering of food. Something could be achieved if the traveller could be persuaded simply to utter the name of the dead man as he came by the tomb; for 'to speak the name of the dead is to make them live again'. In the very ancient mortuary inscription of Nezemib we read, therefore:

> O ye who love life and hate death, say ye, 1,000 loaves and beer, 1,000 poured out for me, for I was a master of secret things. Let a mortuary offering of that which is with you come forth for me, for I was one beloved of the people.

The inscription of Amenemhet virtually begins with the words:

> O ye who love life and hate death, say ye, 1,000 loaves and beer, 1,000 oxen and geese for the *Ka* of the hereditary prince.

It becomes apparent on occasion that the dead and the living can oblige one another by mutual services; and this is brought out in a much later document, the Great Abydos inscription of Rameses II, who tells his father and predecessor what he has done on his behalf:

> Awake, lift thy face to heaven, that thou mayest see [the divine] Re, O my father Merneptah [the Pharaoh Seti I], who art [thyself] a god. Behold, I make thy name quicken into life; I have protected thee, I have taken care of thy temple; thy offerings are provided. . . . How [happy] for thee . . . since now thou comest as one who has returned to life. . . . Speak to Re and ask him to grant lifetime upon lifetime . . . to [me, Rameses II]. It would be well for thee if I were to be king for ever . . . for, while I go on reigning thou shalt be . . . as if thou livest.

The dead father, Seti I, is made to reply:

> Let thy heart be very glad, O my beloved son. . . . Behold, out of a loving heart I said to Re: 'Grant to him eternity upon earth. . . .' I said again to Osiris when I went into his presence: 'Give to [Rameses] twice the lifetime that thy son, Horus, enjoyed. . . .' I [Seti I] am magnified because of all the things that thou hast done for me. I am placed at the head of the abode of the dead . . . I am become a god more beautiful than before, since thy heart has inclined to me, while I am in the nether world.

It implied a particular malignity, therefore, when, at a later date, an attempt was made to erase the name of Tutankhamen from all his monuments after his death – to wipe him out of memory, and harry him in his after-life.

One of the texts already quoted makes it apparent that the dead man, when he presents his appeal to those who pass by, sets out the claim that he has upon the consideration of other people. Part of the object of the monument itself is to present the case that he has for special treatment. And Nezemib, who has already been mentioned, himself went on to say: 'Never was I beaten in the presence of any official since my birth; never did I take the property of any man by violence.' Another official, Henker, tells us:

O ye people of the Cerastes-mountain; O ye great lords of other nomes, who shall pass by this tomb . . . I gave bread to all the hungry of the Cerastes-mountain; I clothed him who was naked therein . . . I was lord and overseer of southern grain in this nome . . . I rose then to be ruler in the Cerastes-mountain . . . I settled every district with men and cattle . . . I speak no lie, for I was one beloved of his father, praised of his mother, excellent in character to his brother, and amiable to [his sister]. . . .

Such texts were capable of indefinite expansion; and it was upon this pattern that the earliest biographies and autobiographies that we know were produced in ancient Egypt. Whether explicitly or implicitly, they show that they are governed by the same motive – they are not 'lives' or 'histories' or even 'narratives', but statements of a dead man's claim to the sympathies and good offices of the living. Once again, therefore, we are confronted with texts that are not historical in intention, but which are capable of developing into history. There is an account of a certain Methen, which has been called 'the oldest biography we possess', and it goes back almost to the year 3000 B.C., so that it is earlier than anything that we have so far considered. It presents us with one of the characteristic features of this whole class of early Egyptian writings; for, instead of describing the man's actions or adventures or achievements, it enumerates the claims that he has on the reader's attention, basing them on the assumption that everything depends upon the esteem in which a man was held when he was alive. The document reads, therefore, like a fantastic expansion of the driest part of an entry in *Who's Who* – the part that simply lists the offices bestowed on a man, the titles conferred and the honorary degrees received. Even the presents that were given to Methen by the ruler are enumerated; for the fact of having been honoured by the Pharaoh during his lifetime is what precisely constitutes his right to be cared for when he is dead. The point becomes more explicit in the inscription of Ptahshepses, which comes a century or two later; for this man was 'educated amongst the king's children' and therefore 'more honoured before the king than any child'. He married the king's daughter, and came to be 'more honoured than any servant'. In the days of king Neferirkere 'His Majesty permitted that he should kiss his boot and . . . not kiss the ground'. Not because of his achievements in themselves, therefore, but because of the light they kindled in Pharaoh's eyes, is a man valued after his death. As time proceeds, one gathers the impression that the writers of these inscriptions were seeking to outdo one another – that each in fact was trying to create a record. 'The king loved me more than any official of his,' says Uni, 'more than any noble of his, more than any servant of his. . . . Never before had any one like me heard the secrets of the royal harem. . . . I was "master of the footstool" of the palace, and sandal-bearer. . . . Never before was this office conferred upon any servant.' But later examples go further still and a man will claim that he had been more loved by Pharaoh than statesman or noble or even son had ever been before.

Because they were so far from being historical in intention, these biographical sketches carry much less of the real stuff of history than we might expect; and a modern reader will be puzzled by their artificialities. If Methen gives a lengthy list of the offices, the honours and the presents conferred upon him, Ptahshepses is really concerned to describe his relationship with successive Pharaohs. Another man gives copies of royal commands that he had received – gives them not because they will be informative but to show the complimentary terms in which they are couched. Uni is remarkable for the amount of narrative that he supplies and he tells us the part that he played in a campaign against 'the Asiatic sand-dwellers';

> His Majesty sent me at the head of this army. . . . I was the one who made . . . the plan. . . . Not one [soldier] plundered – [?] or sandals from the wayfarer; not one took bread from any city. . . . This army returned in safety [after] it had destroyed the land of the sand-dwellers; this army returned in safety [after] it had overturned its strongholds; this army returned in safety after it had cut down its figs and vines . . . this army returned in safety [carrying away] a great multitude of living captives.

Even Uni, however, is equally anxious to describe how his ruler had procured for him a sarcophagus from Troja – 'never was the like done for any servant'. He will tell us how he was sent to dig canals and superintend the construction of ships; but it is a matter of still greater pride to him that he was the man commissioned to fetch the sarcophagus for the queen. It would be more particularly from about 2000 B.C. that these private monuments tended to throw more light on the general conditions of the time. Henu, for example, describes his journey to the Red Sea for myrrh, the building of a ship and the transport of blocks of stone for statues – 'never was the like of this done by any king's confidant sent out since the time of the god'. Amenemhet mentions a military campaign and an expedition to procure gold ore. His troops returned in safety, 'having suffered no loss. I brought the gold. . . . I was praised for it in the palace. . . . All the imposts of the King's house passed through my hands. . . . There were no arrears against me. . . . There was no citizen's daughter whom I misused. . . .' The Stela of Sebek-Khu (or Zaa) makes the only known mention of an invasion of Syria by any Pharaoh of the Middle Kingdom. But he tells us very little about it – what matters to him is that 'I captured an Asiatic. . . . My face was to the front, and I gave not my back to the Asiatic. As Sesostris [the Pharaoh] lives, I have spoken the truth.'

Even the producers of this kind of memorial came to have the desire to show on occasion how an objective had been achieved and how obstructions had been overcome; and even when sometimes it did not serve the obvious utilitarian purpose, it would be difficult on occasion to avoid being seduced into telling a story. The tremendous list associated with the Palermo Stone had been calculated to raise an interest in the past and was evidence of the existence of official records – evidence of the passion of the Egyptians for putting everything into writing. From about 2000 B.C. the existence of a general interest in the past is illustrated by the appearance of popular short stories, some of them about well-known historical personages. These could be wonderfully flexible and easy in style, showing sympathy, human understanding and humour. The most famous of all, the story of Sinuhe, was ancient; but at a much later date (in the region of 1100 B.C.) the narrative of The Voyage of Unamuno throws light on contemporary conditions and might well be an account of actual travels. It is the royal annals, however, which, in Egypt and elsewhere, seem to represent the climax of historical writing in the second millennium B.C. and even for some centuries afterwards. They gave the impression of emerging independently – evolving over again from the same kind of primitive beginnings – and in one after another of the pre-classical empires; and in all cases they seem to have been of mixed origin, their antecedents somewhat anomalous. They may take their rise in the dedicatory inscriptions attached to buildings. But there are also signs that they are regarded as reports made by rulers to the gods. An interesting feature of their development is the fact that they reach their maximum extension and their highest artistry when an empire comes to the climax of its military success.

In Egypt, the royal texts that are associated with the construction of buildings and the erection of statues illustrate the extravagant boasting which remained the permanent feature of the annals. A very wordy inscription, poetic in form, not long after the year 2000 B.C., commemorates the building of a temple in Heliopolis; and it illustrates a further feature of these Egyptian writings, namely, the inclusion of actual dialogue – in this case, the exchanges between the Pharaoh and his servants before the enterprise was begun. The Pharaoh, Sesostris I, speaks as follows:

... Behold, my majesty is executing a work,
And taking thought on an excellent matter.
For the future I will make a monument,
And set up an abiding stela for Harakhte.
He begat me to do that which he did,
To execute that which he commanded me to do,
He appointed me shepherd of this land. . . .
I conquered as a lad,
I was mighty in the egg,
As a child, before the swaddling-clothes were loosed for me,
He appointed me the lord of mankind. . . .
My fame has reached to the height of heaven.
I have established the offerings of the gods,
I will make a work, namely a great house,
For my father, Atum. . . .
My beauty shall be remembered in his house. . . .
The king whose achievements are talked about does not die.

A succeeding monarch, Sesostris III, a little later extended his territory
and erected a statue of himself at the new frontier. He told his sons that
this was 'in order that you might prosper because of it, and in order that you
might fight for it'. It would appear to be for the sake of his sons, therefore,
that he says in his inscription:

I have made my boundary beyond [that] of my fathers; I am a king who
speaks and executes; that which my heart conceives comes to pass by my
hand. . . . He is truly a craven who is repelled upon his border. . . . I
captured [the] women of the Nubians; I carried off their subjects; went
forth to their wells, smote their bulls. I reaped their grain and set fire to
it. As my father lives for me, I speak in truth. . . . Every son of mine who
shall maintain this boundary, he is my son. . . . As for him who will relax
it and not fight for it, he is not my son.

Some two hundred years later, it is Neferhotep who has something like
a constructional achievement to record the fashioning and the installation
of a new statue of Osiris. And because he is recounting a single piece of
story, he can be specific in the unfolding of it — anticipating that most
remarkable feature of the annals: the organic development of the single
episode. He describes the researches that he had to undertake in order to
discover the proper form to give to the statue: he enumerates the stages in
the accomplishment of the project; and he even summarises the things that
he said. His concluding speech runs as follows:

Be ye vigilant for the temple, look to the monuments which I have made.
[I] am the great king, great in strength, excellent in commandment. He

shall not live who is hostile to me, he shall not breathe the air who revolts against me. . . . They shall be cast out . . . [who do not] give me praise at every feast of the temple.

The really famous historical writings of ancient Egypt, however, are the things which are sometimes called 'campaign-annals' — a self-conscious attempt on the part of the Pharaohs to provide a report on what happened, sometimes year by year. At their best they are produced on a considerable scale, but their virtue will lie in the development of a single episode that is of human interest — a single piece of narrative remarkable for its particularity, its natural flow and its continuity. Here, as in some of the commemorative pieces already noted, there would be included even accounts of speeches that had been delivered and discussions that had taken place. One feels that something of the virtue of the Egyptian short story passed into the annals, when the best of these episodes was being recounted; for, taken as a whole, the rest of the reporting is not as satisfactory as might have been expected. There are one or two places where the lay-out of a battle can be reconstructed and the modern scholar can gain a notion of the strategy that was adopted; but only very rarely are the military events described in a way that will explain them; and the very full annals that cover a famous siege of Megiddo give no idea of the manner in which the victory was achieved. Sometimes it is not possible to be sure whether we are reading an account of a military expedition, or merely the circuit of a ruler into the lands of subject peoples for the receipt of homage or the collection of tribute. The boasting is extravagant, there are occasions when victory seems to be won because Pharaoh laid about him with his sword.

Such narratives would seem to be associated in some way with the exhilaration of military success; and not much of this existed in the region of the pre-classical empires for some time after the downfall of the first Dynasty of Babylon in the eighteenth century B.C. An important early example (or perhaps a precursor) of the annals comes at a famous moment in the history of Egypt, when, after the country had long suffered from the invasion and the predominance of the 'Asiatic' northerners — the famous 'Hyksos' régime — there emerged a monarch called Kamose, who, in about the year 1600 B.C. determined to make a fight for freedom. He gives the following account of the way in which he undertook the task :

In year 3 of the mighty king in Thebes, Kamose, whom Re had appointed as the real king, granting him power in very sooth, His Majesty spoke in his palace, to the council of the grandees who were in his suite : 'I should like to know what is the use of this power of mine, when there is a chieftain in Avaris and another in Cush and I sit together with an Asiatic and a Nubian, each of us in possession of his slice of Egypt. . . . No man has respite from this spoilation. . . . I will grapple with him and

slit open his belly. My desire is to deliver Egypt and smite the Asiatics.'
Then spoke the grandees of his council: 'See, all are loyal to the Asiatics
as far as Cusae. We are quiet in our part of Egypt. Elaphantine is strong
and the middle part of the country is ours as far as Cusae. The finest of
their fields are tilled for us. Our cattle pasture in the papyrus marshes.
Corn is sent for our swine. Our cattle are not taken away.'

The grandees clearly preferred a policy of cautious inaction, but Kamose
overrode their wishes; and he describes how he took his troops down-
stream, turning aside to deal with an Egyptian who was helping the
'Asiatics'.

I spent the night in my ship, my heart happy. When the earth became
light, I pounced upon him like a hawk. . . . I overthrew him; I razed his
wall; I slew his people.

He copies out for his readers a letter from one of the 'Asiatic' chieftains
to another, which he had intercepted. His story ends with his triumphant
return to his capital.

We may be inclined to underestimate the importance of the fact that
wars were so often commissioned by the gods. It may be a matter of significance also that some of the famous annals of Egypt explicitly describe
themselves as written for the gods. This is a point that must not be dismissed as a mere formality, if only because it helps to explain a peculiar
feature of these literary productions. They often disappoint us because they
deal so perfunctorily with the actual warfare, but then they will be amaz-
ingly detailed and specific in their account of the plunders taken. Much of
the booty would in fact be dedicated to the gods and temples – a point that
is significant on occasion in the Old Testament. There would be a call,
therefore, for something like a rendering of accounts. Sometimes the narrative of a campaign will in fact be a kind of preface to a list (or a ceremony)
of sacred offerings.

The victories of Kamose and his immediate successor led to the inaugura-
tion of the eighteenth dynasty in which the military successes of Egypt and
the artistry of the annals came to their climax. And a little over a hundred
years after the time of Kamose, perhaps the greatest of all the Egyptian
conquerors, Thutmose III, produced some of the most famous of all the
annals of this country. Even the oldest record of his first campaign, however
one which includes the well-known siege of Megiddo – is addressed to
the god, Amon Re, and might well have been simply the preface to a list
of offerings. The same is explicitly true of his fuller annals, where he opens
his account of his first campaign with a statement which reappears on other
occasions in these writings:

His Majesty commanded that a record of the victories which his father

Amon gave him should be placed in the temple (which) His Majesty made for him, setting forth each expedition by its name together with the plunder which [His Majesty carried away] . . . [it was done according to the command] given to him by his father, Re.

He then tells us explicitly that he undertook an expedition to extend the boundaries of Egypt, 'according as his father, Re, had commanded'. When he comes to the account of his third campaign he says :

I swear as Re [loves me and] as my father Amon favours me, all these things happened in truth : I have not presented fictitious things as things that happened to me. I have engraved the excellent deeds . . . from a desire to put them before my father, Amon, in the great temple of Amon [as] a memorial for ever and ever.

Towards the end of these annals, he provides another clue to his motives :

Behold, His Majesty ordered the recording of the victories which he won between the 23rd year of his reign, and the 42nd, when this inscription was placed in the sanctuary, that he might be given life for ever.

Mingled with all this, however, there must have been an interest in the reporting of contemporary history for the sake of the tale itself, and we know that, behind the annals themselves, there was some annotating of the things that happened, some collecting of data for the sake of the record. If we wish to know what really happened at the siege of Megiddo, for example, the annals tell us that 'all that His Majesty did to this city, to that wretched foe and his miserable army, was noted daily . . . [and is recorded] upon a roll of leather [kept] in the temple of Amon to this day'. In the case of the seventh campaign, there are goods furnished to the harbours, and the details of these 'remain in the daily registers of the palace' and are not reproduced in the annals themselves, 'in order not to multiply words'. Breasted points out that Thutmose spoke of 'recording for the future', and he quotes from the monument of an official called Thaneni, who tells us :

I followed the Good God, Sovereign of Truth, King of Upper and Lower Egypt, Menkkepere [Thutmose III]; I beheld the victories which he won in every country. . . . I recorded the victories which he won in every land, putting them into writing, according to the facts.

Thutmose's account of his first campaign possibly shows the Egyptian annals at their best. He mentions the anarchy that had fallen upon the 'Asiatics' and describes the tribes that had risen in rebellion against him. He tells us how, on the fourth day of the ninth month of the twenty-third year of his reign, he arrived in Gaza, departing on the following day with his army and reaching Yehem on the sixteenth of the month. He then 'ordered a consultation with his valiant troops', and told them how the

Prince of Kadesh and the chiefs of the other rebelling peoples had come to the city of Megiddo. The troops were anxious at the idea of having to travel on a narrow road, with the enemy lying in wait for them – their advance guard bearing the brunt of the fighting, while the rear would be out of action, far behind. Thutmose chose to keep to the narrow road, however, lest the enemy should think him afraid of them; and his troops followed him, though, later, they seem to have induced him to bring up his rear, so that all could be led into action.

> Then was set up the camp of His Majesty and command was given to the whole army, saying: '. . . Prepare your weapons, for we shall advance to fight with that wretched foe in the morning'. . . . The king rested in the royal tent, the affairs of the chiefs were arranged and the provisions of the attendants. The watch of the army went about saying 'Be steady of heart'. . . . Information was brought to His Majesty that 'the land is well and the infantry of the South and the North likewise'.
>
> Year 23, first [month] of the third season [ninth month], on the 21st day, the day of the feast of the new moon . . . early in the morning, behold, command was given to the entire army to move. . . . His Majesty went forth in a chariot of electrum, arrayed in his weapons of war, like Horus, the Smiter, lord of power; . . . while his father, Amon, strengthened his arms. The southern wing of this army of His Majesty was on a hill south of the [brook] of Arna, the northern wing was at the northwest of Megiddo, while His Majesty was in their centre, with Amon as the protection of his members. . . . Then His Majesty prevailed against them, they fled headlong to Megiddo in fear, abandoning their horses and their chariots of gold and silver. The people hauled them [up], pulling them up by their clothing, into this city. . . . Now if only the army of His Majesty had not given their heart to plundering the enemy's property, they would have [captured] Megiddo at this moment, when the wretched foe . . . were hauled up in haste. The fear of His Majesty had entered their hearts, their army was powerless.
>
> Then were captured their horses; their chariots of gold and silver were made spoil; their champions lay stretched out like fishes on the ground. The victorious army of His Majesty went around counting their portions.
> . . . His Majesty [said to them] 'Had ye captured this city . . . behold I would have given [very many offerings?] to Re this day; because every chief of every country that has revolted is within it; and because it is the capture of a thousand cities, this capture of Megiddo. Capture ye mightily.'

Thutmose enclosed the city with a wall, but he does not tell us what happened at the crucial moment, though he describes the surrender of the insurgent chiefs. He is more concerned to give an inventory of the booty –

'340 living prisoners; 83 hands; 2,041 mares', so many chariots, suits of armour, head of cattle, etc.

Another high moment in the series of Egyptian annals is reached early in the thirteenth century B.C., in the time of Rameses II, and here the interest must concentrate itself on another famous battle, that of Kadesh in about 1280 B.C. – a conflict with what are called the Khatti, the Hittites. The most successful piece of literature on this subject is part of an official record and represents an excellent example of limpid Egyptian story-telling of the kind which is essentially human in its appeal. As Rameses moved northwards with his troops, two men, who claimed to be connected with the greatest families amongst his enemies, came to say that their countrymen were willing to surrender, since the chief of the Khatti was skulking in Aleppo, afraid to meet the forces of Egypt. Rameses, therefore, marched ahead, until he learned from enemy scouts that he had been tricked – the chief of the Khatti, with all his allies (more numerous than the sands of the sea) were drawn up against him behind Kadesh, on the Orontes. They took the Egyptians by surprise, and Rameses and his bodyguard were left in the lurch through the retreat of his infantry and cavalry. 'I charged [the troops of] all [the] countries, my infantry [and] my cavalry having forsaken me,' says the Pharaoh. When further troops arrived, they were able to save the situation and claim a victory, though it would appear that Egyptians and Hittites soon came to a compromise.

There had long been extravagant hymns to successful Pharaohs, and victory poems – one to Thutmose III for example. But the battle of Kadesh seemed to call for epic treatment, and now – late in the day – Rameses was given the kind of celebration that could only be expressed in verse. In one of them, he reproaches the God, Amon, for neglecting him in his terrible predicament.

Have I done ought without thee? Have I not moved or stood still in accordance with thy command? I never swerved from the counsels of thy mouth. . . . What are these Asiatics to thee, Amon – wretches that know not god. Have I not fashioned for thee many monuments and filled thy temples with my captives? . . . I cause tens of thousands of oxen to be sacrificed to thee. No good thing do I leave undone in thy sanctuary.

He apostrophises also his own troops:

How faint-hearted ye are, my chariotry, and it is useless to trust in you. There is not one among you to whom I had not done good in my land. . . . I caused you to be notables and daily you partook of my sustenance. . . . I remitted to you your dues and gave to you other things that had been taken away from you. Whosoever came to me with a petition, I said at all times, 'Yea, I will do it'. Never has a lord done for his soldiers what I have done according to your desire, [for] I made you dwell in your houses and cities though you did no soldier's service. . . . But, behold, you all with one consent do a coward's deed; not one of you stands firm in order to give me his hand while I am fighting.

But, above all, the story of the battle of Kadesh, expanded in the annals at the point where Rameses is deceived by a ruse, has now become the epic of the single-handed encounter between the monarch and a host of 2,500 chariots. His own charioteer, who is at his side, loses heart, but according to one poem, he himself reports: 'I shoot on the right hand and I fight on the left. I am as Baal . . . I find that the 2,500 chariots in whose midst I stood now lie hewn before my steeds. . . . Their hearts are become faint in their bodies for fear.'

From this time the annals begin to decline in quality, for it seems to have become the convention to treat battles and victories in poetic style – indeed in poetry that is oriental in its figurativeness, and ruined by hyperbole. It has been suggested that the poetical handling of the battle of Kadesh may have had an unfortunate influence – in other words, when the epic spirit finally appeared, it spoiled the writing of history. No longer is there the continuous narrative which itself stands as a piece of exposition. From much of the extravaganza it becomes impossible to extract genuine information at all. In the annals of Rameses III, in the twelfth century B.C., we can vaguely make out the story of the defeat of invading forces, but it is necessary to know that 'the full flame' means the Egyptian fleet, and 'the wall of metal' means the Egyptian army. Rameses says:

I was prepared and armed to [trap] them like wild fowl. . . . I equipped my frontier in Zahi. . . . The chiefs, the captains of infantry, I caused to equip the harbour-mouths, like a strong wall, with warships, galleys and barges. They were manned from bow to stern with valiant warriors . . . like lions roaring on the mountain-tops. . . .

Those who reached my boundary, their seed is not. As for those who had assembled before them on the sea, the full flame was in their front, before the harbour-mouths, and a wall of metal upon the shore surrounded them. They were dragged, overturned and laid low on the beach; slain and made heaps from stern to bow on the galleys.

Elsewhere in these annals we have more poetical effusions:

Lo, the northern countries which are in their isles, are restless in their limbs; they infest the ways of the harbour-mouths. Their nostrils and their hearts cease breathing breath when His Majesty goes forth like a storm-wind against them. . . . Capsized and perishing in their places, their hearts are taken . . . and their weapons are cast out on the sea. His arrows pierce whomsoever he will among them, and he who is hit falls into the water. His Majesty is like an enraged lion, tearing him that confronts him with his hands.

Yet we have an opportunity of seeing how the same Rameses III could narrate the history of his reign when he was not constricted by the conventional form of the annals or the need to write in the epic style. The tremendous Papyrus Harris is a utilitarian document, produced at the end of his life – an inventory of the gifts and endowments that he had conveyed to the gods and temples – especially Amon in Thebes, Re in Heliopolis and Ptah in Memphis. A subordinate section of this document is an account of the history of his reign, and it shows that he could produce something like a work-a-day narrative. He begins by telling us that, at an early date:

Egypt was overthrown from without, and every man was deprived of his right. They had no chief mouth [no Pharaoh] for many years. . . . The land of Egypt was in the hands of chiefs and of rulers of towns; one slew his neighbour. . . . [Then] Yarsu, a certain Syrian became their chief. He set the whole land tributary before him. He joined his companions to plunder the possessions of the Egyptians. They [treated] the gods like [the] men and no offerings were presented in the temples.

He then describes how, 'when the gods inclined themselves to peace and to set the land right, according to its ancient manner', they appointed a Pharaoh who 'set in order the entire land, which had been rebellious' and 'established the temples in possession of divine offerings'. He himself, Rameses III, succeeded to the crown.

I made Egypt into many classes, consisting of butlers of the palace, great princes, numerous infantry and chariotry by the hundred thousand . . . attendants by the ten thousand, and serf-labourers of Egypt.

He tells how he 'extended the boundaries of Egypt' and overthrew invaders; 'slew the Deneu in their isles' and 'destroyed the people of Seir'; then 'laid low' the Libyans and the Mishevesh, 'who were dwelling in Egypt, having plundered the cities of the Western shore. He describes an expedition across the Red Sea for myrrh, another to copper-mines, probably in the Sinaitic peninsula, and another in quest of malachite. Then he writes:

I planted the whole land with trees and verdure, and I made people dwell in their shade. I enabled the women of Egypt to go . . . wherever they desired, [for] no stranger, nor anyone upon the road molested her. I made it possible for the infantry and chariotry to live [at home] in my time . . . [for] there was no enemy from Kush, [nor any] foe from Syria. Their bows and arrows reposed in their magazines while they lived in satisfaction and were drunk from joy . . . I took a man out of his misfortune and I gave him breath; I rescued him from oppressors more powerful than he. I set all men in security in their towns. . . .

The formality of the annals had clearly become something of an obstruction to historical writing, and better history could be produced outside the conventions of the commemorative tablet.

3 THE HITTITE ACHIEVEMENT

One of the surprises of the history of historiography – and one of the most interesting results of the researches of recent decades – has been the discovery of the significant position held by the Hittites in the literature of the subject, and the realisation of the sympathetic features of their life and thought. Thousands of their cuneiform tablets were unearthed in the first dozen years of the twentieth century at what proved to have been their capital, Boghazkeui, in the heart of Asia Minor; and when their language came to be deciphered, it ultimately proved to be Indo-European in its basis. Somewhere in the region of 2000 B.C., they invaded Asia Minor from the north, imposing their rule upon a pre-existing kingdom of Khatti (from which we derive the name that we give to them) – the original Khatti speaking a non-European language, and forming an important substratum of the population after the conquest of their country. By about 1800 B.C. the new Hittite régime extended itself over Asia Minor and began to undertake expeditions on a wider scale. One of these, in the eighteenth century B.C. – though it may have been only a highly ambitious raid – helped to put an end to the first dynasty of Babylon which we have already noted, the dynasty associated with the famous name of Hammurabi. There followed a chaotic period, both for Egypt and for the countries of Western Asia, in which the arts of civilisation, the production of inscriptions and the development of historical writing were to a serious degree suspended. But from about 1600 B.C. the Hittite monarchy was being reorganised; this was approximately at the time when Egypt, too, was expelling the 'Hyksos' and making its great recovery and its rise to empire. From 1385 B.C. the Hittite system – controlling a tremendous confederacy of vassal-states – was the great power in Western Asia. From about 1340 B.C. it had a ruler, Murshilish II, who was one of the imposing monarchs of the ancient world. Through his activities in the west of Asia he made contact with the *Akhkivavâ*; and these were presumably the Achaeans. In other words, he touched some settlement of the Greeks.

Once again, the climax of political and military success seems to have been attended by a remarkable development in the compilation of royal annals; and those of Murshilish II possess features which give them a special place in the history of the *genre*. No doubt it is a judgement of their quality which has induced some scholars to regard the Hittites as the real founders of historiography. So far as annalistic writing is concerned, the work of Murshilish is not quite so ancient as that of Thutmose III in Egypt, which we have noted. Royal autobiography has even its analogies and precedents in Western Asia; for a 'grotesquely ugly' statue of Idri-mi of Alalakh, in an inscription which runs across arms and shoulders and even down one side of the beard and whiskers, gives an account of the way in which this ruler, round about the year 1400, was driven into exile for seven years and then managed to assert his rights. The writings of Murshilish II come rather later than this – and there may be other pieces of this kind still awaiting discovery – but they are anterior to the famous Assyrian annals, which, at a still later date, were only at the crude beginnings of their development. At this point, the Hittite historiography may have influenced the Assyrian.

The work of Murshilish exists in two forms – an account for the first ten years of his reign (called the Decennial) and the Complete Annals, which in fact are more detailed, more picturesque and in some respects wider in scope. For certain periods both narratives survive, but for the very beginning the text of the Decennial must be used:

The following are the words of the Sun-[God] Murshilish, the Great King, the monarch of Khatti, the hero, [Son of Shup]iluliuma, the Great King and hero. I had hardly succeeded to the throne of my father when the hostile neighbouring countries came out as my enemies. As soon as my father became a god [i.e. died] Arnuandash, my brother, took the throne of his father; but then he became ill. And when the hostile countries heard that Arnuandash, my brother was ill, they took to war against him.

When Arnuandash, my brother, became a god, however, even these hostile countries which had not risen against him took to war. These hostile neighbours said: 'His father, who ruled us as King of Khatti – he was a monarch of heroic stature. He prevailed over enemy countries. But then he became a god. His son, who succeeded to the throne of his father, was also a war-hero but then he, too, became ill, and now he himself has become a god. The one who now sits on his father's throne is a mere child. He will not be able to hold Khatti and its [territories].'

Because my father was left in the Mitanni land so long, his return was delayed and he could not keep the festival of Arinna, the Sun-goddess, my Lady.

However, when I, the Sun, succeeded to the throne of my father, my hostile neighbours having started war against me, I did not move against any of my enemies until I had taken care of the overdue festival of the Sun-goddess, Arinna, my Lady, and I celebrated her. To the Sun-goddess,

Arinna, my Lady, I lifted my hand, and I spoke in the following manner: 'Sun-goddess, Arinna, my Lady, the hostile lands round about have despised my smallness, and over and over again they have striven to capture your provinces, Sun-goddess, Arinna.

Come down to me, Sun-goddess, Arinna, my Lady, and drive my hostile neighbours before me.'

And the Sun-goddess, Arinna, heard my cry and came down to me.

And I was victorious, after I had set myself on the throne of my father; and the surrounding enemy countries I broke in ten years.

The passage is typical of Murshilish in that its constant reference to the deity does not prevent him from clearly describing a political problem and a human situation, the total result being a self-standing story, which could in fact dispense with mythology. Murshilish is often perfunctory in his military narrations – ready to say that the Sun-goddess and the Weather-god gave him the victory – but he is interested in political action, and he presents the whole conjuncture; also he is particularly concerned to describe the considerations on which human beings adopt one policy or another. In this particular case he sees the subject-peoples of the empire ready to take advantage of his own youth and of his family's misfortunes. It is possible that he sees his kingdom suffering because the festival of the Sun-goddess had been neglected. He likes to show the motives on which he himself takes action – even to explain how another policy, which he might have been expected to adopt, would have been less satisfactory. To achieve his purpose, he inserts speeches and gives the gist of documents – quotes offers of help, offers of submission, military discussions, reports from agents and spies. He does not merely itemise events and actions after the manner of a chronicle, but draws them together, sees casual relationships and achieves continuity. The annals, therefore, carry a good deal of explanation; and if in a sense they may have been reports to the gods, that purpose seems submerged in the sheer concern for the telling of a story. Numbers of people must have been intended either to read the annals or hear them recited, and at one point Murshilish addresses his audience, saying: 'You, who are listening to [the reading of] these tablets, send somebody to look at this city of Ura and see how it is laid out.' Perhaps Hittite historiography is affected by the fact that the monarch is not by any means a solitary tyrant, but more like an overlord, limited by institutions and needing the support of some sort of public opinion. Constantly he feels the need to explain his actions and policies; and, surprisingly often, he effects his exposition by narrating a piece of history. As somebody has said, he presents himself not as a proud and remote autocrat but as a 'hard-working, battle-begrimed feudal King'. In the annals there is not the boasting which fills up so much of the space in the Egyptian and Assyrian equivalents. Failures are confessed. And not merely the campaigns of the monarchs but those also of princes and generals are described.

The following is a passage from the Complete Annals of Murshilish:

Manapa-Dattash, who had driven his brother out of his land
   and whom I had recommended to the Karkishäer people,
   and moreover I had given him the Karkishäer country – this Manapa-Dattash
   did not come to serve on my side. And when Uhha-Lú-Ish began to make war on me, he became the partisan of Uhha-Lu-Ish. So I, the Sun went to the Sehu River.
   As soon as Manapa-Dattash, son of Muwa-Ur-Mah heard that I, the Sun was
   coming, he sent a messenger to me and wrote to me as follows: 'My Lord, do not kill me; take me as a vassal; and the refugees who come to me I will surrender unto my lord.' I, however, answered him as follows:
   'Once, when you drove your brother out of your land, I recommended you to the Karkishäer people.
   Furthermore, I gave you the Karkishäer land. But in spite of this
   you did not come to fight on my side. On the side of my enemy, Uhha-Lu-Ish did
   you fight. And now shall I accept you as my vassal?' I should in fact have
   moved against him and destroyed him, but he sent his mother
   to me. And she came and fell at my feet, and she spoke as follows: 'Lord of ours,
   do not destroy us; accept us, Lord, as vassals.' And because it was a woman who
   came to me and fell at my feet, I welcomed her and decided not to go to
   the land of the Seha River. Then I returned to the land of Mirā and I put the land of Mirā in order. Then I built Arshani, Sharawa and Impa
   and fortified them, and occupied them with garrison troops. After that I established Mashhuiluwash
   in the lordship of Mirā and I spoke in the following manner to Mashhuiluwash: 'You, Mashhuiluwash,
   Came as a refugee to my father; and my father adopted you,
   and made you his son-in-law and gave you Muwattish, his daughter,
   my sister, in marriage. But he was not in a position to look after you then,
   and he could not fight for you against your enemy. Now I have built cities
   and fortified them and occupied them with garrison troops.

And I have established you in the lordship of Mirā.'
Furthermore I gave him 600 men as his personal guard
and spoke in the following manner to him: 'Because the people of
Mirā are wicked, These 600 men shall be your personal guard. You shall
have no truck with the people of Mirā
and you shall not enter into conspiracy against me.'

Perhaps not in chronology, but logically beyond a doubt, it is the Hittites
who come nearest to the ancient Jews, bringing us in some ways to the brink
of the Old Testament, while in some ways they seem to stand closer than
anybody to the ancient Greeks. They learned the art of writing and drew
much of their mythology from Mesopotamia, taking over (amongst other
things) the Sumerian epic of Gilgamesh. Translations from the Akkad
language of Mesopotamia played an important part in the development of
their culture, and from the same tradition they caught a certain sense for
history, including apparently a love of the epic and a desire to connect themselves in a similar way with the epic tradition. Here, as in Mesopotamia
itself, the history and the legends of Sargon and Naram-Sin seemed to
acquire a special importance; and scholars speak of the existence of early
writings that stand half-way between epic or legend and actual history.
They seem not to have produced the cuneiform royal inscriptions and the
King-Lists which are familiar in Mesopotamia, so that, down to a certain
date, it is not easy to be sure of the succession of their rulers. They interested
themselves somewhat in the historical moralising for which the priests of
Babylon had set an example, but almost a speciality of theirs was the
historical 'cautionary tale' – the historical example used to point a warning
– and they appear to have produced collections of such anecdotes. Scholars
have tended to be carried further and further back in their search for the
antecedents of the historical work of Murshilish II. Some of them would
go as far as the Anitta-inscription of the eighteenth century B.C., and would
see in it remarkable signs of the narrative art. Though it exists only in an
imperfect state, it speaks as from the ancient Khatti people rather than the
Hittites themselves, and it was produced at so early a date that it could only
have been written in the old Assyrian language. We are on surer ground
with an Instruction issued in about the year 1600 B.C. by King Telipinish.
This ruler began the restoration of the monarchy after a period of disorder
at about the time when Khamose in Egypt attacked the 'Hyksos' and so
inaugurated a great development also in his country. The proclamation of
Telipinish seems to have been part of his attempt to re-establish authority
amongst the Hittites, for its purpose was to regulate the succession and put
a stop to palace revolutions. It was itself, however, a kind of expansion of
the 'cautionary tale', and its remarkable feature was a preamble not merely
narrating recent events but surveying a considerable period of Hittite

history. For this purpose it partly used a previously-existing chronicle which has also come to light. It is an interesting example, therefore, of a specific call on recorded history for the public explanation of an act of royal policy. Concerning one important predecessor of his, Telipinish writes as follows:

When Murshilish [I] reigned in [the Hittite capital] he was surrounded by his sons, brothers, blood-relations, marriage-connections and troops; and he held the hostile countries down by the might of his strong arm, and kept the land in order, extending it till it reached the sea.

And he went to Aleppo and destroyed it bringing prisoners and their property back to [his own capital]. After that, however, he marched to Babylon . . . and carried prisoners and property from there to [his capital].

And Chantilish was the vizier and he had married Murshilish's sister, Charapshulish.

Then Zidantash worked on Chantilish and they did a bad thing, killing Murshilish and starting a bloodbath. [The broken text seems to tell how Chantilish took the throne.]

Then, as Chantilish was getting old and near to death, Zidantash killed his son [Pishenish] and also this man's sons, and put to death his chief servant.

And Zidantash became king.

From about the year 1400 B.C. we see an interesting extension of this use of history as an introduction to a policy document and as an explanation of governmental action. The treaties of the Hittites – and particularly those with vassal-states – differ from all the others of the time that are known to us in that they are preceded by a very considerable historical preamble. These were not perfunctory in character, and it has been noted that, when a renewed conflict led to a further treaty, the old historical summary was not mechanically taken over as the basis of the new preamble, but a fresh narrative was produced. Also, the other party to the treaty seems to have been allowed to insert his own version of the history in his own copy of the document. In other words, he was not forced to subscribe to what his successful enemy chose to regard as the story of the origin of the trouble – not compelled (somebody has said) to sign a war-guilt clause, like the one imposed on Germany after the end of the First World War. These preambles are so specific and they so illustrate the pragmatic and expository character of Hittite historical writing, that it may be useful to see, as an example, the narrative in the treaty between Murshilish II and Manapa-Dattash which confirms the King's account in the Complete Annals:

Thus speaks Murshilish, the Sun, the Great King, ruler of the Khatti land: You, Manapa-Dattash, were left by your father [as a minor]

When you were still a boy; [and Gal-Dattash] and Ura-Dattash, your
brothers, sought on many occasions to kill you.
[And they] would in fact have killed you [but you] took flight
and you went over to the people of the Kar [kishäer country];
and they took the lands and the houses of your father away from you,
capturing them for themselves. [I, the Sun, however, recommended you,
    Manapa-Dattash],
to the people of Kar[kasha] and on many occasions sent
the people of Kar[kasha] a gift; and my brother called to the gods on
    your account;
and the people [of Karkasha] took care of you at our desire.
When, [however,] Gal-Dattash came and broke his oath
the gods who were guarantors of the oath deserted him and the people
of the Seha-River land drove him out.
    They allowed you to remain there at our command, however, and at
our command they took care of you.
Then when my brother [Arnwandash] became a god
I, the Sun, set myself on the throne of my father
and I took trouble for your sake.
I made the people of the Seh-River land do homage to you
and they defended you at my command . . .
When, however, [Uhha-Lu-Ish, the King of Arzawa] came against the
    Sun,
making war on him, you, Manapa-Dattash,
sinned against the Sun, and put yourself
    behind Uhha-Lu-Ish, my enemy.
I, the Sun, went to war and you did not
    fall in behind me.
But as I went into action against Uhha-Lu-Ish
and against the people of Arzawa
who had broken his oath to me,
the gods, guarantors of the oath, turned
    against him, and I, the Sun,
smote him to the ground. And because you had
    put yourself on the side of Uhha-Lu-Ish,
I might have smitten you to the ground in
    the same way; but you put yourself at
    my feet
and you sent old men and women to me
and your messengers fell down at my feet
and you sent the following message to me,
    'My Lord, spare my life,
and smite me not to the ground

take me into your service and defend
  my person;
and I will deliver to you the prisoners of
the land of Mirā, the refugees from Khatti,
and the refugees from the Arzawa country
  who have come over to me.'
And I, the Sun, bestowed my grace upon you
and gave you my favour and accepted you
  as a friend . . .
. . . If you fulfil all these conditions
  I will take you into my service
and you shall be befriended by me.
  And for the future, the following shall
be the terms of your treaty with me . . .

It is now clear that Murshilish II was not the first Hittite king to produce annals, and in 1957 there was disovered a set by Hattushilish I which belongs to the first half of the sixteenth century B.C. It was written in the Akkadian language and was later translated into the Hittite tongue by Murshilish II himself. Some of the successors of Murshilish also produced annals, but one of the most remarkable of the literary productions of the empire – work of somewhat the same kind – is the 'Autobiography' or 'Apology' of Hattushilish III in the early part of the thirteenth century B.C. His story appears in three versions: first of all a short one in the document in which he expresses his gratitude to the goddess Ishtar by instituting endowments on her behalf and establishing an hereditary priest-hood through one of his sons. A longer version is more apologetic in character. Then, thirdly, there is a further narrative, in a document which confers privileges on the family of Middanuvas, a former chancellor who had helped this ruler.

When Murshilish died he had been succeeded by his son Muvatallis, the brother of Hattushilish with whom he remained on good terms. When Muvatallis died, however, Hattushilish, though he had been a powerful governor under him, did not claim the throne for himself but established the man's son, his own nephew, Urhi-U-as, as king. The young man, jealous of his power, began to turn against him, however, and he felt sufficiently provoked to go to war, in which he claims to have been assisted by the gods, the elder statesman Middanuvas and the chief vassal-lords. The upshot was that he himself acquired the throne; but he evidently recognised that his conduct would be open to misinterpretation, and it is interesting to see that he felt it useful to explain himself, behaving as though it were necessary to conciliate public opinion as well as to account for his conduct to the gods. The quality of the apologetic is the remarkable feature of the work, for it must have owed its success to its moderation, and it showed greater subtlety than is often seen in the propaganda of modern governments. It is carefully factual, and possibly one can presume that, since many of its readers must have lived through the events in question, it will not have departed too radically from the truth. Hattushilish does not even attack his nephew in an unreasonable way; indeed he defends him on occasion – defends him perhaps on secondary matters, while reserving his ammunition for the main issue. He seems to take care not simply to overwhelm his enemies with insults. In a sense, he even exonerates his nephew at the finish and puts the blame on heaven – it was a young man's god who led him astray. To a modern reader he seems far-fetched in the way in which he depicts himself as the favourite of the goddess. But in this he is only like Murshilish II, and he may have had special reason for this, for it would seem that he had been a sickly creature in his youth. He, too, had had the feeling that the recovery of his fortunes was a special sign of divine grace.

Some people have been tempted to think that, because Hittite historical writing is often so factual and objective, it must be in general more secular in character, more remote from religious preoccupations. Yet the very documents in question have puzzled some scholars because they so often bring the gods into the story and they seem so sincere in their piety. They are in some respects like the historiography of a thousand years earlier; for the due service to the deity is essential, the gods are consulted before anything is done, and victory will be ascribed to heaven. And, once again, this is perhaps the reason why battles were dismissed in brief stereotype phrases. Perhaps there was no point in describing a battle where the freaks of chance, the incalculability of the issue, so often made the supernatural explanation the most feasible one, especially as war was regarded as in itself a holy thing, fought on behalf of the god – the declaration of war being worded as appeals to the divine judgment – and victory itself as the proof of the righteousness of one's cause. In keeping with all this, treaties were placed particularly under the guarantee of the gods, who would be enumerated by name in the text. Yet, amongst the Hittites, it almost seems as if the religion itself has already become spiritualised to a certain degree. In the histories, the gods do not make a physical entry, a mythological appearance – they operate through such things as the dream or the oracle. Perhaps the royal annalist goes no further than the Elizabethans did when they said that God blew the winds and the enemy was scattered. In the writings of Hattushilish III one seems to have a glimpse of the conception of Providence.

The Hittite historiography is of still further interest to us because of its moral implication; for the people of Khatti had a profounder ethical sense – and were more inclined to connect ethics with religion or with the gods – than the people of Mesopotamia. In some respects they seem to show an advance in the debate between men and gods on moral issues; so that here again, at times, they seem to bring us to the edge of the Old Testament. They inherited the Mesopotamian view that human misfortune came as a judgement upon an offence committed against the gods. Even so, they were ready to wrestle with the gods, as the people of Mesopotamia did, since sometimes it seemed that heaven was not playing fair. In an engaging manner, they could point out to the gods why it was proper to pardon on occasion, and how even a human lord would be willing to pardon a slave, once he had confessed his sin and shown contrition. When they were excusing themselves, they were capable of making the point that, in fact, all men are sinners. And it is interesting to see that one of the most famous of the Great Kings could note in a diplomatic letter, 'We are only men', and then make dispositions for the eventuality of his death.

The Hittites were aware, of course, that the sins of the fathers were visited upon the children to the third and fourth generations. But they found it hard to reconcile themselves to the fact that a king who had committed an offence might be allowed to live a happy and successful life, the punishment falling on his descendants, who had been innocent of crime, had not known that it had been committed, and only discovered its nature after appealing to the oracle to learn what the gods were angry about. Telepinish, when trying to deal with the problem of palace-revolution, had said that a traitor must suffer death, but he thought that the man's children and servants ought to be spared. Murshilish II had refrained from punishing the family of a culprit, though he would have had the right to punish.

It was Murshilish himself who most came to grips with this question in four prayers connected with an outbreak of plague in his country. An extraordinary parallel to this story is found hundreds of years later in the Old Testament, this time in connection with a famine which the Lord tells David is due to his predecessor Saul having broken an oath (2 *Samuel*, XXI, 1–9).

The plague had begun in the time of Murshilish's father, Shuppiluliuma, and had lasted for twenty years. Murshilish was anxious to discover its cause, and found a tablet which provided him with a clue. Then he consulted the oracle, which confirmed the fact that here was the serious offence that had been committed. The Hittites had broken an oath which they had taken before their own Storm-God in connection with a treaty; for under Shuppiluliuma they had attacked Egyptian territory, which they had engaged not to do. Incidentally, Murshilish seems to have come to the conclusion that the plague had been brought into the country by Egyptian prisoners captured in another war, and had then spread by contagion. It was evidently a serious matter, for it carried off a great deal of the population, including priests; and Murshilish warned the gods that they would find themselves without food if the catastrophe went on. He was ready to confess the sin, and he made offerings to the gods; also he showed the genuine contriteness which was regarded as necessary. It was considered possible to alter the purposes of the gods by prayer, and this would sometimes be done in writing. The four different prayers of Murshilish show that, as one scholar has pointed out, it was useful to make varied approaches in prayer, just as it might be useful for a man on trial to have a number of advocates. It is perhaps possible that Murshilish had been himself unfair in one respect; for it would seem that his father, Shuppiluliuma, had made sacrifices in atonement for his sin, while the Hittites – the men of Khatti – who had been involved in the guilt, had failed to do so. Shuppiluliuma's death may even have been held as his expiation for another sin, which was involved in the same episode. The occasion brought the controversy between men and gods to a climax, for the anguish of Murshilish was very great.

It has been noted sometimes that the Hittites were milder in their laws than the surrounding peoples – milder than even the famous Babylonian lawgiver, Hammurabi, or than the ancient Israelites. They seem to have disliked mutilation and the death penalty, though they have been accused of undue laxity in regard to sexual matters. Most remarkable of all is their insistence on the ethical nature of the dealings that took place between heads of government – the way in which they moralise on international relations in both their annals and their treaties. One story after another clearly deals with the ethics of a recent war, setting out the issue in order to show the rights and wrongs of the case. And the treaties with vassal-princes perpetually harp on the generosity of the monarchy – perpetually appeal to the principle of gratitude. These treaties are explicitly described on one occasion as unilateral – they place obligations on the vassal rather than the overlord. But the historical preambles are an account of benefits bestowed already by the latter, and it is in return for these, and in the hope of more, that the vassal makes his promises. Scholars have been showing of late that the Old Testament 'covenant', including the great 'covenant' between God and the children of Israel, is closely modelled on the type of treaty that the Hittites concluded, and here again the motive is gratitude – the things that Yahweh has done in history constitute the basis for the claim to loyalty. It has been argued that the references to the ethical issue in the annals and the talk of gratitude, the harping on moderation, in the peace treaties may only have been a pretence, or that the merciful pose may have been a device to cover political weakness. Even if this were the case, the habit of issuing this kind of propaganda, or even of presenting this kind of self-excuse, is one of the amazing features of the ancient history of Western Asia. It stands in striking contrast to the cruelty and the bullying of the Assyrian monarchs many centuries later. It would seem that the Hittite monarchs were either inclined to mildness, or, being too weak to be vindictive, had a splendid way of making virtue of necessity. Repeatedly we read of the restoration of vassal-princes who had been rebellious or delinquent and had been defeated.

Gurney, in his book on the Hittites, quotes an interesting passage in one of the treaties of Shuppiluliuma. It seems that part of the territory of this monarch had broken away and had submitted to the neighbouring Hurrians. Shuppiluliuma had demanded the return of this land, but the Hurrians had refused to oblige him – they had followed the wishes of the inhabitants, for, they said, 'The cattle have chosen their own stable'. Gurney calls attention to this as the first statement in history of the principle of 'self-determination'. Shuppiluliuma continued the argument, however, and said to the Hurrians : 'If some country seceded from you and went over to the land of Khatti [the Hittite realm], how would that be?' The Hurrians showed themselves consistent – they still said that the cattle should choose their own stable. 'But now,' says Shuppiluliuma, 'here are the people of Kizzu-watua – they have done just this thing. The Hurrians are made to keep to their principle. The people of Kizzuwatua must stay with the Hittites, as they desire.' It is this way of reasoning about international affairs, and confronting the other party with reason – this insistence on the expository method – which marks Hittite historiography as well as Hittite international policy.

4 MESOPOTAMIA

In Mesopotamia, men did not indulge in bright dreams of heaven after the manner of the Egyptians, but brooded darkly upon the nether-world to which all the dead were doomed – a world of grime and misery. The epic of Gilgamesh had shown that the greatest of heroes – even when one of his parents was divine – could not in fact achieve immortality. The fact that he had held the secret of it for a moment, and then let it slip, had only added to the desolation of it. Religion itself seemed to become more earth-bound as a result; and, instead of being the stimulus to great architecture, as in Egypt, the graves in this part of the world were kept unpretentious and low. Here, the nearest equivalent to the pyramid – the Zigurrat – was not a burial place at all. And there was much less impulse for the production of the lengthy funerary inscriptions so common in Egypt.

A separate kingdom of Assyria had been established in the nineteenth century B.C., and it had asserted its independence of Babylon, which had dominated the whole of Mesopotamia. It developed considerably in the fourteenth century, becoming a power, and acquiring the ascendancy over the whole country. Once again, the exhilaration of military success was accompanied by the development of annals, which had their crude beginning at this time. There had already been inscriptions to commemorate the building and rebuilding of temples, and these would be accompanied by a curse against those who should destroy the memorial or blot out the name of the royal benefactor. In the fourteenth century, however, there appeared an inscription of Arik-Dîn-Ilu, which contained disconnected notes about his military successes. In about 1300 B.C. his son, Adad-Nirâri, described himself as

> illustrious prince . . . city-founder, destroyer of the mighty hosts of Kassites, Kutî, Lulumî, and Schubarî; who destroys all foes north and south; who tramples their lands from Lubda and Rapiku to Eluhat; who captures all peoples, enlarges his boundaries and frontiers . . . conquerer of the lands of Turuki and Nigemhi in their totality.

It was in this manner that, both then and later, a monarch would interpolate a description of himself in the dedications that he would attach to the buildings he had had erected. This man's son, Shalmaneser I, in about 1280 B.C., produced the earliest surviving account of Assyrian military operations which was specific enough to stand as a piece of history. The following section of his inscription can be taken as the nucleus or the basic pattern of the Assyrian campaign annals, which greatly expanded the various parts of it.

> At that time . . . the land of Uruadri rebelled, and to Assur and the great gods, my lords, I raised my hands in prayer. I mobilised my armies, went up against their mountain-fastnesses . . . eight countries with their forces I conquered. Fifty-one of their cities I captured and burned. I seized their property as booty. The whole land of Uruadri I brought within three days into submission at the feet of Assur, my lord. Their young men I selected and took for my service. Heavy tribute . . . for all time I imposed on them.

Then, in about 1100 B.C., Tiglath-Pileser I, 'the mighty king, king of the universe', produced lengthy annals in the grand style.

It is generally held that the Assyrian annals developed out of inscriptions which celebrated or dedicated a new building, and which would naturally add a short account of the royal founder. This interpolated piece of description might grow to an inordinate length, and it would acquire independent existence through the ultimate lopping-away of what had once been the essential part of the text. In any case, some of the long narratives of campaigns are found to be connected with the erection of a commemorative building, or they may have been occasioned by a thanksgiving ceremony. The question whether they were influenced in their development by the Hittite annals, which came earlier, is a matter of speculation.

It has been pointed out that there were Assyrian kings who wrote letters to gods rather in the way that any agent, any head of a mission, might communicate with his principal. In one such letter that survives, the monarch has to confess that, as yet, he has not carried out the work committed to him. There exists a letter from a god which seems to be an answer to a royal report of this kind. The suggestion has been made that the Assyrian annals might simply be expansions of these letters to gods – that in fact they may have been addressed to the deity, the announcement of military victory being a form of thanksgiving. And in the case of the Hittite monarch Hattushilish III, an account originally addressed to a goddess was in fact expanded into something like annalistic form at a later time, as we have already seen. We are asked to believe, therefore, that if the boasting in the Assyrian annals is more bombastic than anything else in the whole of world literature, this is not to be taken as an example of self-pride. In reality, it is the god who is being congratulated; and a writer naturally lays it on thick when he is congratulating a god. If one looks at these Assyrian annals, however, one finds Adad Nirâri II saying: 'I am royal, I am lordly, I am mighty, I am honoured, I am exalted, I am glorified, I am all-powerful, I am brilliant, I am lion-brave, I am manly, I am supreme.' Tiglath-Pileser, after each year of his annals, inserts what he calls a paean, a wildly ejaculatory hymn of praise; but it is addressed to Tiglath-Pileser, 'the valiant hero . . . the burning flame . . . the terrible one . . . who humbles all the mighty'. It is all very far removed from the writings of those earlier monarchs who, in their accounts of wars, so often kept themselves out of the picture, and merely reported that their god had prevailed over the enemy. In spite of their references to the deities, the Assyrian annals are surprisingly secular in tone. It is difficult to believe that they were not intended to impress and over-awe human beings.

The annals do not come to a climax, however, until Assyria becomes a great imperial power – that is to say, from the ninth century B.C., which brings us to the very heart of Old Testament times. They are developed with tremendous literary artifice, but they are monumental in character; they declare and declaim the doings of the king, but only at the rarest moments do they attempt the establishment of human contact with the reader. They are almost always purely narrative in character, therefore, and, though the narrative at its very best can also become explanation, there are very few occasions on which the author of the annals adopts the expository manner. Those who are out to trumpet the triumphs of a god or the feats of a king are not easily induced to ask about the way in which things happen in history. The annals manage to recapitulate events without communicating much enlightenment, therefore, except when, in their greatest period, their author becomes intent on their literary effect, and he – like others whom we have encountered – forgets his purpose and loses himself in the desire to tell a story.

The form of the annals remains remarkably consistent. There are cases where they open with a long passage, calling upon a whole succession of gods: 'Assur, the great lord, ruler of the gods, bestower of sceptre and crown, who established sovereignty; Enlil, the lord, the king of all the Anunnaki . . . ; Sin, the wise, lord of the lunar disc . . .' etc. etc. Always, however – and, most generally, first of all – there will be a long and flowery description of the monarch himself, and, perhaps, of some of his ancestors. 'Shalmaneser, prefect of Bêl, priest of Assur, viceroy of the gods, favourite prince of Ishtar, who . . . founder of splendid cities . . . awe-inspiring despot . . . shepherd of all peoples . . . warrior, mighty in battle, who burns up the enemy . . . who bursts forth like a flame of fire . . .' etc. etc.

Often there is no attempt to deal with the politics of a war, and the annals will give no reason for the opening of a campaign, or will merely say that the ruler marched out his army 'at the command of Assur'. The fuller and better annals will be more specific, however, though, as in all this kind of literature, the cause of a war tends to be simply a story about the wicked men of the other party. Of his first campaign, Sennacherib writes as follows:

At the beginning of my reign . . . Merodach-Baladan, [subordinate] king of Babylonia (whose heart is wicked), an instigator of revolt, plotter of rebellion, doer of evil, whose guilt is heavy, brought over to his side Shutur-Nahunden, the Elamite, and gave him gold, silver and precious stones, and [so] secured him as an ally. . . . He gathered together the cities of . . . the lands of . . . all the Chaldeans . . . the tribes of . . . and marshalled them for the fight.

To me, Sennacherib, whose heart is exalted, they reported these evil deeds. I raged like a lion and ordered a march into Babylonia against him.

Of his third campaign, he writes:

The officials, nobles and people of Ekron, had thrown Padû, their king (bound by treaty to Assyria) into fetters of iron, and had given him over to Hezekiah, the Jew – he kept him in confinement like an enemy. They became afraid and called upon the Egyptian kings, the bowmen, chariots and horses of the king of Meluhha [Ethiopia], a countless host; and these came to their aid.

In the neighbourhood of . . . they offered battle.

In connection with his first campaign, Assurbanipal tells us how his father had defeated Tarkû, king of Egypt and Ethiopia, and had made him his vassal. Tarkû, however, 'forgot the power of Assur, Ishtar and the great gods, my lords, and trusted in his own strength'. He turned against 'the kings and governors whom my father had installed in Egypt', marched into the country and 'established himself in Memphis, the city which my father had captured and added to the territory of Assyria. A swift courier came to Nineveh and reported [this] to me.' These annals of Assurbanipal, which came at a later date (in the seventh century B.C.), enlarge greatly upon the political exchanges that preceded a war – the interplay of personalities and the machinations of enemies – particularly the troubles in Egypt and the misbehaviour of his brother whom he had set up as a subordinate king in Babylon. The latter was in fact brought to ruin first of all by the devastations of a plague decreed and predicted by the gods. At times, therefore, we seem to be dealing not with military annals, but with something nearer to the springs of history.

The thing about which the annals are most specific is the journey to the field of battle, and often, at this point, they give a long factual recital, without explanation. We might have no clues as to the meaning of the campaign itself, though the king might tell us where he spent every night – a thing which Adad-Nirâri at a fairly early date gives in nutshell form: 'In my march I kept to the bank of the Habur. In Arnabani I spent the night ... into Shadîn I entered. Tribute and tax and a chariot of gold I received. From Shadîn I departed. In Kasiri I spent the night . . .' etc. etc. This form of daily enumeration soon came to be greatly expanded. It seems to have given special pleasure to the annalist to describe mountain journeys. Sennacherib tells us that, on his fifth campaign,

> I had my camp pitched at the foot of Mount Nippur, and, with my picked bodyguard and my relentless warriors, I like a strong wild-ox led the way.
> Gullies, mountain-torrents and waterfalls, dangerous cliffs, I surmounted in my sedan-chair. Where it was too steep for my chair I advanced on foot. Like a young gazelle, I mounted the high[est] peaks in pursuit of [the enemy]. Whenever my knees gave out, I sat down on some mountain-boulder and drank the cold water from my water-skin [to quench] my thirst. . . . Before my day, none of the kings who ever lived before me had travelled the unblazed trails and wearisome paths which [stretch] along these rugged mountains.

Picturesque accounts exist also of the journeys down rivers, and Sennacherib, writing about his sixth campaign, says, for example:

> Hittite people [by which he means Syrians], the plunder of my bow, I settled in Nineveh. Mighty ships [after] the workmanship of their land they built dexterously. Tyrian, Sidonian and Cyprian sailors, captives of my hand, I ordered to descend the Tigris with them and come to the wharves at Opis . . . they dragged them on sledges [?] to the Arahta Canal [?]. They launched them . . . [I had] my bodyguard of picked foot soldiers, my brave warriors . . . I embarked them in ships and provided supplies for the journey, together with grain and straw for the horses, which I embarked with them. My warriors went down the

Euphrates on the ships while I kept to the dry land at their side. I had
[them] proceed to Bâb-Salimeti. . . . In that place I pitched my camp. The
mighty waves of the sea came up and entered my tent. And they
completely surrounded me while [I was] in my camp, causing all my
men to remain in the mighty ships as in cages for five days and nights.
The ships of my warriors reached the swamps at the mouth of the river
where the Euphrates empties its waters into the fearful sea. I met them on
the shores of the Bitter Sea [the Persian Gulf].

On these journeys the interesting incidental things would occur, and, at
the height of the literary development of the annals, the writer seems to
recognise the interest that they will arouse. Casual happenings will make
the story vivid, as when Sennacherib tells us 'Severe weather set in, uninter-
rupted rains came on, and snow. I was afraid of the swollen mountain-
streams and turned back and took the road to Assyria.' All this is picturesque
and stands as travel story rather than military history; and even when the
battle actually takes place, the annals will break out into hyperbole, giving
no clue to the actual course of events. Battles are in fact mythological occasions and it does not matter whether the victory is a feat of the gods or is
something in the realm of the fabulous achieved by man. Sennacherib himself, when he comes to the actual clash of arms, will declare: 'I raised my
voice, I rumbled like a storm, I roared like Adad. . . . I pressed upon the
enemy like the onset of a storm. All of their bodies I bored through like a
sieve. I made the contents of their gullets and entrails run down on the
ground like the waters of a great river.' As time passes, the language of all
the military history tends to become more formalised, and stock phrases will
even be used to describe mountain journeys or mountain fighting. The
Assyrian troops soar like eagles and pounce like vultures and gore like wild
beasts.

In Assyria, as in Egypt, a vastly disproportionate part of the annals is
taken up by the detailed listing of the booty that has been acquired, and
this may be the evidence of the sacral character of these productions. More
remarkable still in the Assyrian writings, however, are the sadistic accounts
of the punishments inflicted on the defeated enemy. The spirit and the basic
pattern appear fairly early; we see them in a nutshell in the case of the
earliest campaign of Tiglath-Pileser I: 'Like the Storm-god, I hurled down
the corpses of their warriors. I made their blood flow in the valleys and
high on the mountains. I cut off their heads, and, outside their cities I
piled them up like heaps of grain.' Assurnâsirpal writes in one case:

600 of their warriors I put to the sword; 3,000 captives I burned with
fire; I did not leave a single one of them alive to serve as a hostage. . . .
Hulai, their governor, I flayed, and his skin I spread upon the wall of
the city; the city I destroyed, I devastated, I burned with fire.

A little later he writes of another case:

From some I cut off their hands and fingers; and from others I cut off their noses, their ears . . . of many I put out the eyes. I made one pillar of the living and another of heads, and I bound their heads to tree-trunks round the city.

Assurbanipal would put a captured king 'in a kennel with jackals and dogs'. Concerning another he wrote: 'Through his jaw I passed a rope, put a dog-chain upon him and made him occupy a kennel at the east gate of the inner [wall] of Nineveh'.

From a very early date the original building inscriptions would contain a brief curse against those who would destroy the edifice itself and those who would deface the commemorative tablet. One monarch has a curse against the man who blots out his name, but a curse also against the man who 'prevents the gods . . . from entering my palace at the feasts or directs them to another palace'. It was this (sometimes in a greatly expanded form) which constituted the closing section of the annals and produced the most importunate appeals to the gods. The doom was to fall not only on such of the king's successors as defaced his record, but on his kingdom and his people too. 'May Adad destroy his land with his destructive thunderbolt and bring hunger, famine, want and bloodshed upon his land.'

In spite of the constructions that seemed to be part of their accepted form, the annals at their best embody interesting pieces of narrative. There were long inscriptions which recorded in the same way the king's hunting-feats – wild oxen captured alive, elephants which 'he brought down with the bow', lions killed either from a hunting chariot or on foot. At the best moments, however, the building inscriptions are striking, for here, perhaps more than anywhere else, a man like Sennacherib finds things that he wants to explain, though he may want to explain only in order that he may appear more wonderful to the world. This can be seen in the accounts that he gives of his work on the city and the palace of Nineveh. No one of his predecessors, he tells us, 'had given his thoughtful attention' to Nineveh; 'nor had his heart considered the palace . . . whose site had become too small'. No one had made plans 'to lay out the streets of the city, to widen the squares, to dig a canal and to plant trees'. Nobody had set out to make the palace an artistic structure, and from olden times, the Tebiltu River had come up to its side and worked havoc with its foundation and destroyed its platform'.

The course of the Tebiltu I turned aside from the midst of the city and directed its outflow into the plain behind the city . . . Assur and Ishtar . . . showed me how to bring out the mighty cedar logs which had grown large in the days gone by and had become enormously tall as they stood concealed in the mountains of Sirara. Alabaster [marble], which in the days of the kings, my fathers, was precious enough to be used for [inlaying] the hilt of a sword, they disclosed to me in the darkness of Mount Ammanana [Ante-Lebanon].

Near Nineveh, in the land of Balatai, by the decree of the god, white limestone appeared in abundance.

In times past, when the kings, my fathers, fashioned a bronze image in the likeness of their members, to set up in their temples, the labour on them exhausted the workmen; in their ignorance and lack of knowledge, they drank oil, and wore sheepskins to carry on the work they wanted to do in the midst of their mountains. But I, Sennacherib, [constructed] great pillars of bronze, colossal lions . . . which no king before my time had fashioned. [I did it] through the clever understanding which the noble Nin-ini-Kug had given me, [and] in my own wisdom. I pondered deeply the manner of carrying out that task. Following the advice of my head and the prompting of my heart, I fashioned a work of bronze cunningly and wrought it. . . . At the command of the god, I built a form of clay and poured bronze into it as in making half-shekel pieces.

Continually there is the desire of the king to show that he has broken all previous records, but, in the case of a man so interested in knowing how things work, even that desire may give way to the impulse to the kind of history that is exposition.

As in the case of Egypt, we have reason to know that, outside the restrictive form of the annals, some of these Assyrians had the necessary gifts for the writing of autobiography and contemporary history. In one of his building inscriptions, the reminiscences of Assurbanipal follow a freer course than the official historiography seemed to allow:

Marduk, master of the gods, granted me a receptive mind and ample [power of] thought. Nabû, the universal scribe gave me a grasp of wisdom. Urta [and] Nergal endowed my body with strength . . . and unrivalled power. The art of the master Adapa I acquired – the hidden treasure of all scribal knowledge . . . I was brave; I was exceedingly strong; in the assembly of the artisans I received orders [?]. I have studied the heavens with the masters of oil divination; I have solved the laborious [problems] of division and multiplication . . . I have read the artistic script of [ancient] Sumer and the obscure Akkadian language, which is hard to master, [now] taking pleasure in the reading of the stelae [coming] from before the Flood, [now] being angry [because I was] stupid and addled [?] by the beautiful script. This is what was done of all my days: I mounted my steed, I rode joyfully, I went up to the [hunting] lodge [?], I held the bow, I shot the arrow. . . . At the same time I was learning royal decorum, walking in kingly ways. . . .

When he was not proclaiming official history, this man Assurbanipal, who would put a rope through the jaw of his defeated enemy, could confess his personal unhappiness in a touching manner :

> Since I have instituted offerings in the pouring of water for the ghosts of the kings who lived before me (which had fallen into disuse . . .) [and] so have done good to god and man, to the dead and the living, why is it that disease, heartbreak, distress and destruction are always with me? Enmity in the land, strife in the house always attend me. Disturbances, evil words are continually rising against me. Sickness of soul, distress of body, have bowed my form. I spend my days sighing and lamenting. . . . Death is making an end of me. . . . In anguish and grief I sit lamenting every day and night. I sigh :
>
> 'O God . . . Let me see the light. How long, O God, wilt thou deal with me thus? I am treated as though I was one who feared neither god nor goddess.'

CHAPTER THREE

The Originality of the Hebrew Scriptures

1 THE MEMORY OF THE EXODUS

The literature so far under discussion has been, to an overwhelming degree, the 'history of one's own time', written by men who were intent on their contemporary world, and anxious simply to have their own achievements placed on record. Their writings – many of which were specifically intended to endure and were provided with all possible guarantees (both divine and human) against decay – were bound to become 'history' by the lapse of time; and to readers of a later generation they would come not only as stories about the past but voices from another era. The very intentness with which some men had regarded their own present, therefore, and the strength of their desire to make sure of their future fame, meant the gradual accumulation of a kind of literature which could not help encouraging in the long run a sense for history and a feeling for the past. Yet, hitherto, only very rarely indeed had there been any attempt to write about the past and to produce history as a retrospect, involving the recovery of bygone times. The very few examples that had occurred had been produced for pragmatic reasons, and hardly any of these had extended as far as a century or two behind the date at which they were completed. Most of them, indeed, had been mere dips into the past for the purpose of showing that the monarch of the moment had removed the evils which had existed under his predecessors or had broken all previous records. For the rest, the effective 'past' was the world of epic poetry, and, behind that, the realm of pure mythology.

Then, suddenly, one finds oneself confronted with what must be the greatest surprise in the whole story. There emerges a people not only supremely conscious of the past but possibly more obsessed with history than any other nation that has ever existed. The very key to its whole development seems to have been the power of its historical memory. And the greatest feature of even this – perhaps the clue to its effectiveness – was the fact that it was basically not just a general feeling for bygone things. Everything hung on men's attachment to a single event that could never be forgotten.

Their god, Yahweh, had brought the children of Israel out of the land of Egypt, out of the house of bondage. This is the thought that runs through the Old Testament – explicit in the oldest scraps of record embedded in the present text, but repeated throughout the story, echoed in the Prophets and in the Psalms. We are more sure that this existed in the folk-memory of the children of Israel from very early times than of the authenticity of the fact behind it; for some scholars have doubted the reality of the Exodus, and many today would question whether it took place in anything like the form in which it was remembered. It is difficult to think of any other event in history which had so powerful an effect on the mentality or the tradition of a people. Even the place that *Magna Carta* came to occupy in English history is far from being an equivalent. And both the French and the Russian Revolutions are still recent – they may reverberate so distinctly still, merely because they involve issues that are as yet unsettled. But besides affecting the history of Israel as a nation, the Exodus profoundly influenced the history of their religion, indeed the whole history of religion. It was this which brought Yahweh himself to the forefront and became the very basis of his claim to be worshipped by his Chosen People. Never has any other minor, local god come to such a remarkable transformation, for, though the rise of Babylon to imperial status provoked attempts to give its local god, Marduk, a parallel elevation, this was not so momentous an event in world history, nor did the attempt have anything like the same success.

Nor was this attitude to the past, this attachment to historical memory, itself the result of a historical development, at least so far as concerns the essence of it. The new phenomenon does not emerge in the great cities and the imposing empires – does not come as the crowning phase of that evolution of historical writing which we have so far been considering. It may have emerged even before the year 1000 B.C., and it belongs to a period before the Assyrian annals had made their really interesting development. It arises where one would least expect it – amongst a very primitive people, as they are emerging from a semi-nomadic stage of existence. It goes back to the time when the tribes first came together to form something like a people – the time when the historian can hardly dare to speak of 'the children of Israel' as a body. And, to crown all, it was this historical memory that held them together – working efficaciously even though it might not have been in the first place a part of the tradition of every section, every locality. From one point of view, at least, we can say that it was this historical memory which made Israel a people.

The evidence for this early attitude to the past exists in documents much older than our Old Testament, but preserved in the text – documents which may even have provided the basic pattern for the Pentateuch. The first is an ancient cultic formula – a kind of credal statement to be repeated at the harvest pilgrimage festival after people had presented their offerings to the priest and he had set them down before the altar. What they were instructed to say was by no means the kind of thing that one would have expected on such an occasion. They were told to confess:

A wandering Aramean was my father; and he [the tribe] went down into Egypt and sojourned there, few in number; and there he became a nation, great, mighty and populous. And the Egyptians treated us harshly, and afflicted us, and laid upon us hard bondage. Then we cried to the Lord God of our fathers, and the Lord heard our voice, and saw our affliction, our toil and oppression; and the Lord brought us out of Egypt with a mighty hand and an outstretched arm; with great terror, with signs and wonders; and he brought us into this place and gave us this land, a land flowing with milk and honey. And behold, now I bring the first of the fruit of the ground, which thou, O Lord, hast given me. [*Deuteronomy*, XXVI, 5–10.]

Even a Christian today would tend to associate a harvest festival with the recurring cycle of the seasons. But the children of Israel associated it with a unique event. It did not bind them to nature. It reminded them of their history.

This piece of narrative so imprinted itself on their minds that when, at a later date, they were inclined to ask themselves why they ought to obey the commandments, they could think of no better statement of the reason. Instead of resorting to ethical discourse or philosophical explanation, they appealed once again to history. Moses is described as saying, therefore, at the time when he delivered the commandments:

When your son asks you in time to come 'What is the meaning of the testimonies and the statutes and the ordinances which the Lord our God has commanded you?' then you shall say to your son, 'We were Pharaoh's slaves in Egypt; and the Lord brought us out of Egypt with a mighty hand; and the Lord showed signs and wonders, great and grievous, against Egypt and against Pharaoh and all his household, before our eyes; and he brought us out from there, that he might bring us in and give us the land which he swore to our fathers. And the Lord commanded us to do all these statutes, to fear the Lord our God, for our good always, that he might preserve us alive, as at this day.' [*Deuteronomy*, VI, 20–23.]

The last recorded episode in the life of Joshua is the occasion on which he met the leading men in all the tribes of Israel and asked them to choose between Yahweh and the other gods. They might prefer to go on worshipping the gods of their ancestors, he said, or they might choose the gods of the Amorites, whose territory they had now entered. They followed Joshua in choosing Yahweh, and the result was the making of the covenant at Shechem, or the renewal of a previous covenant. But it is interesting to see (in what was perhaps basically an ancient document) the way in which their leader put the original question to them. He produced the following expansion of the formula that has already been quoted :

And Joshua said to all the people, 'Thus says the Lord, the God of Israel, "Your fathers lived of old beyond the Euphrates, Terah, the father of Abraham and of Nahor; and they served other gods. Then I took your father Abraham from beyond the River and led him through all the land of Canaan, and made his offspring many. I gave him Isaac; and to Isaac I gave Jacob and Esau. And I gave Esau the hill country of Seir to possess, but Jacob and his children went down to Egypt. And I sent Moses and Aaron, and I plagued Egypt with what I did in the midst of it; and afterwards I brought you out. Then I brought your fathers out of Egypt and you came to the sea, and the Egyptians pursued your fathers with chariots and horsemen to the Red Sea. And when they cried to the Lord, he put darkness between you and the Egyptians, and made the sea come upon them and cover them; and your eyes saw what I did in Egypt; and you lived in the wilderness a long time. Then I brought you to the land of the Amorites, who lived on the other side of the Jordan; they fought with you, and I gave them into your hand, and you took possession of their land, and I destroyed them before you. Then Balak the son of Zippor, king of Moab, arose and fought against Israel; and he sent and invited Balaam the son of Beor to curse you; so I delivered you out of his hand. And you went over the Jordan and came to Jericho, and the men of Jericho fought against you, and also the Amorites, the Perizzites, the Canaanites, the Hittites, the Girgashites, the Hivites and the Jebusites; and I gave them into your hand. And I sent the hornet before you, which drove them out before you, the two kings of the Amorites; it was not by your sword or by your bow. I gave a land on which you had not laboured, and cities which you had not built, and you dwell therein; you eat the fruit of the vineyards and oliveyards which you did not plant."

'Now, therefore [continues Joshua], fear the Lord, and serve him in sincerity and faithfulness; put away the gods which your fathers served beyond the River, and in Egypt, and serve the Lord. And if you be unwilling to serve the Lord, choose this day whom you will serve, whether the gods your fathers served beyond the River, or the gods of the Amorites in whose lands you dwell; but as for me and my house, we will serve the Lord.' [*Joshua*, XXIV, 2–15.]

An episode from the past which clearly came home to the people of Israel as a piece of history – a thing with which, therefore, they felt a vivid relationship in their real life – performed also for them the function that was performed by the epic in the case of other peoples. The present-day scholar is likely to find it helpful to treat the narrative of it (at least at times) as though it were an example of the epic. More curious still, perhaps, is the fact that the situation seemed to relieve this people of the necessity of having an elaborate mythology. Religion became profoundly involved with history instead.

2 GOD AND HISTORY

The people of Israel had been semi-nomadic, and at least for those of them who came to dominate the tradition (or to control the memory) of the nation as a whole, this had been the state of things until they came together in the land of Canaan. They remembered that their 'father' had been a 'wandering Aramean', and that their ancestors had once lived 'beyond the River', beyond the Euphrates. The semi-nomads lived on the fringe of the settled lands and kept their flocks, but would also engage in short-term agriculture. Occasionally they would enter for a time into the settled lands, but then would find themselves forced to move on. One of their characteristic features was their desire to possess such lands, to become sedentary themselves, and to engage permanently in agriculture. If they could acquire even territory that was in many ways hard and grim (like Palestine itself), this would be 'a land of milk and honey to them'. Better still if they could live in cities that they had not built and harvest the vine and the olive that they had not planted. It might almost be said that the thing they required from a god was this permanent admission to the life of sedentary people. In a sense it might be said that to them a god authenticated himself by his ability to produce this consummation.

Another feature of the semi-nomads was the peculiar relationship that seemed to exist between the head of the clan and the god to whom he attached himself, the latter being regarded as, in a way, a member of the family. He may not have had a name, or he may really have been named after the leader who had become attached to him – so that we hear very often of 'the god of Abraham', for example. It has been suggested even that the god of Abraham, the god of Isaac and the god of Jacob ought to be regarded as three separate deities. If so, the tradition soon lost sight of the fact, for the whole importance of the god of Abraham depended on his undertakings for a remote future. We also hear the term 'the god of our fathers', which suggests that he held his place from one generation to another. What Israel remembered was the fact that this god had promised her land and had decreed that the seed of Abraham should multiply. By this, the god would establish his genuineness and prove his power. Perhaps his relationship with the clan had something of a contractual character.

In the case of the children of Israel, the fulfilment of the promise was long delayed; and in the intervening period much hardship and anguish evidently had to be suffered. And perhaps the postponement was an important feature of the case, for, if the prize had come too easily and too soon, men might not have made such a song about the ultimate achievement. The promise would no doubt be renewed on occasion, and there is an instance of this in Egypt, where great hopes were held out for the future if the people would faithfully follow Moses. In this case, too, however, the fulfilment was long delayed; and this seems to have become part of the permanent pattern of Jewish history. We cannot even be sure that it was 'the god of Abraham' who watched over Israel in the time of the Exodus; for in this period either they found out the name of the god at last, or, under the leadership of Moses, they attached themselves to a Yahweh who had only been a local god, patron of a tribe that they encountered. Some of their later utterances – including the one of Joshua already quoted – assume that it had become necessary to desert at least the gods of their more distant ancestors. It may have been by a kind of retrospective identification that Yahweh came to be seen as the same as 'the god of Abraham'.

Many circumstances support the view that some of the people who subsequently regarded themselves as the children of Israel had in fact lived for a considerable period in Egypt, and had made an Exodus which led to their entry into the Promised Land. It seems clear, however, that many of the tribes that came to Canaan had arrived by a different route, some of them percolating in a peaceful manner over a considerable period of time. The story of the Exodus seems to correspond with something that happened in history, therefore, but with something which, from a mundane point of view, was less momentous than it came to appear. Perhaps it was even (in a certain sense) a peripheral affair. There may have happened, therefore, something of what we have seen occurring in the case of the epic: the tradition of one group, one locality, achieving a general predominance so that it comes to capture the nation as a whole, and becomes part of the folk memory of the entire people. It may be true that the combinations of tribes that come together in the Promised Land were not all of them groups which had previously known Jacob as their ancestor, nor all even related to one another before this time. But somehow or other they were captured by the tradition, and this tradition kept them politically connected, ultimately turning them into a nation. The whole story, therefore, is a remarkable example of the conquest of mind over matter.

According to all the rules of the game, the children of Israel, when they entered the Promised Land, ought to have adopted the gods of the population amongst which they had come to dwell. Settling down to a life of agriculture they ought to have moved over to the nature-cults which were associated with the life of the seasons and encouraged fertility. To many of them, this would not have seemed a reprehensible policy, and to many, it would not have been inconsistent with the worship of Yahweh, or at least could have been accommodated to it. The people of Israel did in fact take over a number of what had been the sacred places of the Canaanites, and seem to have adjusted the traditions of these to the Yahweh cult. Indeed many of them did go over to the strange gods of either their predecessors or their new neighbours, as we can see from the Old Testament. The resistance, however, was great, and the tradition of the Yahweh who had brought his people out of the land of Egypt proved its tenacity and power in the resulting conflict. The austerer representatives of the Yahweh cause would seem to have been assisted by the survival here and there of the semi-nomadic tradition, which, besides retaining the old view of the relations between the clan and its god, tended to distrust agricultural life and the licence of the cities. The religion of semi-nomads, far from the luxury of great temples and the splendour of imperial capitals, had been a comparatively empty affair – more free of idols and elaborate rituals and complicated mythologies. The memory of this may have affected the whole-hearted supporters of Yahweh, and it meant that there was something in the tradition which encouraged austerity. One thing, however, is sure. The conservatives, the partisans of the old Yahweh, sought to influence their kinsmen by the appeal to history. Their great weapon seems to have been the writing of history. The whole situation was calculated to give an impulse to historiography.

Though the antithesis between the two may not have been a real one and should not be regarded as absolute, it is significant that the tradition which came to dominate in Israel attached itself to the God of History rather than the God of Nature. The Yahweh who brought his children out of the land of Egypt seemed to matter more than even the Yahweh who created the world. Men were warned against the worship of the moon and the stars; they were asked to fix their minds on the god whose mighty acts were evident in human affairs. Israel might take over from her neighbours ceremonies and festivals that had been connected with the cycle of the seasons. But she would give them historical associations, and even end by turning them into celebrations of an historical event. It happened that the nature-cults tended to encourage licentiousness, but the connection of Yahweh with history was calculated in itself to give religion an ethical character. It was believed here, as in Mesopotamia, that public misfortune was connected with offences against the deity; but the God of History was connected more with the world of human relations than with the realm of nature. The covenant that he made with Israel required good conduct on the part of the people as a return for the blessings bestowed; in the tensions that occurred between earth and heaven, the acts of God were themselves judged by human beings – judged on ethical grounds – because he, too, was sometimes felt not to have been playing fair. Men struggled to understand the rationale of this Yahweh, who made himself so important in the realm of current events. Their views of God himself, but also of human personality – indeed their views of ethics and their idea of man's destiny and history – all developed together because they were at grips with the problem of a god who played a part in human affairs. Furthermore, at this point, religion provides a reason why men should interest themselves in history.

The tradition of the children of Israel seems to have begun with an emphasis upon the exodus from Egypt. The wonders that had attended this episode – particularly the crossing of the Red Sea – had produced a great impression on them. Either in the course of that story itself or through the masterstroke of an historical genius, the Exodus came to be particularly associated with a Promise which kept hope alive in the wilderness and seemed fulfilled when the Israelites entered the land of Canaan. This was combined with the stories of the hopes that had been held out to the patriarchs. It seemed that the whole history of the people had been a history based on the Promise. At some time or other, the Promise came to be regarded as a continuing thing; it represented the hope for the future, but it depended on the conduct of the people themselves, the fidelity to the covenant, the obeying of the commandments. All this implied a further bond, fastening men's minds on history, and connecting religion with history.

The people of Israel entered the land of Canaan at an auspicious time, for the great empires around them had come to a period of weakness in the neighbourhood of the year 1200, when the Exodus probably occurred. But this people of the Promise were in one of the danger-zones of Western Asia, and proved before very long to be in fact one of the most unfortunate nations in history. Wedged between ancient empires at a time when Assyria was coming to the forefront, they managed to retain even their independent political existence for only a very few centuries. In a sense they were fated for the longest periods to be the victims, still, of the non-fulfilment of the Promise. Here there occurred a further remarkable example of the triumph of the spirit over the facts of life, the victory of mind over matter. One might be tempted to say that the Prophets set out to save Yahweh's credit, in spite of the non-fulfilment of the Promise; but the doctrine of judgement was available to them in any case and they were too well aware of the sins they were called to condemn. Impelled by the prospect or by the occurrence of disaster, they stressed that judgement of God against sin which effects itself in human events, in the very course of history. They insisted at the same time that the judgement was consistent with the terms of the Promise, which had always been a conditional one. Judgement did not cancel the Promise. The whole panorama of history was still basically the story of the Promise. In other words, behind the succession of ages there was a pattern – the abiding Promise repeatedly punctuated by acts of judgement. In reality, however, the Chosen People, the recipient of all the hopes, had become the plaything of giant forces that had arisen around them. All religion seems to have been driven to a higher level in order to cope with the resulting predicament and to meet the challenge. The future offered no ray of light; but it turned out that even all this was not to be regarded as a case of the non-fulfilment of the Promise; for the Promise itself had been a bigger thing than anybody had realised; it proved capable of expansion with the passage of time, and now its unexpected implications were brought out. Yahweh was ready to make another new covenant with his people, and it was a refinement upon the older one, because it was more subtle and more spiritual. It offered greatness to the Israelitish nation, still – but a loftier kind of distinction – loftier even if one judges it only from a mundane point of view. Involved in all this there was a religious development important in the life of Israel itself, and still more important in world history. And by virtue of the evolution of the Promise, something like the idea of progress is introduced into history by men who are unconscious of what they are doing. For the moment it lies concealed there, but at a later date it will have its effect realised.

The historical ideas of the Old Testament are in fact remarkable in a further way. Because of their religion and because of the Promise, the ancient Hebrews saw history as really going somewhere – they came to feel that there was an end to which the whole of creation moved. They did not share the notion, associated with so many philosophies and creeds, that history was merely an aimless revolving, the wheels always on the move but everything remaining really in the same state. To them, history was not cyclic, but predominantly linear – irreversible and unrepeatable. There was room, still, for novelties in the processes of time, therefore, and they said that their god, who had brought them out of the land of Egypt, was still capable of doing new things, just as he had done them at the Creation. All this does not imply the modern 'idea of progress', which emerged for special reasons, and partly as an inference from observed data (at a comparatively recent date) but, unlike the cyclic view, it provided a framework within which an idea of progress could develop. And it would seem that in the development of the Promise, in the passage from one covenant to a higher, in the transition from the Old Testament to the New, there is material from which some notion of progress does emerge – a progress taking place in spiritual things. In any event the Old Testament view of the whole sequence of things in time was one which had the effect of giving the study of history greater significance and real point.

In the higher regions of ancient Hebrew thought – particularly the kind of thought which arises out of the non-fulfilment of the Promise – there emerges an idea which brings the notion of Promise to a kind of climax where the concept of Promise is in itself in a way transcended. It turns out that even the sufferings of Israel – even the judgements upon her – have their place in a higher economy of Providence; for they are connected with a mission that she has to fulfil. Through her, all nations are to be blessed, in fulfilment of the prediction made to Abraham. She stands in history as the 'Suffering Servant' precisely because she has this mission; it is to be her function to lead every other country to Yahweh. This is the first appearance of the idea of the 'historic mission' of a nation; and it would not be easy to say how far the national 'mission' of modern peoples – of England in the time of Cromwell, for example – was indebted to the Old Testament for the idea. It was a great transformation – in some ways almost a reversal – of the implications of being God's 'Chosen People', for now, in a sense it meant being chosen for suffering in order to achieve a higher purpose.

The concepts that help to characterise the religion of ancient Israel are those of the Promise, the covenant, the judgement, the national mission. They are concepts particularly associated with history.

3 THE HISTORY OF A NATION

Amongst the great empires themselves there had emerged no hint of anything like the history of a nation – no sign that the idea of such a thing had entered men's minds. Nor had the royal annalists (or anybody else, so far as we know) produced even the history of a dynasty – a thing which in those days might have seemed more relevant. There had been texts that were hardly better than dynastic catalogues – the Palermo Stone and the Sumerian King-List being the most distinguished examples of such literature. The priests of Babylon had strung together a number of episodes in order to show the disaster that fell on any monarch who had neglected their god, Marduk. Perhaps they had come nearer than anybody else to producing an historical retrospect, but the result was nothing like the history of a country. The Hittite, Telipinish, had dealt with a short series of successive rulers, but only for the purpose of illustrating the evils of palace-revolutions. It seemed to require the stimulus of a religious prejudice or a moral-political issue to send men's minds running over the past, looking for correlations.

Israel, however, provides us for the first time with something that we can call the history of a nation. When the books of *Samuel, Kings* and

Chronicles are reached it may seem to stand rather as the story of a monarchy or of a dynasty. And the moralising in these writings might make them seem only a considerable development (or a considerable expansion) of what the priests of Marduk had attempted to do over a thousand years earlier. But, long before the narrative reaches the establishment of the monarchy in the time of Saul, it is clear that it is being envisaged as the history, rather, of the people of Israel. Even when it deals later with the monarchy itself, we are not allowed to lose sight of the fact that what is envisaged is really the story of a nation. So far as our present knowledge goes, it represents the first emergence of such an idea.

All this may be partly the result of the fact that, though the Israelitish people established itself (and seems actually to have been 'formed') comparatively late in the day – at a time when the civilisations in its neighbourhood had reached a remarkably advanced state – it comes before us, and moves on to the stage of history, while still in a primitive condition. Partly, perhaps, through the overwhelming impression produced by an event in the rear – the exodus from Egypt, in particular – partly perhaps through juxtaposition with sedentary populations already advanced, already familiar with writing and with literature, amongst other things – the children of Israel seem to have reached a consciousness of history without having to go through the intermediate stages that made progress so slow in other countries. And the fact that they acquired a sense of their position as a people in the stream of time meant that their historiography proved dynamic – in a very few hundred years they progressed much further than the royal annalists had done in a millennium.

After they had come into the light of day and clearly arrived on the stage of history, they maintained for a long time much of the attitude of the tribe and clan; and neither in Mesopotamia nor in Egypt are we able to catch men at such an early point in their development. One of the characteristics of the tribal state is the ability to see oneself as a 'people' – to envisage not merely a monarchical leader, but the whole extended family as a collectivity. In the case of the people of Israel, the names Abraham and Jacob themselves stand not simply for an individual but often for the group that has accumulated behind them. For this reason, it was possible for them to say : 'A wandering Aramean was my father, and he went down to Egypt and sojourned there, *few in number*.' In the case of Israel, we can come closer than hitherto to the effective origins of historiography, because we can have a nearer view of the reminiscences of men in the tribal state – a more definite picture of what had been the oral tradition. It is possible that, amongst the nomadic and semi-nomadic tribes, the sense for the past was encouraged by the fact that their religion was not a local cult – tied to one place – but was connected rather with the god of their ancestors.

Patched into our Old Testament are a number of passages which go back to a time when conditions were essentially tribal, and they present us with historical writing in its most simple and primitive state. They include battle-songs, tribal stories and the local traditions of sacred places; and to these may be added early lists and genealogies, early laws, and the kind of cultic formula that has already been noted. Historical scholarship has made considerable advances in recent decades because, instead of merely trying to recover the literary productions of one author and another whose narrative contributed to the formation of the present Old Testament text, it has concentrated attention on those smaller units of poetry, saga, etc., which are to be regarded as the original nuclei.

There is a 'Song of Miriam' (*Exodus*, XV, 21):

Sing to the Lord, for he has triumphed gloriously;
The horse and his rider he has thrown into the sea.

It may go back to the time of the crossing of the Red Sea. It is quoted in the 'Song of Moses', which celebrates the same event and will itself be of very considerable antiquity. A beautiful example of a battle-song is the 'Song of Deborah', about the defeat of Sisera – a piece which survives (with certain alterations, no doubt) in the fifth chapter of the book of *Judges*. It belongs to a time when the children of Israel were not quite a united people – not yet a body politic – and the fact that they were only a loose association of tribes is illustrated by the way in which these latter were in a position to choose whether they would take part in the warfare or not:

From Ephraim they set out thither . . .
From Maehir marched down the commanders . . .
The princes of Issachar came with Deborah . . .
Among the clans of Reuben there were great searchings of heart.
Why did ye tarry among the sheepfolds,
to hear the piping for the flocks? . . .
Gilead stayed behind the Jordan;
And Dan, why did he abide with the ships? . . .

That the Israelites were in a primitive condition compared with their enemy is shown in the previous chapter of *Judges* – for their enemy had nine hundred chariots of iron, and against these they could only cry to the Lord for help. It was 'the Lord' who 'routed Sisera and all his chariots', apparently by the flooding of the River Kishon, which rendered the chariots immovable.

From heaven fought the stars,
from their courses they fought against Sisera,
The torrent Kishon swept them away.

A modern writer tells us that the Kishon is a river which rises suddenly, 'a heavy flood of liquid, flowing through a quagmire'. The prose text in *Judges* IV says that Sisera 'alighted from his chariot and fled away on foot'; and both texts describe how Jael, the wife of Heber, killed him with a tent-peg when he had taken refuge in her tent. Then this 'oldest remaining considerable fragment of Hebrew literature' describes the way in which Sisera's mother waited for his return, expecting to hear of his victory.

> Out of the window she peered,
> The mother of Sisera gazed through the lattice;
> 'Why is his chariot so long in coming?
> Why tarry the hoofbeats of his chariots?'
> Her wisest ladies made answer,
> nay, she gives answer to herself,
> 'Are they not finding and dividing the spoil?
> a maiden or two for every man;
> spoil of dyed stuffs for Sisera,
> spoil of dyed stuffs embroidered,
> two pieces of dyed work embroidered for my neck as spoil?'

Samples of the tribal stories can best be seen perhaps in the same book of *Judges* – an extraordinary miscellany, which deals with the time between the settlement in Canaan and the establishment of the monarchy. An editor has attempted to string them together in an historical chain, and he envisages them as an account of Israel as a whole, when in reality both the stories and the wars may well have been more local in character. Above all, he has tried to turn them into a series of 'cautionary tales' – disaster is avoided only when a Judge, a charismatic leader, rouses the proper fervour for Yahweh. On this point the editor's verdict may have been correct and his moralisings may have needed in fact no distortion of history. In that loose amphictyony of tribes, only a general zeal for Yahweh would be likely to produce the public spirit and the combined action that were necessary for military purposes. Here, then, are heroic stories, many of them rooted in history but liable to gather legendary accretions; and they are not so radically edited as to conceal the barbarities of the times. They show that Yahweh, the desert god, very much the mountain god, had become the God of War, directing operations, performing mighty acts, frightening the enemy into a state of paralysis before a human being had touched them, claiming the booty after the battle and prescribing the cruelties of the Holy War (the killing of all prisoners, for example) – all this after the manner of the God of War amongst Israel's neighbours at that period. In this aspect, too, Yahweh appears as a god who is essentially concerned with the events of history. The stories now in question were at least not invented at a later date to illustrate more civilised, more highly developed concepts of Yahweh; though *Deuteronomy*, which appeared long afterwards, itself contains ancient material connected with the Holy War. A cycle of Samson narratives in the book of *Judges*, however, belongs more definitely to the realm of saga; and the memory of this people had been encumbered with a considerable amount of legendary material.

The traditions of sacred places were not peculiar to Israel, but they were liable to be important and they would be likely to be carefully preserved, since it was held to be so necessary to maintain the cult unimpaired. The children of Israel took over altars, and some of the associated stories, from their predecessors in the land of Canaan; though in these cases they might well feel that adaptation was needed – that both the cults and the stories really belonged to Yahweh on the one hand, and to Abraham or Jacob on the other hand. It is sometimes held that it was through the traditions of these sacred places that the stories of the patriarchal age were handed down; and there are those who believe that such stories were manufactured in these shrines late in the day – after the settlement in Canaan – or that anecdotes originally about other people came to be transferred to the patriarchs. It is true that, at a local shrine, there would often be a piece of narrative to explain how this had come to be regarded as a sacred place; but it would be crude to infer that all the traditions of the patriarchs were invented late in the day merely to provide such explanations. We possibly tend to underestimate the superstitious tenacity with which an ancient and primitive people – and particularly one as history-minded as this – would cling to anything that remained from the past, regarding it as a rare survival from a shipwreck. Similarly, we can easily overestimate the element of conscious manufacture or deliberate invention in those cases where tradition did actually become distorted. Some of the patriarchal stories are now known to conform to very peculiar conditions that existed in the upper-middle Euphrates region, a few hundred years before the settlement in Canaan. The authors who ultimately put them into writing are likely to have repeated old traditions faithfully, for they could not have known anything about the context to which they had once been related. They could hardly have understood what we now know to have been the import of what they were reproducing – material which, as they saw it, could hardly have been to the credit of the patriarchs at times. They also place the patriarchs in the regions in which nomads moved, and they name in this connection only the cities which existed in those earlier centuries of the second millennium B.C. – things which archaeology has made clear to us, but must have been known to Israelites at the time of the settlement only through the continuity of these traditions. Some of the patriarchal narratives may have to be discounted but, even so, it would be implausible to deny the antiquity of the patriarchal tradition in its entirety. After the settlement in Canaan, and in the period of the book of *Judges*, there is a certain unity of faith, and a kind of demand or expectation of common political action which can hardly be explained save by the existence of older bonds between the tribes and an older tradition common at least to a number of them. It is possible that some of the general traditions of a single tribe would be in the custody of the keepers of one of the sacred places, and, once again, modern scholarship has greatly profited from the attempts to identify these traditions and trace what happened to them – to learn in particular how one or another of them might have come to achieve the predominance in the nation as a whole. In all probability an annual meeting of the tribes for the purpose of covenant-renewal in Shechem would assist the process (probably in operation for other reasons too) by which the local traditions were ultimately fused into a national one. Those tribes which had taken part in the exodus from Egypt might end by inducing all the rest – even those who had been in the land of Canaan at that very time – to feel this as also a remembrance from their own past.

The children of Israel turn out to be unique in a further sense, therefore, for they stand alone amongst the people of the ancient world in having the story of their beginnings and their primitive state as clear as this in their folk-memory – in having traditional connections reaching back to such a simple stage of things. The memory of ancient Sumer did not reach behind the origin of the state; the Hittites did not tell stories about the time before they had entered Asia Minor; and the ancient Greeks seem to have lost their connection with their own remoter antiquity. Apparently, before there had been an exodus so overpowering in its effect on them as to be unfor-gettable, they had acquired some feeling for history, and they may have been helped by the fact that, as early as in the patriarchal days, they moved amongst more advanced peoples, whose literature already revealed a sense for the past. The existence of a certain continuity of tradition had an interesting effect on the notion the Israelites had of their remoter antiquity. Other peoples seem to have been able to imagine for themselves an ancestry consisting of gods and heroes, though their tradition did not quite tell them what happened after that. Even at the beginning of modern times, Euro-pean nations pretended to trace their origin to those Trojans who had run far afield after the downfall of their city. Real contact with the past had been broken somewhere; but Israel retained some remembrance of the miss-ing stages, however this might be affected by the aberrations to which the folk-memory is subject. This people said: 'A wandering Aramean was my father', and much of the work of the archaeologists supports rather than undermines this tradition. Their past was an unpretentious one, and they would not allow themselves to overlook its humiliating side – to forget Egypt, 'the house of bondage'. And compared with the heroes of epics, Abraham, Isaac and Jacob seem to belong to a world of familiar things.

Yet it was amongst these people – for whom the past was not a golden age at all but was a thing to escape from – that somebody had the idea of producing a history of the nation and turning it into a great theme. One can hardly imagine how this could have happened if the Exodus had not made such a tremendous impression on the folk-memory and had not demanded to be connected with both before and after – both the promises to the patriarchs and the acquisition of the Promised Land. Because we start with the primitive historical material that has been described, we can trace over again in the case of the Israelites the emergence of historical writing from the very beginnings of it – the passage from oral traditions to a continuous literary work. Ancient Israel provides, therefore, a pocket-size example of the very rise of historiography. These people may have needed to learn very little from the great civilisations that had grown up around them and had been producing history of a sort for well over a thousand years. They may have needed to learn nothing except the fact that the past could be marshalled into a story and history could be a form of literature and also the fact that the story could be so constructed as to show the judgement of heaven on human sin. Modern trends in scholarship have not overthrown the long-accepted view that there emerged amongst the people of Israel a writer who put together a continuous story and whom it may be correct to describe (in the way that some have described him) as an 'historian of genius'. It would generally be held that he completed the labours of one or more predecessors who had begun to work the materials into a continuous narrative before his time; and, though he crowns the whole endeavour, considerable merit belongs no doubt to those who prepared the way for him. The total result was a text which is only one of the components of the Pentateuch as we have it today. Its producer is designated as 'the Yahwist' because he was identified as the writer who, in the book of *Genesis*, used the name 'Yahweh' to describe the god of Israel. The text itself is known as 'J' because of the German spelling of 'Jahve'.

It is perhaps likely that the production of a wider kind of narrative history had become fairly advanced before the establishment of the monarchy, that is to say, well before 1000 B.C. But it may be the case that not until the monarchy was on its feet would the tribes of Israel see themselves assuredly as an organised people; and it often happens that historiography makes its real development after the institution of the body politic, the emergence of some consciousness of 'belonging to the state'. If any people other than the children of Israel were in question, one would not expect serious historical writing earlier than the reign of David, which ran into the first few decades of the tenth century B.C.; and his amazing military success – his extension of the monarchy to the scale of an empire – would have been sufficient in itself to create an appetite for historical writing. Perhaps a work like that of the 'Yahwist' was more likely to appear after the death of Solomon, a few decades later still, and the splitting of the country into two kingdoms immediately afterwards. For 'J' seeks to promote the unity of the people through the influence of the Yahweh cult; and its production might well mark the time when unity had been lost but the loss had not yet come to seem irretrievable.

The text supplies us with the story of Moses and the Exodus, together with the narrative of Joshua and the entry into the land of Canaan. It connects all this with the promises of the patriarchal period and it still carries something of the exhilaration which attends the fulfilment of these promises. The total result is not yet a completed national history, but the beginning of such a thing – the greatest of all the steps calculated to lead to its accomplishment. 'J' stands rather as a magnificent theme – it is something like the epic of the Israelitish people. It combines a number of traditions – the promises to the patriarchs, the escape from Egypt, the wanderings in the wilderness, the covenant at Sinai and the entry into the Promised Land – bunches of anecdotes which may have been connected with particular localities, some scholars holding that originally they had had nothing to do with one another. They would be becoming grouped into cycles of story before the time of the 'Yahwist', and some of us may feel that there was a wider kind of Israelitish tradition which brought them together and made the Exodus so powerful a feature of the folk-memory. But the story as we possess it undoubtedly owes something to the constructive power of the 'Yahwist' himself, as so often happens in the case of epics; so that even the over-all result may have a vague kind of historicity without allowing us to be sure that particular parts of it are authentic.

To all this the 'Yahwist' has prefixed the narrative of times more primitive still, including an account of the Creation and the Flood, the larger canvas giving him scope for a wider vision of history. In various ways the influence of the Babylonian epic becomes apparent here, though it may be an influence coming from Mesopotamia at an earlier time, not necessarily mediated through the Canaanites after the settlement in the Land of Promise. The 'Yahwist' also collects aetiological stories – myths of origin – to account for the division of mankind into nations, the separation of tongues, the beginning of arts and crafts. He likes to tell us that his stories explain why snakes crawl on the ground, why men must gain their bread by the sweat of their brow, why women must suffer in childbirth. The children of Israel at a certain stage became curious about things which seem to interest all peoples when they begin to acquire a sense for the past; the question of the origins of the names of rivers and mountains, of individuals and tribes – the origin also of sacred wells, sacred stones, sacred trees. Many of the preoccupations of primitive peoples – and indeed of ancient Israel throughout its story – would help to account for the passionate interest in genealogy, of which the Bible supplies so much evidence. This has its parallel all over the world at one time and another; for the interest in genealogy often precedes any interest in history.

The 'Yahwist', then, gathers together the old stories and traditions, including the legends and sagas already in oral circulation amongst the people. His own hand shows itself in the joints between the stories, the transition from one set to another, and the establishment of a presiding structure. His mastery was greatest of all in the distinctive theological inter-pretations that he brought to the whole, and in this he raised himself above his predecessors. He undoubtedly performed a great service for the cause of 'Yahwism' itself, and, through an interpretation of history, the actual faith received an impulse and a development. He set out to present a Yahweh who did not limit his activity to sacred occasions but kept his hand on the whole course of secular history. The Old Testament was to become a treatise on the connection of God with the ordinary history of a tumultuous, obstre-perous nation.

It was something of a novelty to have anybody writing history at all, instead of merely recording his own deeds of prowess. It was novel for a man to be writing the history of a nation, and, as we have seen, it would have been novel to produce even the history of a dynasty. But the 'Yahwist', starting from the Creation, adumbrates also the history of mankind itself. He puts the story of his own country into this context, so that the 'universal history' merges into something more local; but this is what tended to happen with 'universal histories' until very recent times. Down to only a century or two ago – and throughout by far the biggest part of the Christian era – the book of *Genesis* was the stimulus to the writing of universal history, and it set the initial pattern of it, provided the opening section.

At a certain point in the story, then, a peculiar religion gave a great stimulus to historiography. For a very long period, politics, in ordinary circumstances, led to the study of one's own city-state, one's own nation, one's own empire. It tended to be religion, and the wider interest in human destiny, which encouraged 'universal history'. In the case of Israel, as in that of Babylon, it was in some senses an advantage that historical writing, instead of being dictated by kings, came under the influence of priests.

4 PROMISE AND FULFILMENT

In the ancient world we start with the view that events are things which 'happen'. They impinge on men like the thunder-storm, they drop from heaven ready-made. They are viewed as discrete particles, and some of the earliest history merely lists them. It was natural to feel that where they did not come from the arbitrary wills of men they sprang from the equally arbitrary wills of gods. In Mesopotamia there was a notion of destiny, but even this had no logic or continuity: we saw in Chapter I that a fresh meeting of the gods took place annually to make new decisions about the fate of human beings during the next year. If correlations were made between one event and another these were at first of the simplest kind. The earliest attempt at a connected history is really the telling of a story – the sort of story in which one thing simply happens after another and nobody knows what is going to happen next. The priests of Marduk may have preceded the 'Yahwist' in the policy of recapitulating historical data in order to present an interpretation. But even they did not have his over-arching theme – first the promises, then the preparatory period and finally the fulfilment. The Old Testament introduces this kind of large-scale interpretation. But it provides more than one example – it is not confined to a single, uniform mode of exegesis. The Old Testament presents complications to the scholar because the whole problem of interpreting history now becomes an issue.

The issue is raised initially for us by the famous 'Court-History' or 'Succession Story' of King David, which must have been reproduced, virtually as it stood, in II *Samuel*, XI to XX, 22 and I *Kings*, I to II, 10. It may well have been written earlier than 'J', for many scholars regard it as almost contemporary with the events it narrates. They base their judgement on the intimacy with which it treats its subject matter, the knowledge it reveals of individuals, and the character of the details it supplies. It is perhaps the earliest example that Israel offers of conscious historical writing handed down in something like its original form. The ancient world, at least down to the time of the Greeks, produced no historical narrative that was more distinguished than this. It requires special consideration because, even if it were held that material of this texture could have been transmitted by word of mouth for a short period, it is virtually an account of contemporary affairs.

The rulers of the Israelitish monarchies do not appear to have produced the kind of annals, written in the first person singular, which are found in the neighbouring empires. It is strange that their dynasties should be the ones for which royal inscriptions are so lacking. A 'building inscription' that has been discovered records the boring of the Siloam tunnel for the carrying of water, but it does not mention the name of the king concerned. The 'Court-History' of David shows an amazing impartiality and independence, and could hardly have been produced by the king himself, or for him, or on his behalf. It describes the peculiarly human rôle of the man amongst his relatives, advisers and leading subjects, making no attempt to hide his weaknesses. Some scholars feel that it is possible to identify the person in the court circle who may have been responsible for the narrative. Nothing could be further removed than this from the history typified by the commemorative tablet.

The long quotation from this narrative in *Samuel* and *Kings* begins with the treachery of David's conduct when he acquired Bathsheba, later the mother of Solomon. It ends with the king in his humiliating old age; the attempt of his oldest surviving son, Adonijah, to seize the crown; and the successful installation of Solomon. The bulk of the text deals, however, with Absalom, the previous heir to the throne, and tells how he had gone to Hebron, and raised the standard of revolt. 'The conspiracy grew strong, and the people with Absalom kept increasing', while David, in Jerusalem, said, 'Let us flee, or else there will be no escape for us'. David first ascended the Mount of Olives, 'weeping as he went, barefoot and with his head covered'. He heard that Ahitophel had joined Absalom and he instructed Hushai the Archite to pretend to offer his services in the same way, so that he could defeat the councils of Ahitophel, but also betray the rebel plan, using the sons of two priests as his messengers. David then fled to the Jordan, while Absalom entered Jerusalem, taking over the king's concubines in order to make it clear that he was now in the saddle – this on the advice of Ahitophel, for 'in those days the counsel which Ahitophel gave was as if one consulted the oracle'. Ahitophel further advised immediate military action.

> Let me choose twelve thousand men, and I will set out and pursue David tonight. I will come upon him while he is weary and discouraged, and throw him into a panic; and all the people who are with him will flee. I will strike down the king only.

Hushai the Archite, however, advised Absalom to wait until he had gathered more forces – counsel which Absalom adopted, and which was to prove his undoing, as had been intended. Hushai presented his arguments in a very plausible way:

> You know that your father and his men are mighty men and that they are enraged. . . . Besides, your father is expert in war. . . . Behold even now he has hidden himself in one of the pits, or in some other place. And when some of [your] people fall at the first attack, whoever hears it will say, 'There has been a slaughter among the people who follow Absalom'. Then even the valiant man, whose heart is like the heart of a lion, will utterly melt with fear: for all Israel knows that your father is a valiant man, and that those who are with him are valiant men. But my counsel is that all Israel be gathered to you, from Dan to Beersheba, as the sand by the sea for multitude, and that you go into battle in person. So we shall come upon him in some place . . . and we shall light upon him as the dew falls on the ground; and of him and all the men with him not one will be left. If he withdraws into a city, then all Israel will bring ropes to that city, and we shall drag it into the valley, until not even a pebble is to be found there.

Having advised a delay which would enable the king to collect his forces, Hushai the Archite warned David of the policy that Ahitophel was anxious to adopt.

Then David arose, and all the people who were with him, and they crossed the Jordan; by daybreak not one was left who had not crossed the Jordan.

When Ahitophel saw that his counsel was not followed, he saddled his ass, and went off home to his own city. And he set his house in order and hanged himself. . . .

Then David came to Mahanaim. And Absalom crossed the Jordan with all the men of Israel. Now Absalom had set Amasa over the army instead of Joab. Amasa was the son of a man named Ithra the Ishmaelite, who had married Abigail the daughter of Nahash, sister of Zeruiah, Joab's mother. And Israel and Absalom encamped in the land of Gilead.

When David came to Mahanaim, Shobi the son of Nahash from Habbah of the Ammonites, and Machir the son of Amniel from Lodebar, and Barzilai the Gileadite from Rogelim, brought beds, basins and earthen vessels, wheat, barley, meal, parched grain, beans and lentils, honey and curds and sheep and cheese from the herd, for David and the people with him to eat; for they said, 'The people are hungry and thirsty and weary in the wilderness'.

Then David mustered the men who were with him, and set over them commanders of thousands and commanders of hundreds. And David sent forth the army, one third under the command of Joab, one third under the command of Abishei, the son of Zeruiah, and one third under the command of Ittai the Gittite. And the king said to the men, 'I myself, will also go out with you'. But the men said 'You shall not go out. For if we flee, they will not care about us. If half of us die, they will not care about us. But you are worth ten thousand of us; therefore it is better that you send us help from the city.' The king said to them, 'Whatever seems best to you I will do'. So the king stood at the side of the gate while all the army marched out by hundreds and by thousands. And the king ordered Joab and Abishai and Ittai, 'Deal gently for my sake with the young man Absalom'. And all the people heard when the king gave orders to all the commanders about Absalom.

So the army went out into the field against Israel; and the battle was fought in the forest of Ephraim. And the men of Israel were defeated there by the servants of David, and the slaughter was great on that day, twenty thousand men. The battle spread over the face of all the country; and the forest devoured more people that day than the sword. . . .

This section of the narrative, culminating in David's grief at the death of Absalom, would seem to have taken its rise in the region of the court, for it shows a knowledge of what was happening behind the scenes. More important still is the fact that here – strangely enough, at the heart of the Old Testament – is a signal piece of history which is communicated as sheer human story; and the human story stands on its own feet, as though its author was concerned only to show the way things work, the way things happen in the world. Constantly he selects the facts which will contribute not only to the narrative but also to the explanation. He is interested to see how the things that men think will affect the story – interested in the argument that if a few of Absalom's men are killed at first, the undecided people will easily persuade themselves that his forces are being annihilated. In the pithiest kind of short speeches, he summarises a debate or shows the sort of considerations that have moved men, or brings a paradox to light. With the utmost brevity he depicts a human situation, explains a policy or describes a scene.

It seems that, amongst the scribes employed in the palace, there would soon be some who would have the task of recording events for their own sake. The reign of Solomon marks a period of great cultural change; for the Old Testament itself bears witness to some of the international contacts which resulted from the range of his empire, and which transformed the intellectual atmosphere in Jerusalem. He would need to learn much from the practices of more ancient courts, and he would even make considerable use of foreigners. The 'Wisdom' literature, which was to be found in both Mesopotamia and Egypt, and which had itself become quite an international affair, must have extended its influence to the capital city; and this may explain why Solomon came to be regarded as himself so important a representative of it – associated with the Proverbs which are one of its chief manifestations. The writings of this movement show its interest in the workings of human nature, the technique of mundane life and the conduct of public affairs.

The 'Wisdom' school might well have influenced historical writing, therefore; and some of its thinking seems to have extended into the narrative of Joseph, which is one of the problem-pieces of the Old Testament. It has been regarded by some as a piece of carefully contrived fiction rather than the product of genuine tradition. Joseph himself represented a type that is particularly associated with this school – the court official who knows how to conduct the business of the world, knows how to interpret events, how to handle people, how to deliver a speech, above all, how to persuade a king. It would be natural to associate the school (if it was a school) with the palace rather than the temple; and those who were under its influence would not necessarily be irreligious – the 'Wisdom' literature often stresses the fear of God and shows a certain feeling for the activity of divine Providence. In the procedures of life itself they might be more concerned with human nature, more occupied with reading the manifestations of mind and mood in human beings. They would not necessarily have quarrelled with that historical tradition or historical interpretation which culminated in the 'Yahwist', but it was more their concern to deal with contemporary affairs.

The action of God upon the story is a more subtle matter with them; and they see it taking place very often in the interior regions of the heart. If any parallel to the narrative of Joseph exists outside Israel down to the time of Solomon, it is hardly in historical writing as such but rather in some of the Egyptian short stories – those of Sinahu and Wenamun, for example, which may be more historical than they pretend to be, and which certainly reflect in a vivid manner the conditions of the time. The 'Wisdom' movement itself exerted its maximum influence on Israel at a later date, in the reign of Hezekiah, and its influence is not necessary to explain the existence at any time of an interest in human story for its own sake. Some scholars would still connect the 'Court-History' of David with the 'Wisdom' movement because of certain features of its thought and style.

As a writer on Israel's wider history and remoter past, the 'Yahwist' did not stand alone. Much of the same area was covered, in all probability at a later date, by another author. He is called the 'Elohist', because he was first identified through his use of the term 'Elohem' instead of 'Yahweh'. He added something to the story, perhaps because he drew on the traditions of northern Israel while the 'Yahwist' had been connected with the south. In some respects he was more sophisticated than the 'Yahwist'; and the deity tends not to appear physically in the text – not to present himself as a mytho-logical figure – but works in less tangible ways, acting principally through dreams. A significant change in the actual handling of human history occurred in the seventh century B.C. It was connected with an important development in the prophetic movement, which issued in the production of something like our present book of *Deuteronomy*. This would seem to have been the 'book of the law' discovered in the temple in 612 B.C., in the reign of Josiah, and regarded as the work of Moses. It helped to provoke the famous religious reforms of Josiah's reign.

Besides producing this work, the Deuteronomic movement led to some editing of earlier historical writings, and to an overhauling of the whole story since the settlement in Canaan. If 'J' had dealt with the Promise and its glorious fulfilment, the new school was concerned with the conduct of the affairs of Israel since the acquisition of a homeland. It had to deal with some unhappy things – the separation into two monarchies after the death of Solomon; the conquest of the northern kingdom by the Assyrians; and the attacks on the southern kingdom in the time of Hezekiah. The experi-ence of the previous five or six centuries provided the material for a further experiment in interpretation; but the catastrophes suffered, and the cata-strophes anticipated must have been the powerful impulses behind the movement, adding a dynamic to the traditions of the austerer Yahwists. Once again, the result did not conflict with the interpretation of 'J', but its changes of emphasis amounted to a new development.

The re-survey of history arises, then, out of great vicissitudes and a heightened sense of the cataclysmic. It involves an expansion of the ancient doctrine that misfortune follows some offence against the deity, for the moral is now applied on a large scale, and its implications are developed with a severer logic. Also, in connection with the people of Israel, it acquires a peculiar twist which almost turns it into something new. Stress was now laid on the fact that the Promise had always been a conditional thing; and now, more than before, it was realised that this Yahweh was a jealous god, more exacting in his demands than any other deity. He had to be treated in fact as the sole god and as a spiritual being who required not only ceremonial observances but also the inner affections of men. He had chosen Israel – and, as things were now envisaged, had chosen her not in the way that other gods had attached themselves to other peoples, but as one who, while governing all, had determined to make a special case of a special nation. He demanded that this should be answered by a devotion equally remarkable, as well as by the repudiation of what were now regarded as false gods and heathen practices. Beyond this, he would not even allow himself to be worshipped at the 'high places' formerly used by the Canaanites for their own gods, lest his own cult should be contaminated by the idolatries that had taken place there. For centuries, the previous kings – even the more pious among them – had seen no harm in this, which amounted to the capture for Yahweh of the altars that had belonged to other gods. But, henceforward, sacrifices were to be offered only at the Temple in Jerusalem – the Temple which, when Solomon built it, had been regarded by some of the austerer Yahwists as itself a symbol of idolatries and foreign influences.

The new teaching is codified in the long chapter XXVIII of the book of *Deuteronomy* which begins with a tremendous list of blessings and then a parallel list of curses – probably the expansion of very similar material in the ancient covenant ceremony. 'Blessed shall you be in the city, and blessed shall you be in the field. Blessed shall be the fruit of your body and the fruit of the ground and the fruit of your beasts. . . . Blessed shall be your basket and kneading-trough. . . .' Because she has been chosen by God, Israel must live as a dedicated nation, adhering to regulations that make her different from other peoples. If she is faithful, her reward will go beyond anything hitherto known; 'and all the peoples of the earth shall see that you are called by the name of the Lord; and they shall be afraid of you'. But if a dedicated nation becomes faithless, its doom will equally go beyond all precedents. At the end of a mountain of curses there is put into the mouth of Moses a descriptive piece that is too apt in its concrete detail to be pro-phecy – it must arise out of what had been experienced at the fall of the northern kingdom. It must therefore be more historical in character than it pretends :

The Lord will cause you to be defeated before your enemies . . . and you shall be a horror to all the kingdoms of the earth. And your dead body shall be food for all the birds of the air, and for the beasts of the earth; and there shall be no one to frighten them away. . . . You shall betroth a wife, and another man shall lie with her. . . . Your sons and daughters shall be given to another people, while your eyes look on and fail with longing for them all the day; and it shall not be in the power of your hand to prevent it. A nation which you have not known shall eat up the fruit of your ground and of all your labours . . . so that you shall be driven mad by the sight which your eyes shall see. . . .

The Lord will bring you and your king whom you set over you, to a nation that neither you nor your fathers have known; and there you shall serve other gods of wood and stone. And you shall become a horror, a proverb and a byword, among all the peoples where the Lord will lead you away. . . . You shall beget sons and daughters, but they shall not be yours, for they shall go into captivity. . . .

Because you did not serve the Lord your God with joyfulness and gladness of heart, by reason of the abundance of all things, therefore you shall serve your enemies whom the Lord will send against you, in hunger and thirst and nakedness, and in want of all things; and he will put a yoke of iron upon your neck, until he has destroyed you. The Lord will bring a nation against you from afar, from the end of the earth, as swift as the eagle flies, a nation whose language you do not understand, a nation of stern countenance, who shall not regard the person of the old or show favour to the young. . . . They shall besiege you in all your towns . . . and you shall eat the offspring of your own body, the flesh of your sons and daughters. . . . The man who is the most tender and delicately bred among you will grudge food to his brother, to the wife of his bosom, and to the last of the children who remain to him. . . .

Whereas you were as the stars of heaven for multitude, you shall be left few in number. . . . In the morning you shall say 'Would it were evening!' and at evening you shall say 'Would it were morning!' because of the dread which your heart shall fear. . . . And the Lord will bring you back in ships to Egypt, a journey which I promised you should never make again; and there you shall offer yourselves for sale to your enemies as male and female slaves, but no man will buy you.

In this spirit, the stories in the book of *Judges* were put together and edited, as we have already seen. But the books of *Kings* were also produced and they interpret the rest of the history on the same principles. In this latter case, a later Deuteronomistic author has continued the story till the fall of Judah, the southern kingdom and the resulting exile. To a considerable degree they represent what is really a commentary, or something like a

sermon, on the history of the monarchy; and, in a sense, they admit the fact
– they tell the reader where to go if he wishes to find a record that is more
definitely historical. In a similar way, *Deuteronomy* is not exactly a collection of new commandments – for the most part it repeats the ancient decrees,
but amplifies them with explanatory material, providing once again a great
deal of exhortation and sermonising. From the death of Solomon and the
division of the monarchy, in fact, the straight narrative history – of which
there must have existed a great amount – has largely disappeared. What
survives is a specialised kind of religious meditation on parts of the story.

Taken in the large, the centuries of the divided monarchy lent themselves
to the kind of interpretation which was now provided for them. The
northern kingdom, Israel, had broken away from the Davidic dynasty, had
separated from Jerusalem and had preferred the altars in the high places.
Not one of its kings had conformed to the standards which the Deuteronomists insisted upon, and its people had been more open to the influence of
idolatries abroad, those of the Phoenicians, for example. It was the north
which had met its doom, and at the time of its downfall the writer of *Kings*
turns aside to produce a little interpretative essay :

> And this was so, because the people of Israel had sinned against the Lord
> their God, who had brought them up out of the land of Egypt from under
> the hand of Pharaoh King of Egypt, and had feared other gods and
> walked in the customs of the nations whom the Lord drove out before the
> people of Israel, and in the customs which the kings of Israel had intro-
> duced. And the people of Israel did secretly against the Lord their God
> things that were not right. They built for themselves high places at all
> their towns, from watchtower to fortified city; they set up for themselves
> pillars and Asherim on every high hill and under every green tree; and
> there they burned incense on all the high places, as the nations did whom
> the Lord carried away before them. And they did wicked things, pro-
> voking the Lord to anger, and they served idols, of which the Lord had
> said to them, 'You shall not do this'. Yet the Lord warned Israel and
> Judah by every prophet and every seer, saying, 'Turn from your evil
> ways' . . . And they . . . made for themselves molten images of two calves;
> and they made an Asherah, and worshipped all the host of heaven, and
> served Baal. And they burned their sons and daughters as offerings, and
> used divination and sorcery, and sold themselves to do evil in the sight
> of the Lord, provoking him to anger. Therefore the Lord was very angry
> with Israel, and removed them out of his sight; none was left but the
> tribe of Judah only.
> [II *Kings*, XVII, 7–18.]

The conclusion seemed a natural one – by no means forced; and it did
not rest on doctrine which had been devised after the actual event. The

prophets had issued their warnings from the beginning of the story, and their conflict with kings had been on these very issues. Judah herself had committed the same sins, though, by her own account, less consistently; but Judah was spared for a longer period, partly because of a promise made to David and his house. Though the son and grandson of Solomon did evil,

> Nevertheless for David's sake the Lord his God gave [the latter] a lamp in Jerusalem, setting up his son after him, and establishing Jerusalem; because David did what was right in the sight of the Lord and did not turn aside from anything he commanded him all the days of his life, except in the matter of Uriah the Hittite.
> [I *Kings*, XV, 4–6.]

If the system is worked out in greater detail – in terms of short-range judgements on human sin – it begins to appear less plausible. Josiah, the reforming king of Judah, was the most virtuous of monarchs. 'Before him there was no king like him, who turned to the Lord with all his heart and with all his soul and with all his might, according to all the law of Moses; nor did any like him arise after him.' The author of *Kings* seems shy of telling us that he suffered a violent death in a conflict with the Pharaoh Neco before he reached the age of forty, though the fact comes out in parenthesis after a reference to the actual annals of the reign. Josiah's grandfather, Manasseh, committed all the idolatries and 'seduced [the people] to do more evil than the nations had done whom the Lord destroyed before the people of Israel'. He 'shed very much innocent blood, till he had filled Jerusalem from one end to another'. We are not told that he had an enormously successful and prosperous reign, though it is stated (possibly with some exaggeration) that he was king for fifty-five years. It would seem that, even in theory, the divine judgement was not regarded as operating within short periods, except in extreme cases, though it was tempting to write as though it worked in this way on the occasions when the facts seemed to justify the view. In any case the Deuteronomistic system admitted of certain flexibilities, as in the case of Solomon's grandson, who, in spite of his offences, had his dynasty continued out of respect for David. On the crucial issue of the worship at the 'high places', the author seems far from rigid. He was prepared to allow great merit to the ruler who permitted such worship, provided the man had been the enemy of idolatry. Asa, for example, 'did what was right in the eyes of the Lord as David his father had done. He put away the male prostitutes out of the land, and removed all the idols that his father had made. . . . But the high places were not taken away. Nevertheless the heart of Asa was wholly true to the Lord all his days.' It was as though the mere use of the 'high places' for non-idolatrous reasons could be counted as only a technical offence, at any rate in the past; or there was a recognition of the fact that only the newly discovered 'book of the law' had clinched the case against the practice, and an otherwise worthy man was not to be condemned retrospectively for what he had not realised to be a sin. The Deuteronomic writer (or the successor of his who compiled the book of *Kings*) seems chiefly anxious because all the virtues of the great Josiah – all the reforms of his reign – did nothing to mitigate the sorrows of Judah. After recounting the king's merits, he writes:

> Still the Lord did not turn from the fierceness of his great wrath, by which his anger was kindled against Judah, because of all the provocations with which Manasseh had provoked him. And the Lord said, 'I will remove Judah also out of my sight, as I have removed Israel and I will cast off this city which I have chosen, and the house of which I said, my name shall be there'.
> [II *Kings*, XXIII, 26–27.]

Josiah's son and grandson both did 'evil in the sight of the Lord, and, in the reign of the latter, Nebudchadnezzar of Babylon came against Israel to destroy it'. Then the author, as though he were in some doubt about the matter, writes:

> Surely this came upon Judah at the command of the Lord, to remove them out of his sight, for the sins of Manasseh, according to all that he had done, and also for the innocent blood that he had shed; for he had filled Israel with innocent blood and the Lord would not pardon.

To the Deuteronomistic writer, therefore, the sins of Manasseh were the effective cause of the downfall of Judah.

All this does not pretend to be a true history of the ancient monarchy, and even the book of *Kings* offers itself rather as an interpretative essay. At the end of each reign, the reader who wishes to have the real narrative of events – the facts for their own sake – is referred to the standard sources, the Books of the Chronicles of the Kings of Israel or the Kings of Judah. A hint is even given of the important things he will find there – the things which the Deuteronomic writer had made no pretence of telling. In the case of Ahab we read: 'Now the rest of the acts of Ahab, and all that he did, and the ivory house which he built and all the cities that he built, are they not written in the Book of the Chronicles of the Kings of Israel?' In the case of Jeroboam II we must go to the Chronicles to learn about 'his might, how he fought, and how he recovered for Israel Damascus and Hamath which had belonged to Judah'. In the case of Hezekiah it is a question of 'all his might and how he made the pool and conduit and brought water into the city'. Even so, there are strange omissions. Hardly anything is said about Omri, except that he built Samaria and did evil, and that one must go to the Chronicles to learn of 'the might that he showed'; though Omri's importance is revealed in the Assyrian annals, which designate the country itself by his name for a century after the end of his reign and his dynasty. The account of Hezekiah has nothing to correspond with Sennacherib's description of his handling of that monarch.

The Book of the Chronicles in both Israel and Judah must not be confused with the Old Testament books which bear the same name. The references to them suggest that they were available to readers, so they are likely to have differed again from the official records which must have been kept in the palaces. They are unlikely to have been literary productions or running narratives and were probably sketchy accounts of one event after another – any event that seemed worth recording. The account of David's decline at the beginning of the First Book of *Kings* continues the use of the 'Court-History'; and the comparatively full account of Solomon is based on the Book of the Acts of Solomon, and, no doubt, some official sources, especially for the full story of his building operations. The temple-annals would be used both here and (probably) for the reign of Josiah. But the full account of Elijah and Elisha, besides owing something to oral tradition, would seem to depend on written sources – lives of the prophets or cycles of narrative. It is clear that a considerable amount of historical literature was in circulation long before the books of *Kings* were compiled.

Finally, the Deuteronomic school revised the earlier historical writing of Israel and the effects of this are seen particularly in the books of *Exodus* and *Numbers*. The story required only a little pointing to make the required emphases more tangible and the moral more explicit. In *Exodus*, XII, 26–7, it is the editor who inserts

And when your children say to you, 'What do you mean by the service?' you shall say 'It is the sacrifice of the Lord's passover, for he passed over the houses of the people of Israel in Egypt, when he slew the Egyptians but spared our houses'.

Where the second of the ten commandments forbids the making of graven images, the Deuteronomic writer wishes to strengthen the point. He adds the note that Yahweh is a 'jealous god, visiting the iniquity of the fathers upon the children to the third and fourth generation of those that hate [him]' (Exodus, XX, 4).

In many cases the editing process involved the insertion of pieces of Deuteronomic exposition into the story as previously narrated, or the transfer of the same message into the speeches that had been concocted for ancient leaders and prophets – speeches which condensed the presumed views and motives of these personages, but also served the purpose of historical interpretation. The Deuteronomic view that the worship of false gods was the essential cause of defeat in battle was probably read back into the mind of Samuel by a later editor (I *Samuel*, VII, 3) and a later writer – one who, like the Deuteronomists, was hostile to the monarchy, attributing it to a popular demand that had been displeasing to God – put into the mouth of Samuel, at the foundation of the kingdom under Saul, not only his misgivings (I *Samuel*, X, 18–19) but also a solemn warning (touched up by a Deuteronomic editor) of the way in which God would turn against his own people if they rebelled against him (I *Samuel*, XII, 6–18).

In this way the historiography of ancient Israel began to acquire the successive layers which it has been one of the tasks of modern scholarship to identify and disentangle.

5 EXILE AND RETURN

If the Exodus gave a great impulse to historiography and to the religion of Israel, the Exile – the transfer of the leading elements of the population to Babylonia at almost the beginning of the sixth century B.C. – was likely to be equally unforgettable to a people that survived it, a powerful influence upon a nation that reflected perpetually on the things that happened to it. For Israel, a people which had regarded itself as chosen by God and particularly favoured by him, no other kind of tragedy could have produced an impression more overwhelming; and it was a recent event, occurring in the full light of day, but as clearly the fulfilment of prophecy as the entry into the Promised Land. In a way quite unparalleled in neighbouring countries, the children of Israel had early reached the point at which the development of religion itself was almost bound to come as the result of reflection upon their historical experience. There had now occurred a momentous addition to that experience, and out of it sprang new kinds of thought which greatly affected the attitude to the succession of events in time. The return from exile was an event almost equally impressive, producing a new historical situation which greatly affected the development of ideas and the attitude to the past. All the conjunctures, therefore, combined to produce once again amongst the ancient Hebrews intellectual movements that were to resound in world history.

The people had not lost their identity in a foreign country, and, in respect of the politically effective part of them, the Deuteronomic prophecy that they would turn to gods of sticks and stones proved incorrect. The religion survived even after being separated from Jerusalem and the Temple, which had come to be regarded as so important to it; and it may have gained on certain sides by being uprooted from the soil to which it had been attached. It survived in some people as a mere spiritual thing – less concerned with mundane prosperity and national pride – thrown back more upon the inner life. For men of Israel living amongst alien people and alien cults, as well as for that remnant of them which remained faithful while their fellow-countrymen lapsed, religion, at least in one of its aspects, was almost bound to become more individualistic in character – not so tied

to the nation as a corporate unit, but pushing further than before the sum-
mons that it brought to each separate person. It came to be seen more clearly
that in the spiritual life each man has his separate wire to eternity; the law
could now be described as written on man's heart; and there was the promise that, henceforward, a man would be punished only for his own sins.
The development in this direction had been taking place for a long time, as
Yahweh was seen to be in every corner of the earth and attempts were made
to persuade him to be a forgiving god – attempts which tended to emphasise the actual contriteness of the sinner and the state of the inner man. If
all this remained in some sense an ideal – perhaps a minority movement –
it affected the whole development of the Jewish mentality and was destined
to influence the future very greatly.

There was a sense in which, after an experience of such a shattering
nature, the religion of Israel became unhinged from its connection with
history. That connection had helped to keep it down-to-earth; and the tradition of the desert, which had kept the skies clear for Yahweh, had obstructed
the development of mythopœic thought. The hostility to foreign cults and
to the notion of making graven images even of Yahweh, had helped to
prevent the rise of the kind of mythology that existed in other nations.
Perhaps it was the return from exile which proved to be the powerful
immediate influence from the fifth century B.C.; for the way in which this
was effected may have been partly responsible for what came to be almost
a flight from realism. It was as though the mythologies which had been
cleaned out of the past were projected into the future. Alternatively, Israel
was fated to run through the whole gamut of possible attitudes to time and
destiny. There emerged from this date the political messianism and apocalyptic dreaming which have so often occurred in history and have dogged
even the twentieth century.

The wonders of the story never cease; for the Persians defeated the Babylonian empire, and at the end of the sixth and beginning of the fifth centuries B.C., they allowed the exiles to return, and to rebuild the walls and
temple of Jerusalem, on terms that the latter fixed for themselves. The prevailing party of these took the lessons of history – the moral of the whole
story – almost too seriously. The sin had been to have had truck with
foreigners and their pagan cults; the moral of even the book of *Judges* had
been that the children of Israel ought to have obeyed the commands of
Yahweh and destroyed the previous inhabitants of Canaan entirely, instead
of settling down to live amongst them, and being contaminated by their
licentious cults. Inter-marriage with the foreigner had been a root cause of
the evils from the very beginning. The essential thing now, therefore, was
the recovery of the original purity of the nation; and, after exile in a foreign
country, this was all the more difficult but at the same time all the more
important. An almost fanatical determination to keep separate from the

northern part of the country – completely rejecting the Samaritans – helped to reinforce the policy. Since the nation had come to tragedy through the neglect of the law, the adhesion to all the details of the law was to be another aspect of the policy of the new Israel. In a more definite sense than before, the country was to be a religious community, guided essentially by a priesthood. It was still subordinate to the Persian empire, and instead of having a king, it was to be under the direction of a high priest who held almost a royal position. Nothing in the past had suggested that such a system might develop, for the kings had held a sacerdotal position. It was an important stage in the development of what we call Judaism.

This, too, had to be provided with a history; for it was necessary to show that it was the thing that Yahweh had intended from the very first. The need was met by a writer who produced in a single work the present two books of *Chronicles* as well as *Ezra* and *Nehemiah* (some of the chapters of which became displaced), though making use of important earlier material. The work belongs to the latter part of the fourth or possibly even to the third century B.C. The same 'priestly' school edited some of the earlier historical writings, and, for example, provided its own account of the Creation, in many respects unlike that of 'J'. The book of *Chronicles* begins with Adam, but condenses the early history into chapter after chapter of genealogical lists, for genealogy had now become a matter of momentous importance, and this work seems to show that the keeping of such lists had long been a more serious matter than the previous writings had enabled us to realise. The story then moves quickly to the establishment of the monarchy; but Saul is regarded as wicked, and now the significant feature of the narrative is the glorification of David, whose sins and humiliations are generally omitted. The description of him is a picture of the ideal monarch, and even the Temple is really imputed to him – he makes the plans, provides the materials, gives the instructions. The position and power of the priests and Levites, as they existed in the fourth century B.C., are now read back into the past. There was even an attempt at this time to push back their special rights to the period before Moses, and their detailed organisation – the precise distribution of functions etc. – is imputed to David, in whose time they had in fact no special rôle. The book of *Chronicles* is so pre-occupied with this matter, and so interested in the music of the Temple, that its author is thought to have been a Levite, perhaps a member of a musical guild. In the account of the history of the monarchy, the northern kingdom is ignored save in some of its contacts with the southern kingdom, Judah, for it was regarded as having been utterly untrue to Yahweh, and the resolve to have nothing to do with Samaria would harden the earlier prejudices against it. In many ways the accounts of the monarchs are a repetition of the books of *Kings*, but in some cases there is a remarkable expansion and it is clear that the author of *Chronicles* had a wider range of sources, some of which he names. But there is a further sense in which the mind seems to harden and to take things more literalistically than before – as one might expect when a religion is drawing in upon itself or a religious society is fortifying itself against the outsider. The divine judgement on unfaithful kings is now seen as a more immediate affair, and works itself out within a single reign. It is even more detailed than this, for the monarch who has been virtuous for a time and has prospered may turn to evil ways, and then his fortune changes. Even the virtuous Josiah now suffers as a result of sin, and the prosperity of Manasseh can be confessed, for, though he began as an evil ruler he was brought to repentance and he restored the service of Yahweh. It would need no perversion of history to achieve the required correlations in the way that this author achieved them, for those who explain misfortune on this author's principle can always find a corresponding sin. In *Kings* and *Chronicles,* Josiah was so virtuous that the authors of both quoted a prophetess who had said, 'You shall be gathered to your grave in peace'. He suffered death in battle at the hand of the Egyptians at Megiddo; but according to the later author, this was because he took no notice of the Pharaoh, Neco, who said that he was speaking on behalf of God and was coming north to fight the Syrians on God's behalf. The virtuous Asa does not come off scot-free in the *Chronicles,* though first of all he was rewarded with thirty-five years of peace. In a war against Israel he made an alliance with Syria, and the seer Hanani reproached him, 'because you relied on the King of Syria, and did not rely on the Lord your God . . . from now on you will have wars'. Asa treated the man cruelly, and before long suffered from a disease in his feet; yet even in his disease he did not seek the Lord, but sought help from physicians. These longer accounts of the rulers make use of further material that may have been as reliable as the sources underlying the book of *Kings.* The story of Asa's offence clearly goes back to such a source and creates a complication which the writer of *Kings* simply ignored. The repentance of Manasseh might seem less plausible, but the author of *Chronicles,* besides saying that it was in 'the book of the Chronicles' which the author of *Kings* had used and which gave the king's prayer and the words of the seers who spoke to him in the name of the Lord, adds this remark:

> And his prayer, and how God received his entreaty, and all his sin and his faithlessness, and the sites on which he built high places and set up the Asherim and the images, before he humbled himself [i.e. before his repentance and reform], behold, they are written in the Chronicles of the Seers.

After the time of David and Solomon, whose failings are omitted, the books of *Chronicles* are often fuller, and apparently more close to the sources, than the books of *Kings*; and even for earlier periods they draw on older sources – sometimes on traditions that may have survived in oral form. When the narrative reaches the post-exilic period and the return to Jerusalem, it makes great use of contemporary lists and genealogies, but also of the memoirs of Nehemiah, again one of the technically remarkable historical productions of the ancient Jews.

In ancient days there had existed a tradition which cherished the austerities of the desert, the tribal ideal and the holy places that existed in the land of Canaan. Its upholders were calculated to be in the forefront of those who were hostile to the monarchy as such, and who distrusted Jerusalem as a late conquest. At first it had really been David's city rather than the headquarters of the people – a place full of aliens and alien influences, especially when Solomon was building the Temple. There emerged, however, another tradition which tended to idealise David and the monarchy as established by him, and it received a shock when the ten tribes of the north broke away. It was no doubt fortified as a tradition when Judah came into its constant conflicts with Israel. Owing to the special promise that had been given to David – 'Your house and your kingdom shall be made sure for ever before me; your throne shall be established for ever' (II *Samuel*, VIII, 16) – it had even been held that Judah, in spite of its sins, would escape the fate that fell on the sister-monarchy. At the same time, the passion of those who hated idolatry and the interests of those who were hostile to the northern kingdom, brought Yahwism into closer alliance with Jerusalem as the safeguard against the evils of the 'high places'. The return from exile greatly strengthened the cause of Jerusalem and the Davidic monarchy, and made it seem that Yahweh was ready to give it his blessing after all. One of the purposes of historical activity in the subsequent period – in the books of *Chronicles*, for example – was to establish the continuity of the new régime with the old and to give fresh life to this aspect of the tradition. The dream of an independent political status and a glorified monarchy was now stronger than ever, but its fulfilment was repeatedly delayed, and great empires still dominated the eastern Mediterranean and Western Asia. The idea of the Davidic monarchy became intensified but lost contact with reality, without losing its mundane character – without turning into a purely spiritual ideal. Political messianism led to the view that, not by the actions of men or by the ordinary processes of history, but by the direct action of God in the fullness of time, the terrestrial glories of the Davidic kingdom would be established. Eyes were now turned to the future, and if history itself were not to develop to a grand consummation, the hand of Yahweh would produce this result. At least those who lived in history had something to look forward to.

The prophets who had kept close to history and to the diagnosis of contemporary events had themselves become the spokesmen of further promises, and had come to paint poetical pictures of a transcendent future. But the age of the prophets passed; and the attention of the people of Judah seemed to concentrate itself on the refinements of the law rather than on the mighty deeds of Yahweh in past ages. In the latest Old Testament period, accounts of events were produced which are sometimes remote from the real facts of history. Attempts were made to schematise the course of ages, to plot the graph of successive world-empires, and to predict how things would develop or how they would end. The symbolism of some of this writing has kept the whole race of scholars – and men in general – puzzling over the matter ever since. There developed an apocalyptic literature which presented a new heaven and a new earth, visions of celestial powers, a realm that was like a mythology highly transcendentalised. It seemed like a flight from history.

Yet, early in the first century B.C. there appeared the first Book of Maccabees, describing another great episode of Jewish history – the fanatical fight for the faith against Antiochus IV Epiphanes, who had sought to hellenise the Jews and had thrust pagan gods upon them. In a manner that would satisfy modern technicians, it tells a sober story, without divine interventions or messianic fervours. The precision of its details, its dating and its geographical knowledge gives it real narrative power, and makes it forever an important source for the events of two or three generations earlier which it describes. It is fair to the enemy, frank in its account of defeats as well as successes, and restrained in its treatment of the story. It is clearly by a pious Jew; and once again there comes from this people a work that must rank with the best that ever came down to us from the ancient world.

6 ISRAEL'S NEIGHBOURS AND THEIR PAST

It is customary to speak of men being 'tied to a tradition' or wanting to 'preserve the past' when in reality the sense for bygone times is not involved. It may be a question of continuing to use the agricultural implement one already knows or to follow the social custom that one recognises, and the idea of tradition may not have entered into the case. What men so often want to conserve is really the present, the thing that is before their eyes. They will play an inherited violin because it is the instrument before them – not because it has been handed down from the past. And, similarly, in the past, they would read (or would have read to them) ancient authors, not out of romantic sentiment, but because these were the books around them. They might have had the feeling that an ancient author possessed a mysterious authority, but in Mesopotamia and Egypt the old writers were read, and then they went on being read. In Egypt some of the most brilliant literature and art was produced soon after 2000 B.C., and these ancient authors were being taught in the schools hundreds of years later. Men would always have loved a good story, and the epic would give them a notion of a past that had been heroic.

Late in the eighth century B.C., however, the empires with which we have been dealing had come to feel that their civilisation had grown old. There may even have been something decadent in these peoples, or a sense of being decadent. They showed a 'strong archaising tendency' which affected 'language, art forms, literary genres and religious observances'. By this time there had been produced the Assyrian 'Synchronistic History', which went back to the past, summarising the relations between Assyria and Babylon for a number of centuries. It was a dry and factual affair, and it has been suggested that, since it says much about treaties and boundaries, it may really be an archival piece, connected with a controversy over territory. There is a famous inscription of Mesha of Moab in the eighth century B.C. and its attitude to the deity reminds one of the Old Testament, though essentially it is only a record of his own military successes. In the third quarter of the seventh century B.C., Assurbanipal prided himself on his knowledge of the old languages of Sumer and Akkad. It is only through the copies in his famous library that the modern world has recovered some of the ancient literature of Mesopotamia. In that famous institution there seemed to be an attempt to recapture a whole civilisation by the accumulation of all its writings. During this period the Babylonians must have been keeping up their own chronicle of contemporary affairs, but it was more succinct, more purely factual, than the annals of the Assyrian kings:

> In the tenth year, Nabopolassar, in the month of Iyyar, mustered the army of Akkad, and marched up the Euphrates.
> The men of Suhu and Hindanu did not fight against him; their tribute they laid before him.
> In the month of Ab, they reported that the army of Assyria [was] in the city of Qablinu. Nabopolassar went up against them.
> In the month of Ab, the 12th day, he did battle against the army of Assyria and the army of Assyria was routed before him, and great havoc was made of Assyria.
> Prisoners in great number they took. The Mannaeans who had come to their aid and the chief men of Assyria were captured. On that day the city of Quablinu was captured. . . .

This chronicle had been produced for centuries and many parts of it have come to light. But by this time the Babylonians were interested in their own past and were copying or re-compiling ancient chronicles, too, studying the omens of centuries before, recovering ancient literary works, and reviving some of the formalities of earlier religious inscriptions. We could almost say that there was a kind of interest in archaeology – the appearance of something like research. Under Nabodinus of Babylonia it was worked out that Hammurabi lived seven hundred years before Burnaburrash and that a temple which the king restored had not been rebuilt for eight hundred years. The same ruler prides himself on having discovered a memorial to Naram-Sin – one which placed the man 3,200 years before his own time. Assurbanipal of Assyria had boasted earlier that he had recaptured the goddess Nanâ, who for 1,635 years had been 'angry' because she had been held in Edom. It might seem that now, at least, an interest in historical enquiry had been awakened.

It would be wrong to deny such interest, but it might also be imprudent to attach too much importance to it, and at least we possess some information which helps to explain it. The Assyrian kings, for example, liked to boast of the fact that they, first of anybody over a long period of time, had restored a given temple. Already in the eighteenth century B.C., Neferhotep of Egypt had given an account of a piece of historical research. 'My heart hath desired to see the ancient writings of Atum,' he said. 'Open for me a great investigation.' He 'proceeded to the library' and 'opened the rolls', but his real intention was to find the correct way of fashioning a representation of the god.

> Let the god know concerning his creation, and the gods concerning their fashioning . . . [let] me know the god in his form that I may fashion him as he was formerly, when they made the statutes in their council, in order to establish their monuments upon earth. . . . I will fashion him, his limbs, his face, his fingers, according to that which my majesty has seen in the rolls.

Something of the same is still true in the Babylonia of the time of Nabonidus in the sixth century B.C., and indeed during the whole of what is called the neo-Babylonian epoch. There was a sense for the past, and a great desire to restore ancient temples; but it was necessary to follow the rules that had been established in each case – to discover the *temena* which had authenticated the original building and had shown how the god had intended it to be constructed. A breach of this divine decree might bring tragedy, and there were occasions when a temple was pulled down because it was discovered that it did not correspond with the basic document. If the text itself could not be found, some other document might be used to authenticate tradition at a given place; though it was liable to be superseded if something still more ancient emerged. The *temena* was attached to the original building and if the temple was in ruins it might be necessary to institute something like a 'dig'. Mention is made of specialised workers who took part in the investigations. In the process, varied kinds of texts were likely to be uncovered; they would be transcribed and studied and if they contained the name of a ruler, he would be located in the king-lists and the date would be worked out. The effect of this was, in fact, to draw the mind further into the historical field. A religious motive seems therefore to underlie these early researches and to explain why 'the long texts of Nabonidus have such an archaeological tone'.

CHAPTER FOUR

The Rise of Classical Historiography

1 THE GREEK ATTITUDE TO HISTORY

The article on 'History' in the *Encyclopaedia Britannica* points to a group of ancient Greeks whom it describes as 'the first historians'. For century after century it has been proclaimed that Herodotus is 'the father of history', and certainly he is the first historical writer whose work can still be read and can be associated with an author's name. It is held that the Greeks were the first people to deal with the events of the past in anything like a scientific manner, realising that the facts themselves must be the subject of an investigation, and that, when once established, they can be compared and correlated so as to become the basis of such things as political science. Distinguished students of the past who would have found it difficult to reach agreement on the second greatest of historians have often been able to unite in saying that Thucydides plainly holds the first place of all.

Along with all this, however, there exists the insistent view that the Greeks did not achieve historical-mindedness, and never could have achieved it, because they had the wrong view of time and the time-process. Collingwood speaks of 'the anti-historical tendency of Greek thought'. Moses Finley writes that 'on the intellectual level everything was against the idea of history. . . . Of all the lines of enquiry which the Greeks initiated, history was the most abortive.' It has been pointed out that Greek historiography, which really begins in the fifth century B.C., breaks off in the fourth, 'while philosophy rises to its height' – a philosophy 'which takes no account of the work of the historians'. Again, Moses Finley tells us: 'All the Greek philosophers to the last of the Neo-Platonists were evidently agreed in their indifference to history.' The philosophy was a hostile force, drawing the mind away from the changing and the transient and fixing it upon the eternal and immutable. T. F. Driver, in *The Sense of History in Greek and Shakesperian Drama*, describes the complex relationship of the drama with time and history, but notes that 'the Greek historical consciousness is essentially unhistorical'. Even in Homer (in great contra-distinction to the Ænead), 'time figures only as a literary device . . . the event leads from no past to no future'. In the historical play by Æschylus, *The Persians*, 'time is frozen . . . the experience of living in time is not communicated'. The aim in Greek tragedy is to 'minimise the factor of time and reveal the operation of cosmic laws and powers'. With the Greeks, 'time tended to be absorbed into the cosmos in such a way as to be a function of cosmic space rather than a different order of reality. . . . Space is the characteristic mode of thought in Hellenism as time is [amongst the Hebrews] . . . Greek syntax is the reflection of a mentality which approaches time not as a mode of experience but as a material to be measured, cut, arranged, classified. . . . Plato and Aristotle pondered time so much because it presented such a problem to a spatially-orientated consciousness.'

In the first century A.D., the Jewish historian Josephus, who had come to identify himself with the Roman Empire, delivered a famous attack on the Greeks, and especially on their treatment of history. It was his thesis that 'this custom of transmitting down the histories of ancient times hath been better preserved by those nations which are called Barbarians, than by the Greeks themselves'. He described how the Egyptians, the Babylonians and the Phoenicians were the people who, by general consent, had 'preserved the memorials of the most ancient and lasting traditions of mankind'. These peoples belonged to regions unusually exempt from destructive cataclysms, he said; but also they had taken care to put everything on record – 'their history was esteemed sacred and put into public tables as written by men of the greatest wisdom they had among them'. The same had been true of the ancient Jews; and, in fact, he wrote (though we might be inclined to think that he went wrong in his counting): 'we have the names of our high priests from father to son set down in our records for a period of two thousand years'.

But, as to the Greeks, he said: 'almost all which happened to the Greeks happened not long ago, nay is of yesterday only. I speak of the building of their cities, the inventions of their arts and the description of their laws; and as for the writing down of their histories, it is very near the last thing that they set themselves to.' He turned to the question of the preservation of historical records or traditions:

As for the places where the Greeks inhabit, ten thousand destructions have overtaken them and blotted out the memory of former actions; so that they were ever beginning a new way of living and supposed that every one of them was the origin of their new state. It was also late, and with difficulty, that they came to the letters they now use.

Josephus was rather fond of saying that these ancient Greeks had found it difficult to learn their letters, their alphabet. But, in any case, he said, they had failed to produce records in the way that had happened in Egypt and in Mesopotamia.

> For . . . we [must] remember that in the beginning the Greeks had taken no care to have public records of their several transactions preserved. . . . This original recording of such ancient transactions hath not only been neglected by the other states of Greece; but even among the Athenians themselves also, who pretend to be aborigines and to have applied themselves to learning, there are no such records extant.

Whatever view we may take about the relations between the ancient Greeks and their history, we can hardly say that, at the earliest recognisable stage of the story, they were at all deficient in what, at that stage, was the appropriate form of piety towards the past. Because they reached that stage thousands of years later than some of the peoples whom we have been studying, they have been able to leave us at least glimpses of evidence which throw light on something elemental, though its equivalent must in all likelihood have existed in Egypt and Mesopotamia before the emergence of 'the state'. It has been pointed out that 'if ever a race had a genius for commemoration, the Greeks had. . . . Reverence for the great individuals of the past was part and parcel of the primitive religious concepts of the Hellenic peoples. The commanding place occupied in religious belief by hero-worship has more and more clearly revealed itself.' Farnell thinks that some form of ancestor-worship may well go back to an 'indefinite antiquity' in Greece, whence the 'reverential affection' for the reputed founder of a tribe or clan or family led to the establishment of periodic rites, if the man's grave was sufficiently near at hand. 'We have indirect evidence that the tendance of the family dead was growing into actual worship from the eighth century, B.C.' Some of the hero cults 'must be dated to a remotely early period', and the epic – which itself embodied a certain piety towards one's ancestors – no doubt gave encouragement to this. 'It is indisputable that the post-Homeric Greeks were worshipping [the] epic heroes in the full conviction that they had once lived a real human life.' The Greeks were 'heroising real individuals in the sixth and fifth centuries B.C.'; and 'certainly some time before the fifth century the founders of new cities were normally worshipped after their death'. All this is not to be equated with a sense of the past, since on the one hand the fear of the dead, the fear of ghosts, had some effect on men, while on the other hand there was a hope and belief that the person worshipped was still actually present – still able to make himself felt in the world – 'the tomb of the hero was a talisman, effective as a palladium in time of war'. Combined, however, with what we know of the attitude of the Greeks to the epic, we cannot separate it entirely from a more general sort of piety towards the past – especially if there is any truth in the view that tragedy itself developed, if only in part, from mimatic celebrations, representing the actual deeds and vicissitudes of the hero who was being commemorated.

An attitude to the past may seem a simple thing but clearly it may have developed from a multiplicity of factors; and the problem of the ancient Greeks is likely to confront us with some of the complexities involved. It may be useful to try to see whether the anomalies that have revealed themselves are related to anything in what we might roughly call the Greek experience.

2 THE CYCLICAL VIEW OF TIME

We now know that, behind Homer – behind the history of what we call classical Greece – there existed a brilliant civilisation which has left a great mass of records (business notes, for example), decipherable in recent years as a result of the script known as Linear B. This Mycenean realm collapsed not very long after the date which is generally assigned to the famous fall of Troy, and, as it weakened, new populations moved across the country, inaugurating an entirely new era of history there. They were apparently unlettered; nor do they seem to have been civilised by the subject population in the way that happened with some conquering races. Circumstances were apparently so desperate that everyone was absorbed in the material side of life for a long time, and, somehow or other, a culture withered. The collapse of the old order was so complete that the Greeks of the classical period knew practically nothing about it. The pattern of a shield in Homer belongs to that earlier Mycenean age, and this may mean that some of the poetry of the time came through the screen, or that an actual shield had survived, almost perhaps as a museum piece. The classical Greeks were unable to read Linear B, and show no signs of having met it even as a problem to be solved. I am told by a classical scholar that if they had seen a tile or tablet inscribed with Linear B, this would have been meaningless to them and they would have kicked it to one side. The Jewish writer Josephus, in the first century A.D., describes the Greeks of his own day as making great researches in order to discover whether writing was known at all in those older days – in the period of the Trojan war, for example – and he says that there was great doubt about the matter. So far as one can see, all knowledge of writing disappeared after the Mycenean age, and for centuries the new populations were without anything of the sort. When we meet it again, it is a new sort of writing, a new alphabet, skilfully developed from a basis that the

Phoenicians had supplied. It is surprising to see how little of the earlier history of the Greeks passed through to the future even by oral transmission; though the conquest by the newcomers, the Dorians, was remembered (a thing that the victors would not easily forget) and the later Greeks remained convinced that the predecessors of the Dorians had spoken Greek.

A kind of iron curtain was drawn, therefore, between the classical Greeks and the remarkable Mycenean civilisation that lay behind them. A far bigger gulf was produced than that which occurred in what the Europeans call the Dark Ages – the centuries after the fall of Rome's Western Empire. In this latter case, at least the treasures of civilisation remained in considerable quantities in the safety of monastic libraries, and the ability to read them did not entirely go out of the world. As the centuries succeeded one another, Western Europe was able gradually to recover the thought and something like the history of the Graeco-Roman world. But the classical Greeks seem to have been virtually unable to get behind the iron curtain that lay in their rear. It has been suggested that there is no fundamental reason why they should not have developed the archaeology – they had the tools, and at least some of the required detective-work must have been well within their grasp. They learned later how to use inscriptions that were in their form of script and there are one or two occasions on which Thucydides seems to make what we should call an archaeological inference. The men of Mesopotamia were able to dig for the purpose of investigation; and in the days of classical Greece the Mycenean civilisation could not have been buried so deep as in the nineteenth century A.D. Discussing the later Greek proverb which charged the inhabitants of Crete with 'romancing', Gilbert Murray wrote:

> Was it that Crete was full of stories of a past greatness which to the ordinary forgetful world seemed merely incredible? . . . So near had Minoan Crete come to complete oblivion.

In the case of the Minoan and Mycenean civilisations – so close at hand – the first stage of the story provides us with a remarkable failure of historical memory.

This helps to explain the significance of what one or two people regarded as an unusual experience in the fifth century B.C. In that century the Greeks only knew of a comparatively short history behind them – they thought that the historical past extended back for only a very few hundred years, and that before this was the time when the gods walked and stalked on the earth. Hecataeus of Miletus, in the early part of the century, went to Egypt and told there how he could trace his ancestry back for sixteen generations, which would bring him to one of the gods. The Egyptians showed him the statues of priests – son succeeding father for thousands of years – a vast extension of what was to be regarded as historical time. Herodotus records very much the same experience somewhat later; and it is clear that the experience made a great impression. The result was to create a great respect for Egypt and perhaps even too great a respect for anything the priests had to say. Egypt was the place to be referred to for the most difficult historical questions of all, questions about Helen and Paris, about the Trojan war, about Hercules and the earliest gods. Hecataeus and Herodotus were at least not lacking in awe when they encountered the evidence of a past that was really remote. The ancient Greeks became sensible of something catastrophic that had cut them off from so much of their own past.

One finds in Greek literature further places where the mind seems to have reverted to that original situation and emphasis is put on the notion of a recurrent catastrophe that destroys a civilisation, leaving a remnant of mankind to start everything at the beginning again, with hardly even a memory of the things that had been achieved before. The words of Josephus show that even in the first century A.D. there remained the notion that in Greece 'ten thousand destructions' had occurred and had 'blotted out the memory of former actions', each producing the impression that now the nation was really only just starting its history. The experience of Hecataeus and Herodotus is recalled by Plato's account in the *Timaeus* of the way Solon in Egypt 'had taken the opportunity of consulting the leading experts among the priests upon ancient history and had made the discovery that he himself and his fellow-Hellenes were in a state of almost total ignorance on the subject'.

> On one occasion he sought to lead them into a discussion upon Antiquities by entering upon an exposition of the most ancient traditions of Hellas relating to the so-called Phoróneus and Niobe, whence he descended to the period after the Deluge, narrated the legendary history of Deucalion and Pyrrha, recited the genealogies of their descendants and attempted to supply a chronological basis for dating the events in his story. This drew from an extremely aged priest . . . the words : 'Solon, Solon! You Hellenes are perpetual children. Such a thing as an old Hellene does not exist. . . . All of you are young in mind. Your minds contain no thoughts handed down from Antiquity by ancient tradition and no knowledge hoary with age. . . . A series of catastrophes in a variety of forms has befallen, and will continue to befall, the human race, the greatest being those effected through the agency of fire and water. . . . In Hellas you have a tradition of Phaeton . . . it preserves the fact that, at immense intervals of time there is a declination in the orbit of the heavenly bodies revolving round the earth and a catastrophe which overtakes life on this planet in the shape of a vast conflagration. At this juncture the inhabitants of regions with a mountainous relief, a high altitude or an arid climate pay a heavier toll than those of riverain or

maritime zones; and on these occasions we in Egypt are rescued by the Nile. . . . There are other occasions on which the gods cleanse the earth with a deluge of water, and in these circumstances the shepherds and herdsmen on the mountains survive, while the inhabitants of your towns in Hellas are swept away. . . . In Egypt, however, water never descends upon the fields from above – not even in these diluvial epochs – but rises from below by a law of nature which never varies. Thus, for the above reasons, traditions preserved in Egypt are the most ancient in the world. . . . Glorious or important or in any way remarkable events in the history of Hellas or of Egypt itself . . . are consequently recorded and preserved in our shrines here in Egypt since a remote antiquity. On the other hand, human society in Hellas or elsewhere has always just arrived at the point of equipping itself with written records and the other requisites of civilisation, when, after the regular interval, the waters that are above the firmament descend upon you like a recurrent malady and only permit the illiterate and uncultured members of society to survive, with the result that you become as little children and start again at the beginning with no knowledge whatever of ancient history either in Egypt or in your own world. Let me tell you, Sir, that the genealogies which you have recited in your account of your Hellenic past are scarcely above the level of children's fairy-tales. In the first place, you have only preserved the memory of one deluge out of a long previous series, and in the second place you are ignorant of the fact that your own country was the home of the noblest and highest race by which the *Genus Homo* has ever been represented. You yourself and your whole nation can claim this race as your ancestors through a fraction of the stock that survived a former catastrophe, but you are ignorant of this owing to the fact that, for many successive generations, the survivors lived and died illiterate.'

If Plato himself did not hold this view of the course of things in time but produced the whole rather as a kind of parable, it is interesting to see that he thought by such means to meet something that existed in the minds of the people around him. It is as though the Greeks had made almost a pattern case of the earliest thing they really knew about themselves – made almost a myth of remembering that they were a people who had forgotten the past. But Plato makes other references to this view of history, and in the *Laws* he talks of old traditions which tell of 'many destructions of mankind by flood, disease and other causes from which only a remnant survive' – 'a few hill-shepherds, tiny sparks of humanity, surviving on mountain-peaks', with a few goats and oxen, but without tools or any skill in the use of them. Aristotle in his *Metaphysics* declared that in all probability the arts and the various kinds of philosophy had been discovered and rediscovered over and over again, but repeatedly lost as a result of successive catastrophes. J. B. Bury once wrote:

If the Greeks had possessed records extending over the history of two or three thousand years, the conception of causal development would probably have emerged. . . . The limitations of their knowledge of the past to a few centuries disabled them for evolving this idea.

They may have had almost an inkling of the idea of progress, for they soon arrived at the view that mankind has to rise from a primitive stage, gradually learning the various arts and sciences. What really held them up was their theory of catastrophe, bringing the human race perpetually back to the beginning again. Time, as they thought they experienced it, was cyclic therefore, and utterly pointless for them. In his *Politics*, Plato makes a different kind of picture to represent what happened. He sees a god who puts the whole world into rotation, guiding it for a time and keeping it in happy and prosperous ways, but then withdraws his hand, so that everything turns into the opposite direction, everything going to the bad until another era is completed, and he takes it into his care, revolving it in the other way again. Polybius in the second century B.C. still connects the cyclic view of history with the notion of recurrent catastrophe. He writes:

When a deluge or a plague or a failure of crops or some similar cause has resulted in the destruction of much of the human race, as the records tell us has already happened, and as reason tells us may often happen again, all the traditions and arts will simultaneously perish, but when in the course of time a new population has grown up again from the survivors left by the disaster, as a crop grows up from seed in the ground, a renewal of social life will begin.

If for the Greeks on so many occasions and for so long a period this was the pattern of the whole course of things, it must have corresponded with something which they felt to be their experience, and it put them in a position very different from that of the children of Israel who saw their history as based on the Promise. The Stoic doctrine of World-Periods, and the view that after innumerable ages the whole universe would be consumed and a new one would come into existence, is based on the same kind of pattern and seems like a cosmic extension of the same view. If this was the underlying notion of the time-process, it is easy to understand why time as such had no meaning for the Greeks, or indeed was really the enemy — not itself a germinal thing, not capable of offering hope for an indefinite future. In these circumstances it would be more natural to turn one's mind and affections to philosophy, and to the notion of something eternal and unchanging. Greek historical writing taught men the mistakes to avoid in life. It did not help them by further revealing the existence of latent potentialities in life, or by giving them the impression that they might really be going somewhere.

3 THE HOMERIC MEMORY

The Greeks come gradually into the light of day, and they possessed no historiography until the fifth century B.C., but already they had the epic, which they regarded as history. It would be the general view today that the siege of Troy, which provides the background for Homer, is an authentic part of the Greek story, and must belong to the Mycenean age, not far from the year 1250 B.C. Even this point is still a matter of debate, however, and it has been suggested lately that the writer of the epic may have sent the Greek expedition to the wrong destinations. There is Egyptian evidence for what appears to be a Mycenean attack on Egypt, and this has prompted the thought that here, rather than in Troy, may be the proper background of the *Iliad*. It is perhaps significant that Homer seems to have had no knowledge of the Hittite Empire, which was in retreat in Asia Minor during the period of the Trojan war; and there is an alternative hypothesis which would see the epic as possibly connected with Hittite evidence of a conflict in that region – a conflict of Achaeans (Greeks) who came not from the mainland but from the island of Rhodes, with forces led not by Troy herself but by the wilder people of Assuwa. It has been held that in any case some of the stories that are to be found in the *Iliad* concern battles that must have taken place on the Greek mainland. If Troy really was besieged by the Greeks, the subsequent sagas were so powerful that other heroes were drawn into them, and songs or traditions about an attack on Thebes by a combination of Greek forces would seem to have been transferred to Asia Minor. It has been conjectured that if Troy had really fallen before a Greek attack, the exultation in such a victory would have made itself felt in the epic from the very start; but the news of the success comes late in the development of the *Iliad*, and the story of the wooden horse seems added as an afterthought. One writer suggested not long ago that Homer, or one of the authors of the epic, must have visited the site of Troy, since the description of the general area is correct in so many of its details. But this scholar argues that the poet was five miles out in his location of the actual city.

Assuming that the Greeks besieged Troy in the region of 1250 B.C., and that the affair was being turned into songs and stories not very long afterwards, a great stretch of time had to pass before the *Iliad* took shape in about the ninth century B.C. Moreover, during that tremendous interval, catastrophes and overthrows had put an end to the Mycenean order of things. Stories were likely to have been twisted almost beyond recognition after they had been transmitted orally through so many centuries; and any major theme that the epic might possess would be just the thing that would come from the artistry of the poet, stringing separate episodes together. It would be held that there are passages in the *Iliad* which go back to Mycenean times: for example, the catalogue of the ships that were sent by the various states of Greece – a document which conforms to the geography of the earlier period rather than to the map as it existed a few centuries later. Beyond this, there have been interesting attempts by scholars to discover what miscellaneous things may have leaked through into the epic from the Mycenean world, in spite of the iron curtain and the great lapse of time. Professor Denys Page cites the description of the shield of Ajax – a kind which was 'obsolete from the thirteenth century' – and says that Ajax must have been 'sung' long before the Trojan war. He argues that a name ending in '*eús*' could not even have been invented in the later period – '*Achilleús*' must go back at least to the twelfth century. In his view Homer tells us things about the Trojans which nobody could have discovered after the fall of Troy – things about the Achaens which could only have been learned in the Trojan war. Professor Nilssen said that the only genuine Mycenean things mentioned in the epic are a gold cup carried by Nestor, a moveable metal collar to hold a spear-head firm, a frieze adorning a palace and a helmet made of wild boars' tusks. But in his view, all of these, except the last, would be open to effective challenge. Dr Rhys Carpenter says that

> true survivals from pre-Hellenic times seem to me to be e.g. the tendency of gods to take on the guise of birds, the confused tradition of the use of chariots in battle and the uncertain conviction that bodies can be preserved from decay by some sort of embalming. These are all likely to be the poets' inheritance and prove no direct familiarity with Mycenean conditions. Homer did not know what battle chariots were for, since his own community did not use them. Hence he depicts them as mere means of transportation.... [He] makes too much mention of iron.

According to Dr Reichel, 'the Homeric heroes all fight in Mycenean armour'. Gilbert Murray said that 'the surface speaks of the Ionian or Athenian kind of fighting' but that 'when the real fighting comes it is as a rule purely Mycenean'. In so far as he was correct in this judgement, he would tend to confirm the view that some hard core of story, representing an original nucleus, could keep its shape while everything around it might have changed.

In general, it seems clear that Homer did not reproduce either the Mycenean age or the world of his own time, but something that had come down as an accepted or recognisable picture of an 'heroic age' – something which might comprise certain features of the actual past, and other things inherited from earlier epics, but which also might have developed as a poetic convention. He communicated this in a style and metre which were also the result of a long development, and were calculated to produce the appropriate atmosphere. And, since people really believed in the gods who appeared in the story, the result would have the flavour of genuine history. There was something in it that would answer to the piety of the Greeks for their ancestors and for the heroes of former times. There was something also which awakened a sense of national pride and enabled a collection of city-states to see themselves as a single people with a common tradition. Even Thucydides, we are told, 'did not doubt the reality of a Hellen [eponymous ancestor of all the Hellenes], of a Pelops, an Agamemnon or the Trojan War'. There were many local traditions too: but if any of these were inconsistent with Homer they would be likely to die out, or they would tend to be trimmed and twisted into conformity with the epic. And partly because this latter was so beautiful a substitute for history, partly also, perhaps, because men had come to depend upon it so much, it may even have ended by becoming in one respect an obstruction to the development of history.

It was precisely because Homer was regarded as serious history, and because men had an interest in the past, that there occurred further developments which bring one nearer to genuine historical study. There had existed other epics besides the *Iliad* and the *Odyssey*, touching other aspects of tradition and legend besides the Trojan War; and the production went on after the time of Homer, though now it acquired a tendency of its own. Amongst the overseas Greeks, where the main poems had developed, there existed in Ionia a school of poetry which was attached to the Homeric tradition, though it interested itself in the entire field of legend and heroic story. While it 'refrained from cultivating the ground tilled by Homer', it produced tales of Troy which came earlier than the *Iliad* or threw light on the after-period; it also covered the gaps in the existing narrative. It may have drawn upon existing traditions or older epic material to answer the questions which Homer had failed to answer, and to satisfy the thirst for knowledge which he had evidently provoked. Men were anxious to learn more about the Trojan war itself, the way it ended, the things that happened to the heroes afterwards. Apparently to meet this need, a body of poetry was produced which, together with the *Iliad* and the *Odyssey,* purported to give complete coverage to the Trojan war as a great historical episode. And this series of writings was regarded as Homeric too, though the Greek tragedians took their materials from this source, and avoided purloining from the two main epics, to which alone the name of Homer was attached after about the year 350 B.C. The same group of later writers took hold of other legends and local traditions and epic material, ranging back to the early days of the world – the origin of the Greek people and its various branches, the wars between the gods. They produced a conspectus extending from the very beginning to the death of Odysseus, as though they felt the need to have the past put into order by the use of the best materials that were available. In all this one even finds something like a critical endeavour – an attempt to explain or smooth away the inconsistencies of Homer himself, for example, or to straighten out the chronology which a poet might well neglect. In a similar way there was an attempt to clear up the genealogies which Homer had left in a confusing state. Hesiod tried 'to work into a consistent system the relationship of gods and heroes, linking actual families with reigning heroes'.

The traditions that lay behind this literary work would owe something to priests and temples, but would live also in noble families, particularly those which claimed royal and heroic descent. The pride or the ambition of these latter would stimulate the manufacture of further sagas as long as the oral transmission was carried on through great houses and courts, for the audience itself is in a sense a collaborator in the production of the epic. Even the *Iliad* may have received expansion at times in order that local demands and aristocratic claims should be satisfied. Here, as elsewhere, the interest in genealogy would precede any wider interest in history, and the nobles seemed anxious to be able to trace their ancestry to Homeric heroes and to the gods themselves – anxious to have narratives that would authenticate their claim or enable them to counter the pretensions of a rival. For us, if not for the men in question, this would seem to be the point where legend and history met.

If the epic in various parts of the world awakened at any rate an interest in the past, the Chadwicks, in their work on the Homeric Age, have shown that it is attended by a desire to have the answers to certain questions. In Greece, as elsewhere, men wanted to know how the world had originated, and how the different peoples – or the subordinate groupings, the Aeolians, Ionians, Dorians, etc. – had come into existence. They were interested in discovering how places acquired their names, and how some of them had come to be sacred. Like other peoples, the Greeks would cling to fabulous explanations or create a legend out of a crude piece of etymological interpretation; but there is an appointed way of explaining these matters – it has to be done by telling a story. The results of these first attempts at historical enquiry or conjecture, therefore, are liable to be highly questionable, adding to the amount of fabulous matter that is in circulation. Even at the Renaissance, when so many new classes of people in Western Europe awoke to an interest in history and asked the self-same questions, the result was still an increase in the weight of legend that was current in the world.

Perhaps the fact that there had been a gap in their genuine memory made the Greeks, at the beginning of the story, seem to be rich in what we must call their legendary history.

4 'SCIENTIFIC' HISTORY IN ATHENS AND IONIA

The Greeks, who had so lost contact with their Mycenean predecessors, surprise us still further by their failure to remember their history for four or
five hundred years after the Trojan war. Josephus's complaint that they had
failed to keep records becomes relevant at this point in the story, for even
today we lack the materials for an adequate treatment of these centuries.
Nor is the deficiency likely ever to be made good. We are without the
records that would enable us to fill even the fifth-century gap between the
Persian wars described by Herodotus from oral tradition and the Peloponnesian war described by Thucydides from something more like experience.
Josephus appears also to have been not entirely off the mark when he
directed his taunts against Athens in particular.

That city appears to have been unlucky from the start, for it has little
place in the *Iliad* or the *Odyssey*. The few mentions of it are generally inter-
polations, but it was late in interesting itself in the Trojan story, and, by that
time, the form of the epic was too well-established to permit of serious
change. It has little place in the other so-called 'Homeric' writings, or in an
epic like the *Thebaid*. All this literature had been concerned with Pan-
hellenic activities, while the Athenian heroes had no great part to play outside their own city. Perhaps this was why they were unable to make so much
out of even their own mythical material as was achieved in the case of some
other cities. Their narratives of Theseus contain too little of real tradition,
and this is submerged under a mass of wild mythologising. The great tragedians dealt with Pan-hellenic heroes and only at moments succeeded in
connecting them with Athens. Some other places fared better at the beginning of the story, and, since there were no records here for a long time, the
earliest historians of the city had to fabricate what they could out of unreliable material.

Even when kings ruled in the cities of the Greeks, they did not put their
achievements on record in the way that the oriental monarchs had done.
They produced nothing equivalent to the annals, which, as we have seen,
appear to have been a product of successful imperialism. There is a great
dearth of early inscriptions, and if the art of writing was introduced before
the eighth century B.C., it does not seem to have been used for state documents or public records till much later. One or two facts may have been
handed down along with many fictions, but 'there is no well-established
Greek date before the seventh century', while for the seventh century itself,
or even for the sixth, there are still only a few – they come with a certain
continuity only after the middle of the fifth century. Oral tradition provided
the main material for the historian, therefore, and, once again, this was even
more true of Athens than of certain other cities. Lists of early kings were

worked out but the information attached to these was meagre – there was generally one single exploit or one single institution attributed to a given monarch. Much of the tradition about the early days consisted of 'aetiological' stories, which would explain the origin of arts, institutions and customs by reference to a particular creator or a particular event. Even the story of the tyranny of Peisistratus in the latter half of the sixth century had to be reconstructed largely from oral tradition, and on this kind of source Herodotus himself depended very much for his account of the war with Persia that took place in the first half of the fifth century.

The earliest documents were mere lists of officials and priests; and before the end of the fifth century – but apparently after the time of Herodotus – the most famous of these, the list of archons in Athens (a list possibly going back to 683/2 B.C.) became available to historians. It was to be a reliable instrument for the establishment of a chronology, which hitherto had depended too much on genealogy and on the calculation that three generations were equal to a century. But it did not in itself solve the general problem of Greek chronology – the difficulty resulting from the fact that other cities measured time by other lists. Some of the laws of sixth-century Athens were known, but it was only at the end of that century that the decrees of the people began to be preserved in inscriptions. In the course of the same century some officials may have had to hold documents in private archives, but the tyrants and archons of that period are unlikely to have kept records. By the end of the century it would be difficult to carry on the government without the keeping of documents; and records of the Council were now being preserved. The régime of Cleisthenes in this period provided something firmer for historians to work upon. But in dealing with a report on the reform of the Athenian constitution a century later than this, Jacoby points out how little the document contains of anything like an appeal to the past or of historical-mindedness – how much it reveals the lack of knowledge about 'the foundations of state life' and the absence of any conviction that, by research among documents, one could discover what happened before Cleisthenes. By this time, however, Greek historiography had been born, though it emerged far away from Athens.

It arose in Ionia, the region on the Western coast of Asia Minor and the neighbouring islands where Greek colonists had been established for centuries. Hitherto it had been more advanced than Athens, where some of its thought had shocked the religious prejudices of the people. For this was the area where the epic had had its great development; here emerged the first prose-writing in the Hellenic world, the first philosophers, and the first moves towards a scientific method. For a time, also, Ionia was ahead of the mainland in the arts. In this place, and at the moment we have now reached, we are confronted, not perhaps with the very birth of Western culture, but certainly with one of the greatest turning-points in the history of civilisation.

The region had enjoyed commercial success, and an era of prosperity had no doubt brought in greater leisure. Bury held that the Ionians profited from 'the absence of a politically powerful priesthood' which might have alleged moral reasons for checking speculation about the cosmos. In the seventh century B.C. the cities made a remarkable political development – the famous Greek *polis* was assuming its well-known character – and perhaps it is surprising that, in view of this, so little documentation was produced. Then, in the middle of the sixth century, the region lost its liberty – it was conquered first by the kingdom of Lydia in Asia Minor, only to fall (along with that kingdom) to the Persian Empire, against which it vainly rebelled just after the year 500 B.C. Earlier than this, however, the cities had contacts with the cultures of Egypt and Western Asia; and, at the stage they had now reached, the contact was an electric one – they were ripe for receiving the maximum stimulus from such influences. Even when they submitted to the Persians, their horizon was widened – they were part of an empire that stretched to the frontiers of India. Besides acquiring a tremendous amount of knowledge about the world, they came into touch with the oldest civilisation of the world and with cities that had been the very seats of ancient culture. The influence of the East upon the West affected the realm of literature, and it is no longer possible to say that the Greeks were the creators of the epic. We have already seen something of the impression produced on Hecataeus and Herodotus by their conversations with Egyptian priests. Thales, who lived considerably earlier, dividing his life between the seventh century and the sixth, had been described as the first thinker of Western civilisation, and was the leader of the Ionian movement towards philosophy and science. He learned his geometry in Egypt, and, according to Hieronymus of Rhodes (quoted by Diogenes Laertius), 'he never had any teacher except during the time when he went to Egypt and associated with the priests'. He predicted an eclipse of the sun and it is difficult to see how he could have acquired his astronomical knowledge save through the Babylonians. The Ionians owed most of all, perhaps, to the fact that they stood at the meeting-place of civilisations. They were in the position which induces men to make comparisons, analyse differences and hunt for the explanation of things that are fairly fundamental – a position which encourages one to see things with a certain amount of relativity. It is this that produces an atmosphere congenial to the development of a sort of rationalism.

The older civilisations had produced a fairly massive recording of events, and in recent times had acquired something of an interest in even the historical past. One would expect their influence to be felt in the field of history, but their actual example may have been less important to the Ionians than the subjugation first to Lydia and then to the vast Persian empire – an experience calculated to evoke a certain historical consciousness. Clearest of all is the fact that the Ionians became accustomed to moving amongst the Lydians and Persians, with whom their fate had become connected, and began to show an interest in these neighbouring peoples, as well as in Egypt, which seems to have impressed them most of all. They set out to explain alien manners, institutions and ideas, and also to learn about the territory of these peoples. This was so important a feature of the development which occurred that history in Ionia seems to emerge as almost a by-product of geography or ethnography. It would probably be better to say that knowledge had not yet been divided into compartments, and that something which was a mixture of geography and history was the first to differentiate itself, before these two subjects had themselves become quite separated from one another. One of the peculiarities of the Greek story is the fact that, at the very start, the Ionians are interested in the past of nations other than their own.

The new tendencies would not diminish the interest of the Ionians in the history of the Greek people. Till the seventh century the continued writing and revision of the epics had shown the persistence of their preoccupation with the heroic age; but henceforward they ceased to produce this kind of literature. The conquerors of this region (and the tyrants who now ruled under them in the cities) would have no use for writings which tended to awaken a national spirit and remind Ionians of their former glories, their former liberty. Political and economic developments had brought about social changes which must have had their effect on the character of the literary man's audience. Owing either to a change of patronage or a change in taste, poetry began to take a different course, and become more lyrical, more private and personal in its appeal. Now there was a greater desire for information and perhaps it was in connection with this that prose-writing had begun to appear. It has been claimed that historiography emerged at this point to take the place of the epic – a view possibly supported by the fact that historical writing took over the Pan-hellenic outlook which had been so evident in Homer. At least, it took up the special functions which the supplementary Homeric writings had been performing – it set out initially to complete the task of systematising the genealogies, straightening out the myths of the gods and solving the chronological problems.

The attempt to range the deities in proper order and to establish the relations of heroes both with gods and with families still living in the world, had meant that, from the first, 'history' had presented itself to the Greeks as a kind of 'investigation'. Here, as in the case of the ancient Hebrews, though for a different reason, it involved something more than mere fidelity to an original record that was hard and rigid and intended to be perpetual. The very fact that the resurrection of the past had been in the hands of the poets – who left so many loose ends, so many questions unanswered – had proved a stimulus to critical endeavour, a desire to make the story square with itself. Criticism had been directed first of all upon the poems and in a sense it had been initiated by poets who had solved outstanding problems by producing further epics. When the historians – the writers in prose – emerged, they carried on with the same task for a time, but there was also a further sense in which they were compelled to see history as 'investigation'. They had to enquire into the past of other countries, where their Homer could be of no use to them, and there was no epic that would serve as a fountain of knowledge. In foreign countries they had to seek solutions to problems, and it was in this way that the Greeks trained themselves in what was to be their chief contribution to historical method – the questioning of living people and the cross-examination of witnesses. The Ionians contrasted the alien nations with their own, and the fact that they were forced to consider resemblances and differences contributed an added drive to their thinking. They reached interesting conclusions, for example, after comparing their mythology with that of Egypt – conclusions which reinforced the view that it was the Egyptians who possessed the wisdom of antiquity. Above all, historiography arose in Ionia in that period of intellectual awakening which followed the appearance of something like the philosophy of science. The fact that it emerged in connection with ethnography and geography may have helped to give it a more scientific flavour and turn it into 'investigation'.

Hecataeus of Miletus, who lived between the sixth and fifth centuries B.C., is the first assured historian and might be called the founder of geography. He sought to disentangle from the poets the genuine traditions of ancient Greece, but also he collected local traditions and tried to collate them with the literary evidence. His visit to Egypt is an important moment in his intellectual history, and there he collected information from the priests, questioning them even about the Trojan war. He seems to have had great faith in Homer and to have been fairly conservative in his treatment of myths. But in the first sentence of the oldest Greek historical work that we can have any assurance about, he says in about 490 B.C. : 'I write down what I consider to be true, for the things that the poets tell us are in my opinion full of contradictions and worthy to be laughed out of court.' The scientific character or critical spirit of even his successors ought not to be exaggerated: they did not eliminate the gods but sought to rationalise such of the stories as seemed to be too implausible. The geographical literature, which appears to have developed out of something like guide-books, achieved a scientific flavour more easily, and Herodotus, though his knowledge is inadequate, speaks most like a scientist when he is discussing the rôle and the workings of the Nile. We can gain some idea of the reasoning of the geographers if we look at the things that Hippocrates had to say in that region where geography and history meet, for, though he comes later – after Herodotus – at the very end of the century, the kind of thought that is attributed to him goes back to an earlier date. Writing on the influence of atmosphere, water and situation he says:

> We have still to consider the problem why the Asiatics are of a less warlike and more tame disposition than the Europeans. The deficiency of spirit and courage observable in the human inhabitants of Asia has for its principal cause the low margin of seasonal variability in the temperature of that continent, which is approximately stable throughout the year. Such a climate does not produce those mental shocks and violent bodily dislocations which would naturally render the temperament ferocious and introduce a stronger current of irrationality and passion than would be the case under stable conditions. It is invariably changes that stimulate the human mind and prevent it from remaining passive. These, in my view, are the reasons why the Asiatic race is unmilitary, but I must not omit the factor of institutions. The greater part of Asia is under monarchial government; and wherever men are not their own masters and not free agents, but are under despotic rule, they are not concerned to make themselves militarily efficient, but on the contrary [want] to avoid being regarded as good military material, the reason being that they are not playing for equal stakes. . . . Whenever they acquit themselves like men it is these masters who are exalted and aggrandised . . . it is also inevitable that the inactivity consequent upon the absence of war should have a taming effect upon the temperament. A strong argument in favour of my contention is furnished by the fact that all the Hellenes and non-Hellenes in Asia who are not under despotic rule but are free agents and struggle for their own benefit, are as warlike as any populations in the world – the reason being that they stake their lives in their own cause and reap the rewards of their own valour. . . . You will also find that the Asiatics differ among one another, some being finer and others poorer in quality, and these differences also have their cause in seasonal climatic variations.

It is hazardous to speak of the emergence of anything that is absolutely new in history. We ought on occasion to remind ourselves of the fact that there never was a time when man might not know how to put two and two together. Without some ability to correlate data, our distant ancestors could never have developed agriculture or produced the pyramids or devised the alphabet. That Herodotus should discuss the reason for the flooding of the Nile need cause no great surprise, after Thales had predicted an eclipse of the sun, and so much had already happened in the realm of technology. But, that the behaviour of men in history should become the subject of a continuous disquisition which gave climate a rôle in the story, and that then the influence of institutions should be discussed in the same terms as the influence of climate – all this is of real significance in a world previously accustomed to thinking that events came from the arbitrary wills of men and gods. It does not matter if in any of the cases that have been mentioned – the case of Herodotus and the flooding of the Nile, for example (for Herodotous could not believe that there might be snow in the sultry upper regions of that river), the 'science' was very defective; for the whole course of procedure is self-rectifying, and 'bad science' is necessary before one can have 'good science'. The great achievement of the overseas Greeks in the fifth century B.C. was the introduction of this kind of thinking into the discussion of the things that happen in history, and its establishment on such a basis that it proved capable of development in the future. It may have meant no more than translating into the realm of the literary historian the kind of things that men had come to say in the politics or war that they conducted in real life, though, even so, the transfer enabled them to bring the thinking to a higher degree of organisation. But it meant taking the biggest hurdle that had to be surmounted if history were to be rescued from the world of mythology and brought down to earth, so that the mind could come to a deeper understanding of its workings. And the contribution of the Greeks to historiography was precisely at this point – the development of a scientific way of treating the historical data that had been established, rather than the devising of the means for their establishment, or the production of a technique of 'discovery'.

An important feature of the movement in fifth-century Ionia was the interest in a history much more recent than that of the epic poets – the interest in a 'past' of a very different nature, involving the ordinary work-a-day world. Something – possibly the consciousness of the international situation and of the need to see onself in relation to outsiders – made it relevant to learn of events that lay more directly behind the present-day scene. The desire to know about neighbouring peoples had been prompted by issues of real life, and, here again, it was the immediate past that would have application to current problems. In the fifth century the writing of history seems to have had a special association with the occurrence of great events. At the very opening of the century there took place the unsuccessful rising of the Ionian cities against the Persian domination. Next there occurred the great attack on Greece by the Persians under Xerxes, when Athens played the leading part in the defeat of the invader and rose to a dominating position. Hecateus happens to coincide with the first of these events, while Herodotus made it one of his objects to describe the second, though he worked a few decades later. Then there occurred the Peloponnesian war, and Thucydides determined at the time to describe it, completing his *History* just before the end of the century. As in the case of the two wars of the twentieth century, resounding events gave a stimulus to the writing of what was almost contemporary history.

But, this time, it was not the work of a boastful emperor who was out to commemorate himself. Both the author and his audience can be seen to have stood on an entirely different footing. The writings assume the existence of political consciousness in their readers, and it was understood that the men concerned were not like those Asiatics who could be indifferent to victories in battle because they were profitable only to their masters. The birth of Greek historiography is connected with the rise of the Greek city-state and the establishment of a broadly based government inside the various cities. Great developments had taken place in Athens, leading to the age of Pericles in the fifth century. The Ionian cities themselves recovered their freedom after the defeat of the Persians under Xerxes. Men felt that their own lives and interests were tied up with the fate of their city and of the Greek people; and it is significant that Hippocrates should have made so much of this point in making the comparison with the people of Asia. The fortunes of one's state became a major preoccupation, therefore, and the place occupied by one's city in the given region and the given time – the city viewed as the historian would view it – was a principal conditioning factor in one's life. Where men are citizens and not merely subjects, their political consciousness carries with it also a consciousness of history – on the one hand a realisation that they are living in history, creatures of time and circumstance, and on the other hand a feeling that the past of the body politic is really their own past. Something of this had been apparent in the Old Testament, even in the time of the monarchy, for all were concerned if Yahweh were goaded to anger. But now, though the gods did not disappear from the scene, one began to study history for a different purpose – with the idea of getting a better command over it. The scientific approach which the Ionians of Asia Minor bequeathed to the Athenians, the conscious individual desire to discover the rational causes and effects of what men were doing now and what they had done at other times and in other places, enabled the great Greek historians – Herodotus from Asia Minor, Thucydides of Athens and their successors – to achieve for the first time what we can recognise as the writing of a history, and in spite of the general Greek lack of historical-mindedness to do so with an insight and an understanding which many modern scholars consider has not been surpassed.

CHAPTER FIVE

The Chinese Tradition of Historical Writing

1 THE ORIGINS OF A UNIQUE ACHIEVEMENT

In the various regions which we have examined, the interest in the past had emerged fairly spontaneously, coming on each occasion in its own way, appearing as a native thing, and owing much of its character to the kind of experience which had led to its rise. The form which it took and the direction in which it developed were affected to a certain degree by those factors or conditions which in each case had originally awaked the concern for history. At the same time, the resulting historiography – the literature actually produced – owed something to the influence throughout Western Asia of those ancient centres of civilisation which had been the original source of writing on this subject in this sector of the globe. Not only the Hittites, the people of Israel and the Greeks, but also a host of other nations in the vicinity – the Moabites and the Phoenicians, for example – had been influenced by the imposing work of these older civilisations, the empires of Mesopotamia and Egypt. Over that very considerable area where three continents come together, there was a general movement, a development of historiography which in the future was to decide much of the character of Western civilisation itself. And the movement was one which hardly had a parallel elsewhere.

It was not quite unique, however, for in one other quarter of the globe – in China – historiography had acquired a similar importance, and had also emerged at a very early date. And here the spectacle was to become still more impressive: the beginnings very remote; the resulting tradition unparalleled in its length and its internal consistency; the prestige of the subject quite exceptional; and the literary output of incredible bulk. Most imposing of all was the way in which the classical values, the established techniques and the organisation of the profession were able to maintain themselves for century after century, and almost down to the present day. Over a century ago, Hegel wrote in his *Philosophy of History* that 'no other people has had a series of historical writers succeeding one another in such close continuity as the Chinese'. Then, speaking of the situation as he saw it in his own day, he went on :

> A matter of particular surprise is the accuracy with which they carry out their historical work. In China the historians are amongst the highest functionaries of the state. The ministers, constantly in attendance on the Emperor, are commissioned to keep a journal of everything he does, commands and says. Their notes are then worked up and form material for the historian. We cannot go further into the minutiae of the annals that are produced; for they themselves fail to show any development, and for that reason they would only hinder us in ours.

Whatever initial influence Mesopotamia may have had upon the early development of civilisation in China, the historiography of this latter region must be regarded as having been spontaneous in its origin. During the long period in which the tradition of its historical writing was taking shape, China was so cut off from the West that it took an entirely independent course, achieving the extreme of what we call 'insularity'. For the same reason the productions of the Chinese are not a factor in the development of Western historiography. Yet all this does not make the Chinese achievement a whit less important to us. Those who try to relate the rise of historical writing to men's early beliefs, and to the historic experience of the nations concerned, will find in this example a basis for comparisons which carry the argument to a deeper level. In such a matter it is possible that one can never properly envisage one's own tradition until one has found another with which to make comparison and contrast.

'Universal History' is such a formidable affair that the student who surveys it in its width will hardly reach sufficient depth for the attainment of interesting results. It is possible, however, to make a boring at a strategic place and gain a glimpse of something like the structure of an alien civilisation. A comparison of either the natural science or the historiography of China with that of Europe is an appropriate starting-point for this kind of investigation. Though the two traditions are independent in both their origin and their growth, they are not so locked away from one another as to be incapable of inter-communication. If the Westerner may miss some of the subtleties of Chinese historiography, he can also recognise some of its beauties. An attempt to see what lies behind the differences between the two systems may give us an insight into the nature of 'Universal History' and a glimpse of what is involved in the comparative study of civilisations, especially as, in both cases, the passage of centuries brought the culture to an advanced stage.

A curious feature in China is the fact that, whereas in the West we have for such a long time a historiography but no reference to 'historians', in the East the rôle of the individual writer is very quickly brought to our notice. The function itself was recognised at an early date; it acquired prestige; it achieved a certain independence.

Not many years ago, two scholars, working widely apart – one of them a Japanese writer – arrived independently at the view that the Chinese character (*shih*) which represents an historian originally depicted the posture of the man who kept a record of hits in archery contests. The Chinese themselves have sometimes described the character which they used for the *shih* (and which might mean archivist as well as historiographer) as a hand holding not a record of hits but simply a record of events. They talk about 'a hand holding the middle', by which they mean keeping the balance, achieving impartiality, really getting at the truth. Sometimes they seem to have used the character *shih* simply to represent a scribe.

The term itself goes back for over three thousand years, that is to say, to a period well before 1000 B.C. The German scholar, Otto Franke, while accepting the view that originally it meant a priestly scribe, thought that – still at a very early stage – a more adequate translation would be 'temple archivist'. That is to say, it stood for the man in charge of the writing and the documents in the place where the sacrifices were made to one's ancestors. Each family would have its ancestral temple or hall; and this would contain the family trees, the registers and inventories, the decisions of the oracle and the record of treaties or contracts made. In other words, it was the repository of the archives. The temple-archivist would produce short pieces of writing on bones or on pieces of tortoise shell, thousands and thousands of which have been discovered in comparatively recent decades. They would record the results of divinations, the answers to oracle-enquiries and the genealogical data; or they would set out brief prayers for the sacrifices or compose dedicatory inscriptions. In the case of the princely houses these functionaries acquired particular importance. They came to be the people who drew up treaties, recorded edicts and drafted the documents granting feudal enfeoffment. Examples of this aspect of their work are preserved in inscriptions on bronze.

The mere fact of being a scribe was calculated to give a man peculiar importance in ancient China. The difficulty of reproducing the Chinese characters made writing much rarer in that country than elsewhere, and the art even possessed a certain sanctity. A modern Chinese writer has pointed out that, whether people could read or not, they regarded the Chinese characters as sacred, and as 'establishing contact between the human and the divine'. He tells us that 'Heaven rejoiced' and 'Hades was made to tremble'

when this form of writing was invented, and, according to him, so much
of this feeling survived into the twentieth century that both common people
and scholars in comparatively recent times would frown on the use of newspapers for wrapping parcels. As late as the 1930s, men would go about the
streets and would gather any scrap of paper that had writing or printing on
it, and this they would put into bamboo-baskets that carried the inscription
'Reverence-love-charactered paper'. The collected pieces would then be
burned in Buddhist, Taoist or Confucian temples. In the early stages of
Chinese history, the sanctity of the scribe must have been very much greater,
especially as the desire to communicate with the dead or with the deity
seems to have been one of the reasons for the development of writing itself.
A man's ancestors were supposed to have great influence over his life, and
it was easy to believe that the sacred characters provided a contact with the
other world. Indeed, precisely because writing had this mystic power, there
was a sense in which a thing that had happened was not really fixed as an
event (the fact of its occurrence was not really clinched) until it was placed
on record. It was like the case of making a run in cricket: it is not really a
run unless it has been put down in the scorebook. History had a special
unearthly kind of virtue because of the mere fact that events had been put
into writing.

In the early stages of the story, the temple archivist had charge of divination as well as records. Some have suggested that the word *shih* might be
translated as 'astrologer', but it has been objected that this term would
cover only part of his activities. He would be the man to say which day was
propitious for beginning a journey, the holding of a ceremony or the com-
mencement of a war. In a sense, therefore, he had charge of events per-
taining to the present and the future as well as the past. He reported not
only human events but also the things that happened in nature. It was he
who looked after the calendar, recorded eclipses of the sun and moon and
dealt with the time-table generally. Even at a later date, the account of
droughts and floods and eclipses, together with other freaks and catastrophes in the world and other celestial phenomena, would sometimes have a
disproportionate place in historical writing. And, though this part of the
work was handed over to a separate functionary some time before the opening of the Christian era, the experts in the field have occasionally pointed
out that the texture of historical writing in China was affected by the view
that an intrinsic relationship or a special sympathy exists between the workings of nature and the workings of history.

The earliest attempts to produce pieces of writing about the past seem to
have derived from the need to have something to assist the memory in the
performance of sacrificial rites. The monarchs of the early dynasties, when
they paid honour to their ancestors, would turn to the archivist for guidance.
Sometimes it was necessary for ritual purposes that there should be a short

account of the legends concerning the ancestors – a key to the dances or the kind of pantomime that was performed. Some of the stories of China's remoter past would seem to have been useful for such a purpose, as they are extraordinarily mythical in character.

The *shih*, the archivist, the historiographer, therefore, emerges at first in a half-fabulous world, and is endowed with mysterious forms of power. There was almost a kind of magic in being able to write. A kind of authority accrued to him as the man who 'kept the score'. His connections with the important rituals of ancestor-worship gave him command over the past. Through astrology and divination he held the key to the future too. At the houses of princely families, and most of all at the imperial court, the temple-archivist acquired prestige at an early date, and stood high in the hierarchy of functionaries. He held the documents which carried the decisions of former times, the royal edicts, the treaties, the evidence that a fief had been granted to one person or another. He would be the man to draft contracts and decrees, and would act as the secretary of the reigning monarch. This gave an opening for the exercise of influence and power; and his rôle might become enlarged, just as in England the secretary of the ruler expanded his function and became a Secretary of State. We hear of important government work being confided to the archivist, who was a useful man to send out on diplomatic missions.

Even at an early date, however, he recorded events as they happened, day by day, and in this he seems sometimes to have been regarded as making a report to ancestral spirits. In early centuries from which hardly any writing survives, this aspect of his work seems to have made a great impression, so that he comes down in tradition as having been an important figure. Many tales were told about the sufferings of historians who braved the Emperor himself and were sometimes executed because they had told the truth. There are stories about historian-archivists who, when their protests and advice went unheeded, took up their maps and records and laid them before a new man, who then displaced the old monarch and established a new dynasty. At least in tradition the *shih* was supposed to act as an independent authority and to be a man of great integrity.

Then, for a time, his importance became enhanced in a further way, because there was conferred on him a further important function. He received what is sometimes described in English as the office of Censor. He was recognised as the impartial umpire who should pass judgement on the actions of the monarch himself. It had long been the prevailing view that dynasties fell because of the wicked conduct of the men on the throne, and this idea embodied itself permanently in the very structure of Chinese historiography. The *shih*, observing the signs of the times, did not merely look at the stars, he considered the actual events of the political world and saw if the wicked conduct of the ruler was becoming a danger to the state itself. At a later date the office of Censor was separated from that of the historian, but the original connection between the two throws some light on the imposing status of the *shih*.

2 THE EARLY CLASSICS

The cataclysms of Chinese history seem to have spared little of the historical writings of the pre-Confucian days; and from early times there seems to have been controversy about the genuineness or the textual accuracy of the things that did survive. This did not prevent the establishment of a small group of Chinese classics which everybody was required to study, and amongst these was the *Shoo King*, which we know as the 'Book of History' or 'Book of Documents', a compilation traditionally associated with Confucius, though his actual connection with it is very doubtful. Some of the records it contains purport to belong to very ancient times; but the texts which are earlier than the first millennium must be unauthentic and though there are pieces which go back a few centuries before Confucius (i.e. before 550 B.C.), a good part of the work seems to have been a late forgery. It is a collection of royal speeches, ministerial declarations, edicts, memorials and feudal documents, accompanied by a certain amount of narrative.

It tells us how Kings Wăn and Woo had their Grand Historiographer (or Archivist). It reports one speech in which it was remarked: 'Ye know that your fathers of the Yin dynasty had their archives and narratives showing how Yin superseded the appointment of Hea.' One Grand Historiographer is depicted as a chief officer of state at the funeral of the monarch, and it was he who 'bore the testamentary charge'.

> He ascended by the guests' steps and advanced to the (new) King with the record of the charge, saying: 'Our great Lord, leaning on the gemadorned bench, declared his last charge, and commanded you to continue the observance of the lessons, and to take the rule of the empire of Chou, complying with the great laws and securing the harmony of the empire, so as to respond to and display the bright instructions of Wăn and Woo.'
> The King twice bowed low and then arose and said: 'I am utterly insignificant and but a little child. . . .'

At the same time the *Shoo King* shows that historical interest was not confined to the stories of rulers and the vicissitudes of politics and war. There appears in the text a desire to know the origins of civilised life and to discuss the nature of civil society. We learn how the Emperor Yaou – the first to be dealt with – commanded his brothers, He and Ho, 'in reverent accordance with their observation of the wide heavens, to calculate and delineate the movements and appearances of the sun, the moon, the stars and the zodiacal spaces; and so to deliver respectfully the seasons to the people'. One of

them, He, was to go to Ye-e 'and there respectfully receive as a guest the
rising sun and to adjust and arrange the labours of spring'. The Emperor
said to him: 'The day is of medium length and the star is in Neaou: you
may thus exactly determine the mid-spring.' In a section entitled 'The
Tribute of Yu' there is an interesting geographical passage:

> Yu divided the land. Following the course of the hills, he hewed down
> the woods. He determined the high hills and great rivers. . . .
> The nine branches of the Ho were conducted by the proper channels.
> Luyhea was formed into a marsh in which the waters of the Yung and
> the Tseu were united. The mulberry grounds were made fit for silk-
> worms, and then the people came down from the heights and occupied
> the ground below.
> The soil of this province was blackish and rich . . . its articles of tribute
> were varnish and silk. . . .
> Yu surveyed and described the hills. . . .
> Thus throughout the nine provinces a similar order was effected: the
> grounds along the waters were everywhere made habitable; the hills were
> cleared of superfluous wood and sacrificed to; the sources of the streams
> were cleared; the marshes were well banked; access to the capital was
> secured for all within the four seas.
> A great order was effected in the six magazines of material wealth; the
> different parts of the country were subjected to an exact comparison so
> that the contribution of revenue could be carefully adjusted according to
> their resources. The fields were all classified with reference to the three
> characters of the soil.
> He conferred the land and surnames.

Since the *Shoo King* was one of the classics – its outlook partly the result
of tradition no doubt, but certainly at the same time determinative of future
attitudes – it is interesting to see at this early stage so many of the things
that were to be permanent features of Chinese historiography. There are
sections, for example, which anticipate the treatises on governmental institutions which were to be so familiar at a later date. It seems clear in any
case that the importance of the work lay in its moral and political teaching
rather than its integrity as a collection of 'sources'; and it had a very definite
'tendency', one that must have been very congenial to a Confucian, and a
factor in future developments. Amongst other things, we find here on
repeated occasions the famous doctrine that had a fundamental and permanent importance in China – the thesis that a monarch held the government because he had 'the decree of heaven in his favour', but his successors,
when they sinned, would find the decree transferred to somebody else. We
are told how Heaven 'rejected and made an end of the decree' in favour of
the dynasty of Yin: 'for want of the virtue of reverence the decree . . .

prematurely fell to the ground. . . .' Now, however, the dynasty of Hea must suffer the same fate, and the neighbouring ruler who makes war against it will say: 'I am resolutely executing the judgement of Heaven'; 'I am entrusted with the execution of the punishment of Heaven'; 'For the many crimes of the sovereigns of Hea, Heaven has given me the charge to destroy him'. When he has a moment of doubt, the following homily is delivered in his presence:

Heaven gives birth to the people and gives them such desires that, unless they have a ruler, they must fall into every kind of disorder. Heaven also gives birth to a man of intelligence and it is this man's business to bring them under control. . . . Heaven therefore endowed our King with valour and wisdom so that he would stand as a sign and direct the great number of states and continue the old ways of Yu. You are now only following the standard course, possessing and obeying the appointment of Heaven. The King of Hea was an offender, falsely pretending to the sanction of Heaven.

The teaching was appropriate to a cataclysmic age, for it sanctioned any *status quo* that could preserve itself, or any usurper or conqueror who was able to prevail. Success was the evidence of divine favour, but at the same time there was a judgement of Heaven that was embodied in the actual events of history. We are told that 'Good and evil do not wrongly befall men, because Heaven sends them misery or happiness according to their conduct'.

Yin is quoted as saying:

Of old the earlier sovereigns of Hea cultivated earnestly their virtue. . . . Then there were no calamities from Heaven. The spirits of the hills and rivers likewise were all in tranquillity, and the birds and beasts, the fishes and tortoises, all realised the happiness of their nature. But their descendants did not follow their example, and Heaven sent down calamities, employing the agency of our ruler.

Over and over again it was made clear at the same time that virtue was to be achieved only by following the example of one's ancestors. This teaching, precisely because it was so often reiterated, is of real significance to us, because it provided so strong a motive for the study of the past. Here is the reason often explicitly given for the injunction to examine antiquity. The following is the way in which a king speaks to his younger brother, at the moment when he is giving him power in Yin:

Heaven gave a great charge to King Wan to exterminate the great dynasty of Yin. . . . O! Fung, bear these things in mind. Your management of the people will depend on your reverently following your father, Wan. . . . Moreover, where you are going, you must follow the traces of the former wise kings of Yin, making an extensive search for things that will be useful for protecting and regulating the people. Again, more remotely, you must study the old accomplished men of Shang, that you may establish your heart and know how to instruct the people. Moving a stage further still, you must also find out what is to be learned of the wise kings of antiquity, and you must use this in order to tranquillise and protect the people. Finally, enlarge your thoughts to the comprehension of all heavenly principles. . . . Heaven in its awfulness helps the sincere. . . . The feelings of the people can for the most part be discerned but it is difficult to calculate the attachment of the lower classes.

In all this there is an attempt to discriminate between recent and remoter, local and more general history, as guides to political action.

As a result of all this, the *Shoo King* is remarkably conservative in its political tendency. We read in one place: 'Study antiquity as you enter upon your offices'; in another place: 'Of old, our Kings made it a principal object . . . to employ the men of old families in the work of government'. The ruler is told: 'Follow the course of the Mean, and do not, by assuming to be intelligent, throw old statutes into confusion.' Again, we find the maxim: 'Attend to the springs of things. Study stability.' The theory of the monarchy we have met with already: we find it stated again in the following manner:

The great God has conferred even on inferior people a moral sense, compliance with which would show their nature to be invariably right. But to cause them tranquilly to pursue the course which it would indicate is the work of the sovereign.

For the rest, there are maxims for rulers and statesmen:

Do not slight the occupations of the people.
Do not go against what is right to get praise from the people.
Be careful for the end at the beginning.
Measures of government must be varied according to the manners of the time.
Before you make a movement, take anxious thought about the good it will do. Your movements should also have respect to the time for them.
I do not dare to rest secure in the favour of God or, at the present time, when there is no murmuring or disobedience among the people, to forecast from a distance the moment when terrors will come from Heaven. The issue depends really on men.

It would be a mistake, therefore, to take merely the narrow view of the technical historian when studying the *Shoo King*. The compiler was using the framework of China's past in order to transmit the programme of teaching on politics and history which was independent of the authenticity of the quoted texts, though it carried within itself no doubt the ingredients of a tradition. Morality rather than religion is in the forefront, and, so far as religion is concerned, it is piety toward one's ancestors that is emphasised – another way of turning men's minds to the past. Amongst the host of aphorisms that appear are some interesting reflections on the subtleties or the paradoxes of the moral life. One monarch is told: 'Attend to the sacrifices to all thy ancestors and be not so excessive in the ones to thy father.' We read also:

> Virtue has no invariable pattern – a supreme regard to what is good will provide the necessary model.
> The indulged consciousness of goodness is the way to lose that goodness.
> Officiousness in sacrifices is called irreverence.
> Though we repent, we cannot overtake the past.
> Be not passionate with the obstinate or dislike them. Seek not every quality in one individual.

A still more famous work, another of the ancient classics, is connected with Confucius by evidence still more explicit, yet it is difficult for a modern student (at any rate a Western one) to see the point of the association. It carries the title *Ch'un Ts'ëw* ('Spring-and-Autumn Annals'), but it lacks the ideas which give the 'Book of History' its interest and character. For this reason the latter was sometimes described as dealing with 'thoughts', while the former was concerned with 'actions' – this being at one time a recognised distinction in Chinese historiography, the basis even for a division of labour.

It would seem that, at least as far back as 753 B.C., scribes appointed by princes would be given the definite task of producing a report on the events that concerned their state. For a period of about five hundred years (that is to say, until the third century B.C.), annals were produced in the various principalities of China – principalities dominated by feudal magnates who reduced the central government to a mere shadow. These annals were very thin at first and they appear to have contained a considerable amount of mythical matter. Hardly any of them survives in what can safely be regarded as its original form, though the text of some of them may have been used and even copied in the scissors-and-paste work of later writers. It was the custom to describe these works as 'Spring-and-Autumn Annals' because they followed the course of the four seasons, and the names of two of these were sufficient to indicate the whole series. The set belonging to the principality of Loo came to occupy a special place because this was the country of Confucius, and he was supposed to have been the writer of the work, or to have been responsible for editing it.

The book, as it has been handed down, however, is so dull and inconsequent; and the completed product so apparently pointless, that its association with Confucius has caused some difficulty; and one is left to wonder how he can have been quoted as having said that this was the work by which he would be remembered, the one on account of which men would be bound to condemn him. A tradition established itself that he had written it in a kind of code, evolving a terminology which only his intimates would understand, and which would specify (without explicitly stating) the people and the actions to be condemned or praised. The famous Chinese historian, Ssŭ-ma Ch'ien, writing about 100 B.C., gives the following account of the matter, and gives away the fact that, at this early date, the students of the work had realised the difficulty:

> From the records of the historians, he [Confucius] made the *Ch'un Ts'ëw*, commencing with Duke Yin, coming down to the fourteenth year of Duke Gae, and thus embracing the times of twelve marquises. He kept close in it to [the annals of Loo]. . . . His style was condensed but his scope was extensive. Thus the rulers of Woo and Ts'oo assumed to themselves the title of King; but in the *Ch'un Ts'ëw* they are censured by being only styled viscounts. Thus also the son of Heaven was really summoned to the meeting at Ts'eën-t'oo, but the *Ch'un Ts'ëw* conceals the fact, and says that the 'King by Heaven's grace held a court of inspection in Ho-Yang'. Such instances served to illustrate the idea of the master in the censures and elisions which he employed to rectify the ways of those times, his aim being that, when future kings should study the work, its meaning should be appreciated and all rebellious ministers and villainous sons under the sky become afraid. When Confucius was in office, his language in listening to litigations was what others would have employed and not peculiar to him; but in making the *Ch'un Ts'ëw*, he wrote what he wrote, and he retrenched what he retrenched, so that the disciples of Tsze-Lëa could not improve it in a single character. When his disciples received from him the *Ch'un Ts'ëw* he said: 'It is by the *Ch'un Ts'ëw* that after ages will know me, and also by it they will condemn me.'

It has been impossible, however, to work out a code in which the principles of Confucius can have been carried out with any consistency in the *Ch'un Ts'ëw*. So far as one can see, the work is calculated rather to outrage the teacher of the master, evading the real confrontation with the truth, concealing inconvenient facts (saying that a man died when he was really murdered, for example), and giving cover to those who had been guilty of crimes. There has been a tendency of late, therefore, to conjecture that these dry annals were merely a basic text which Confucius embroidered orally – the mere starting-point for the development of his oral teaching, the thing that really mattered. In the period after his death there appeared a number of commentaries on the 'Spring-and-Autumn Annals', and these claimed to be expositions of his teaching, though they differed from one another and must have gone back to memories of what had been communicated orally.

In many respects there is a remarkable sophistication in the *Shoo King*, which purports to give us texts from a still earlier period, and no doubt philosophical thought (or at least reflection on politico-moral issues) was more advanced than historical thought, or formed the better part of it. But unless we are prepared to cover it with some kind of mystique, the *Ch'un Ts'ëw* takes us back to the crudest kind of annalistic writing, the kind of history that might be produced by copying haphazardly items from a man's engagement book. No wonder Legge, its nineteenth-century translator, wrote: 'We cannot reconcile it with our idea of Confucius that he should have produced so trivial a work, or see how his countrymen down to the present day should believe in it and set it forth as a grand achievement. One would have said that these, whether accurate or inaccurate, must be genuine annals; for it is not easy to think why anybody should have invented them; they show no sign of feeling; they set out to offer no sort of opinion; and they are not characterised by any general tendency. Yet it has been possible to convict them of inaccuracy in points of detail.' Mencius wrote in the fourth century B.C.: 'The world was fallen into decay and right principles had dwindled away. Perverse discourses and oppressive deeds were again waxing rife. Cases were occurring of ministers who murdered their rulers and of sons who murdered their fathers. Confucius was afraid and made the *Ch'un Ts'ëw.*' He 'completed the *Ch'un Ts'ëw* and rebellious ministers and villainous sons were struck with terror'. It is difficult to see how he can have been writing about the book that we know.

We gain a more adequate view of pre-Confucian historiography, therefore, if we examine a distinctly later work, the commentary on the 'Spring-and-Autumn Annals' by Tso Kew-ming, a work brought to light only in the middle of the second century B.C. A later historian, Pan Koo, said that Kew-ming worked with Confucius on the records of the principality of Loo, and heard the oral teaching which the master did not dare to publish. He set out to produce a book which would provide the 'praise and blame' and make good the concealments and suppressions. He hoped in this way to vindicate the master; but he, too, had to conceal the work, because of the persecution that it would be bound to suffer, and, according to the story, it was only after the 'Spring-and-Autumn Annals' had been discovered in the wall of Confucius's house, that the commentary, the *Tso Chuen*, was brought to the attention of the Emperor. It was not until A.D. 99 that it received formal recognition. Until this date, preference had been given to a commentary by Kung-yang which was supposed to be able to trace its course of oral transmission through a period of three hundred years, until it was put into writing in the middle of the second century B.C., that is to say, at the time when the text of the 'Spring-and-Autumn Annals' appeared. Confidence had been given for a time also to a further commentary, by Kuh-Lëang. But these latter were not writings of any real significance. They sought chiefly to associate the Confucian work with the doctrine of praise and blame.

It was Tso Kew-ming who provided the fuller and more accurate account of the 242 years covered by the 'Spring-and-Autumn Annals', and a further period. One later historian described him as having been a historiographer in the principality of Loo, and this may be correct, for he seems to be familiar with the actual records. He must also have worked on the documents or the annals of principalities other than that of Loo, for he knows a great deal about their ruling houses, their leading families and their great men. It is the new material contributed by him that makes him so important, and it is he who both makes the 'Spring-and-Autumn Annals' more intelligible, and shows up their inadequacies. He does homage to the text of Confucius and tries to explain it, but he writes as though he were unaware that he was challenging or correcting the master's narrative. He is not preoccupied with the 'praise and blame' view of history, though he likes to moralise at times, introducing his remarks with the words: 'The superior man will say' – as though he were supplying the judgement of Confucius himself.

A few hundred years later – in A.D. 279 – an important collection of documents was discovered in a tomb, and it must have been in existence for almost half-a-dozen centuries. It seems to have been mishandled at first, so that it was brought into confusion and losses were suffered, and the deciphering of the ancient script may have been carried out too hastily. Included in the collection was a long chronicle, 'The Annals of the Bamboo Books', which began in the third millennium and went down to the year 298 B.C. One of its earliest sections, an account of the Emperor Yaou, provides a further illustration of the character of the early recording in China:

Emperor Yaou: Dynastic Title: T'aou and T'ang.

In his last year, which was ping-tsze (13th of the cycle 2145 B.C.), when he came to the throne, he dwelt in K'e; and commanded He and Ho to make calendric calculations and delineations of the heavenly bodies. In his 5th year he made the first tour of inspection to the Four Mountains. In his 7th year there was a K'e-lin. In his 12th year he formed the first standing army. In the 15th year, the chief of K'eu-suw came to make his submission. In his 19th year he ordered the minister of Works to undertake the regulation of the Ho. In his 29th year the chief of the Pigmies came to court in token of homage, and offered as tribute their feathers which sank in water. In his 42nd year a brilliant star appeared in Yih (?Crater). In his ?50th year he travelled for pleasure about Mount Shou, in a plain carriage drawn by dark-coloured horses. In his 53rd year he sacrificed near the Loh. In his 58th year he caused his son Choo to be sent in banishment by prince Tseih to Taushwuy. In his 61st year he ordered the baron K'wan of Ts'ung to regulate the Ho. In his 69th year he (?) degraded K'wan. In his 70th year, in the spring, in the first month, he caused the chief of the Four Mountains to convey to Shun of Yu his charge to succeed to the throne. In his 71st year he commanded his two daughters to become wives to Shun. In his 73rd year, in the spring, in the first month, Shun received the resignation of the Emperor in the Temple of the Accomplished Ancestors. In his 74th year Shun of Yu made his first tour of inspection of the Four Mountains. In his 75th year Yu, the Superintendent of Works regulated the Ho. In his 76th year, the Superintendent of Works smote the hordes of Tr'aou and Wei and subdued them. In his 86th year the Superintendent of Works had an audience, using for his article of introduction a dark-coloured mare. In his 87th year he instituted the division of the Empire into twelve provinces. In his 89th year he made his pleasure-palace in T'aou. In his 90th year, he took up his residence for relaxation in T'aou. In his 97th year the Superintendent of Works made a tour of survey through the twelve provinces. In his 100th year he died in T'aou.

3 CONFUCIUS AND AFTER

The Chou dynasty had already been ruling in China for six hundred years when, in about the fifth century B.C., it entered its final stage, which lasted till the third century and is known as the period of Warring (or Contending) States. The situation was then somewhat analogous to that which existed on the European continent in the age of feudalism, for the separate principalities within the empire behaved as independent kingdoms, made wars and concluded peace-treaties with one another, and reduced central government to a mere pretence. Yet all this coincided with a tremendous flowering of culture, Chinese thought and literature acquiring an originality and freshness that it never attained again. The philosophical thought of this region now came to its climax. The movement almost synchronised with the rise of philosophy in ancient Greece. Confucius, born probably in 551, died in 479 B.C., well before the birth of Plato.

For a long time before even this there had been in China a movement towards what we should call rationalism. One Chinese scholar traces the tendency back to the thirteenth century B.C. From that time, he says, the tortoise-shell inscriptions no longer carry the ancestor-worship back to remote and mythical times in the way they had previously done. Also the diviners now seemed to become less concerned to ask for predictions about the rain, the harvest, the birth of children, illness and death. The passage of centuries certainly brought the emergence of thinkers who were less ready to believe in spirits or in anthropomorphic gods. Some were prepared to argue that a man made sacrifices to his ancestors not for the sake of any good it did to them, but for the good that it did to himself. They became less inclined to believe even that the decline and fall of a state was due to vindictive action on the part of a jealous god. The state decayed for common-sense reasons, as its virtue declined and it lost its stamina. Or the judgement came from a Heaven which did not necessarily comprise a god, but seemed to stand as a system of an impersonal kind. The *Shoo King* often seems to be taking this point of view, and it tells us that Heaven does not have a 'partiality' for a given ruler – it 'simply gives its favour to pure virtue'. 'Great Heaven has no affection – it helps only the virtuous.' It came to be held that even the 'immortality' which men were so anxious to achieve could be construed in the same humanistic way. It meant being remembered by the world – by posterity – for one's moral character, or one's service to society, or one's published works. Tradition attributes to Confucius the view that men have a longing to survive after death, but to survive in the memory of future ages, that is to say, in historical literature. The whole view was calculated to give added importance to historiographers, who tend to reproduce it explicitly when they are explaining their motives.

In this movement towards a more mundane and rationalistic view of things, 'philosophy' itself came to be an extraordinarily matter-of-fact affair. It did not lead one into cosmological theory or into rarefied realms of metaphysics, but sought the kind of wisdom that is necessary in the conduct of life. It concerned itself above all with the operation of government, the question of the reform of society, the development of what we should call political theory.

The philosophers were interested in the work of general education, but also it would be their ambition to be the advisers of princes. In the period of the Warring States we find these itinerant scholars moving sometimes from one principality to another, trying to hawk their programmes and policies, and to acquire a position of influence. It was their ambition to secure employment at a court, as consultants or advisers. Sometimes we find that they would be sent on diplomatic missions. Confucius had done service for a time in the principality of Loo. He, too, hoped to be adopted by one prince or another. His message was for the world of action.

All this raised the status of history. Philosophy, which in ancient Greece produced an anti-historical effect, became in China the most powerful of allies. This was all the more the case in that, here, philosophy came down to street-level and greatly affected the shape of the general mentality. It did not take its start from abstract concepts and attempts to spin subtle spider-webs out of its inner contemplations. It drove men to the consideration of the concrete world, and made them seize on tangible facts, demonstrable situations. The very mode of argument that was employed differed greatly from the method of the ancient Greeks, for what was needed was not severely logical argument but rather a persuasive power, depending on rhetorical devices. And the most effective of the rhetorical devices was the exploitation (in one way or another) of historical examples. There was a party to be persuaded, a prince to be won over. The object might not be attainable by an austere chain of deductive reasoning. It was more to the point if one could make apt allusions to great men. China differed in a further way from ancient Greece: it had no great inheritance of myth that was suitable for the poets, the philosophers, the orators, to draw upon. Those who had anything to teach found it better to adduce historical personages if they needed names that everybody knew; and ancient kings played the part which in the West so often fell to biblical characters or figures in classical mythology. Some scholars have suggested that, since China stood alone, locked away from other countries and other civilisations of the world, her students of public affairs were unable to compare conditions in other lands. The only comparison they could make was with the China of former periods, or with what they thought had existed in earlier times. It is probably true to say that a whole group of converging forces or associated factors helped to create the general mentality of the Chinese in the crucial period. But it seems clear that this general mentality was particularly congenial to the development of history.

If there had been any doubt about the matter, the personality of Confucius must have decided the issue. His particular interest lay in the kind of thought which has bearings on political action and social relations. He observed all the disorders of the time and saw that they created an urgent need for a man with a message. Like many other people, and in accordance, no doubt, with an existing tradition, he hankered for the state of things which he thought had existed in an idealised past. One could say that the return to the past was the main part of his programme – he called for the imitation of the ancient kings. Going further than so many of the exponents of this kind of conservatism, he insisted upon the enquiry into the past, the collection of the records, the preservation of the annals, the literature, the thought, the ceremonies, the institutions. The famous classics that are associated with his name were connected with the study of bygone times, and were intended to put the records into common currency, so that the present and the future would have them always near at hand. Besides the *Shoo King* and the *Ch'un Ts'ëw*, there was the *Shih King*, a great collection of poems, some of which went back well over a thousand years. There were the *Li Ki*, the Books of Rites, which dealt with ancient ceremonies and institutions. And there was the *Yi-King*, the 'Book of Changes' which provided an explanation of the universe in terms of the trigrams and hexagrams supposed to date back to Fuh-hi, three thousand years B.C. – a work that became important because of its use in divination.

Confucius would seem to have been afraid lest, in a time of confusions and wars, the records of the past would be destroyed and the memory obliterated. There are signs that in his day – and for a period after it – the cause of history was somewhat in decline, needing the administration of a tonic. The warring princes were dissatisfied on occasion with those local annals which exposed and condemned some of their own modes of conduct. The general prestige of the historiographer had been reduced and he had lost some of his independence. It was true that even the schools that were opposed to Confucius valued history and tended to use historical examples as instruments of persuasion. This was the case with the so-called Legalists themselves – the people who wanted to see China turned into a unitary, absolutist state, the embodiment of power, while Confucius was attached to the aristocracy and feudalism, and attached also to the idea of moral example as the key to successful government. Even the school of Mo Ti, which went further than any other in the development of a pure, logical method, fell into the way of appealing to history. All save a few other-worldly Taoists and mystics were inclined in this direction. Confucius was no doubt excessively conservative – unable to see that the 'feudal' order which had endured for fifteen hundred years had ceased to be an adequate ideal. But it was he and his followers who imposed themselves on the future. He had many disciples who clearly did much to spread his teaching in the generation after his death. A surprising amount of the historiography of the pre-Confucian period goes back to the books associated with his name, to the commentaries produced by his disciples and to the labours of men who worked under his inspiration. It was to be a momentous thing for China that the Confucian tradition was officially adopted as a kind of orthodoxy a few centuries later and acquired such influence over education.

Yet the teaching may have owed some of its success to the fact that it was rooted deeply in an ancient and profound tradition. It brought to a culmination that movement by which historiography, which had once been almost a ritual art, was turned into a secular, moralising affair. There had been an ancient belief that a given dynasty received its mandate from Heaven because of the virtues of an original leader, but then lost it when the virtue declined. The process came to be seen as working almost mechanistically: the original virtue itself involving some lack of balance and so leading to a corresponding vice. Alternatively it would be held that ancestors contributed a mystical kind of power to their successors, but this became weaker as one proceeded along the chain, and after a lapse of time it lost its effect. It was not through arbitrary interventions of gods, whose sense of right had been outraged, but by the judgement of an impersonal Heaven, indeed by the processes of history itself, that the wicked met their punishment – we find it explained as being the action of human beings. Morality itself, working almost automatically, explained the ups-and-downs of states, because this was the way in which the universe was constituted. All this – and the consequential view that the primary function of the historian was to distribute 'praise and blame', may go back to an older China, but it was the Confucian teaching-tradition that gave it its power through so many centuries. A Chinese scholar, Ku Chieh-Kang, who was one of the pioneers in the introduction of Western historical methods into his country in the early years of the twentieth century, wrote an autobiography in which he asserts that the principle of 'praise and blame' had distorted historical writing through the ages.

In the year 221 B.C., one of the Contending States of China, the principality of Ch'in, prevailed against the rest and achieved the unification of the whole country. In its own locality, this dynasty had already been attached to an anti-Confucian tradition, namely, that of the so-called Legalists, who wanted in reality a strong state and approved of the pursuit of power with not too much regard for moral considerations. The party was hostile above all to the Confucian idea of a return to a feudal past, and liked neither the freedom of discussion which he favoured, nor the notion of improving the world by mere moral example. The new dynasty, having established its imperial power, sought to increase its authority by attacking the prevailing ideology, and turned against the main traditions of Chinese thought, attempting to destroy everything except its own species of orthodoxy. The persecution was bound to be particularly severe for the followers of Confucius, and, since the mere sentiment for past times was a political danger, much of the hostility was concentrated against the historians, who had suffered much already from the hostility of princes. In 213 B.C. an Emperor of the Ch'in dynasty decreed the famous Burning of the Books – the wholesale destruction of histories, save the ones relating to the family principality, the destruction also of the works that had come to be regarded as classics. He attempted at the same time to abolish even the discussion of the condemned doctrines, and he decreed the penalty of death against those who appealed to antiquity or tradition. It is true that the ban was properly enforced for only six years, and it was actually withdrawn after a trifle more than two decades, but it had been effective, especially as books had been written on strips of bamboo, and so were bulky things, difficult to hide. It is true also that a copy of every work was allowed to be kept in the imperial palace, but this proved an insufficient safeguard, as the palace was soon to be burned down.

In this way China, though she is the country in which one would least expect such a thing, suffered a break with the past which brings to mind the hiatus that occurred in Western culture after the fall of the Roman Empire. It happened that in the same period there was a change in both the forms and the materials of handwriting: more modern characters were devised and the hair writing-brush was improved so that it could be used for writing on silk. The fact that the older script had become archaic seems to have been a factor in the disappearance of the older literature. For one reason or another men came to feel that there had been a great culture of the past, and that the world had lost touch with it – that indeed it would need a serious effort to recover the contact. The result was the nearest thing that China ever had to the Renaissance in Western Europe: not merely a desire to learn from historical writings about the past but an endeavour to recover a culture regarded as classical.

In 206 B.C. China came under the rule of a new family, the famous dynasty of Han. It not only revoked the destructive policy of its predecessor but went into full reverse and gave its patronage to the Confucian school. Now came the attempt to recover the ancient classics and the lost histories, and in one way the task was harder than in medieval and Renaissance Europe, for many of the writings seem really to have disappeared. Since the ban had been so short, it is surprising to see how long it took to recover some things. The stories or the legends of the recovery are sometimes curious – works turning up in mysterious hiding-places – one of them re-written by a man of ninety who had learned the contents by heart. Most curious of all was the difficulty of being sure which was the proper text, since the manuscripts now brought forward were sometimes unreliable. In some cases there would be two or three recensions, each claiming to be the proper text. One is left with the clear impression that the ancient writings of China were in a state of great confusion in the period after the accession of the Han dynasty.

Finding themselves unified under a great imperial dynasty, and feeling society more secure, the Chinese could now more safely look back to the past, romanticising that 'feudal' era when intellectual life had come to a climax. This was particularly true of the Confucian scholars, for whom the temper of the times was more congenial, even apart from the fact that they were now under imperial patronage. It was they who played the principal part in the restoration of the classics, the re-establishment of the tradition and the recovery of the history. And this fact, too, was to be of signal importance: Confucianism had the whip hand at the crucial moment. It must always have had the tendency to read its own ideas back into those ages of the past to which it had attached itself. And nobody ever recovers the past clear and clean – those who restore a tradition may think they are merely remembering but they are also reconstructing. For the historiography of ancient China, a great deal was to depend on the achievements and discoveries of the Han period.

There is one indication of the genuineness of the desire to recover the past. The texts of the older Chinese writings had gone through many vicissitudes, and some trouble was taken to deal with the resulting problems. There was need for a kind of science which would help one to establish the authenticity of documents and even to verify the meaning of words and phrases. For the first time scholars were confronted by an unmistakable challenge of this kind; and they began to devise a technique of textual criticism. From that very period, therefore, the second century B.C., the discipline began to develop, and, as it became elaborated through the ages, it came to be one of the most remarkable features of Chinese historical scholarship. Some forms of documentary criticism which the West was to prize very highly, hardly developed in China. But in the art of dissecting a text and detecting the antecedents of a piece of historical literature they achieved a remarkable degree of refinement.

CHAPTER SIX

The Establishment of a Christian Historiography

Our examination so far of the rise of historical writing has shown how the origin of a genuine interest in the past, as opposed to mere storytelling for its own sake, is connected with the ideas men have about the whole human drama. These ideas, by their very nature, usually belong to the realm of religion. As pointed out in the preface, over very great sections of the globe, philosophies and creeds have flourished which denied significance to mundane events and which saw in the ups and downs of fortune nothing but pointless kaleidoscopic change; so that the historical-mindedness of Western civilisation, like its prowess in the natural sciences, is a remarkable and exceptional thing, which needs to be explained, and which requires us indeed to dig pretty deep in order to reach an explanation. Our whole enquiry is therefore bound to come to a new climax when the religious outlook and the awareness of history come together in a new way with the emergence of Christianity. For Christianity was the religion which from a period of fairly primitive conditions presided for more than a thousand years over the development of the exceptionally history-conscious society and culture of Europe when these were in their formative stages.

At the very beginning of an enquiry into the impact of Christianity on men's perception of the past, we are confronted by a problem. So far as we can see, the earliest Christians were not themselves greatly concerned about the past as such, and certainly not greatly interested in the course of mundane events in bygone times. This is always liable to be the trouble with people who put their heart and their treasure in heaven. In the case of the earliest Christians, the difficulty was aggravated by the fact that they believed the end of the world to be immediately imminent. The saving of souls was therefore an urgent matter. There was no point in brooding on bygone things. In a sense our enquiry must go back to the beginning again, as it has already done in the cases of the Egyptians, the Assyrians, the ancient Hebrews and the ancient Greeks. We have to trace again the actual genesis of an interest in the past, a concern for history, in a people initially without it. In the case of Christianity there are moments when the issue seems to be in doubt, especially since it developed almost from the beginning in close contact with Greek philosophy which, as we have seen, was unwilling to attach any serious value to history. If the balance had been tipped in this direction, if, for example, St Augustine at a later date had remained under the influence of a neo-Platonism which insisted on the pointlessness of the chances and changes in human affairs, the Christian religion itself would have developed differently and would have assumed a rather different shape. On the other hand it is possible to hold the opinion that the nature of the faith itself was bound to bring Christians over to the side of history in the long run. Indeed, this may well be the case. But it would still leave us with two questions. What was there in Christianity which was calculated to have this effect in the long run? And by what stages did Christians come to realise that they were committed to history, committed to seeing significance in human events and undertaking the study of the whole course of things in time? We therefore need to look more closely at the origins of a Christian historiography.

1 THE CHANGED OUTLOOK OF JUDAISM

At the beginning of the story there was a further hostile factor in the case – one so significant that it will be necessary to go back a little in order to understand it. The Jews, whose unique and absolutely original contribution we studied in Chapter III, had been changing the character of their religion. In the centuries before Christ they had brought about another colossal surprise. They, of all peoples, had turned against history. This development is very relevant to our enquiry, because the earliest Christians emerged from this new type of Judaism, and were deeply influenced by some of its most recent developments. The notion that the gods executed judgement in the course of history, that they punished the sins of a government by bringing disaster on the nation concerned, had spread throughout Western Asia before the Hebrew people had come into existence. The originality of the Children of Israel had lain in the fact that they saw all history as based on the Promise, and that after the Exodus from Egypt and the entry into the Promised Land they became a people more dominated by an historical memory, more obsessed by history than any other, either before or since.

The Promise was always conditional on good behaviour, and for this reason the teaching about it could be dovetailed into the older view that God administered His judgements in the actual events of history. And in fact the Jews came under a colossal judgement in the age of the great prophets. This people of the Promise suffered disasters hardly exceeded in the history of any nation – the loss of Jerusalem, the destruction of the Temple, dispersion and exile in foreign lands.

At this point in the story one is tempted to say that the ancient Jews learned the lesson of history far too well, and followed out the consequences with too severe a logic. The faithful remnant who survived and were able to return to their country and to rebuild the Temple in Jerusalem were thoroughly convinced that their disasters had been a judgement from God, and that they had suffered because they had disobeyed the commandments. They now determined to put the commandments first, to obey them in every detail. Consequently, henceforward it was the Law rather than History that became their obsession. They retained their ancient literature, including the great amount of historical writing that we have in our Old Testament, but they now used it in a different manner, not so much for the sake of the history, but rather for the Law that could be extracted from it. And indeed they partly re-edited, partly rewrote, a good deal of their history in order to emphasise that legalistic point of view which had now been adopted. Furthermore, since a great part of their former sins, for which they had been so severely punished, had consisted in their consorting with foreigners, intermixing with them and then being contaminated by their idolatries, they now went to the extreme reverse. They closed their ranks, forbad mixing with the foreigner, paid great regard to racial purity and set out to insulate themselves against the rest of the world. Their policies did not save them from disaster and in practice helped to bring upon them some of the great misfortunes that they suffered. But it might be argued that the long-term results were important, and that the Jews owe to these policies the remarkable preservation of both their religion and their identity as a people. At any rate it was Law rather than History that had become the decisive factor in their development. In this general movement, what we call 'Judaism' developed, with attitudes rather different from anything that had existed formerly.

Apart from this, however, even the notion of history as based on the Promise soon developed implications which had elements of novelty and which themselves may have helped to bring about further disaster. It had always been assumed that God's judgements did not cancel the Promise, but rather that history in reality was the story of a standing Promise, repeatedly punctuated by acts of judgement. Even the great prophets of the exilic period had pointed to a fine future that was in store for the faithful remnant that should return from Babylon – a wonderful consummation to be achieved under a king of David's line. But after the return from Exile, the reward never seemed to materialise; for the Jews were still at the mercy of great empires around them – the Persian, then the one that Alexander the Great established, and finally the empire of Rome. History itself – the conditions of the time – left little room for expectation. So the Jews began to look beyond history, to a final act of God which would signalise the end of all the ages. They turned from history to speculations in eschatology, dreams of a Messianic kingdom and an ultimate vindication of justice; and this led to forms of utopianism, forms of political messianism, even unfortunate adventures in the political realm. Instead of looking at the past, they set their eyes on a future that represented a break with the ordinary realm of historical happening. Instead of glorifying the god of history, they looked to a god whose great accomplishment was to be in the future. There is something deeply inimical to history in this kind of daydreaming with political unrealities. When the earlier Hebrews had talked about the acts of God in history, they meant that they saw the hand of God in concrete events that had actually happened.

In this mood the Jews carried a stage further the age-long controversy with heaven, the wrestling with God, on the subject of the divine judgement that was supposed to operate in history. At an early date there had appeared in Mesopotamia the view that the neglect of a god would be punished by national misfortune; and this view, which might well have come chiefly from reflection on the nature of the gods, had spread throughout Western Asia. But in this simple form it had not quite fitted the facts. No doubt it was by virtue of actual experience, by actual correlations made between data, that there developed the great qualification about divine judgement. The punishment might not be immediate; the culprit might be allowed to live a full and prosperous life, his sins being visited on his successors, even to the third and fourth generation. There had been debates with the deities who were felt to have been unfair at times in this practice of visiting the sins of the fathers on the children, and we have seen how the Hittites, centuries before the time of the Old Testament, had argued with heaven and sought to understand the meaning of the divine policy. In places, the Old Testament moves forward to a rather different interpretation of human suffering, interpreting it as the way in which Yahweh might test even a good man, might chasten or discipline the faithful, or goad the wicked into mending his ways, the object being that the man himself should benefit from the act of judgement, rather than that he should be destroyed by it. At one of its highest points the Old Testament achieves the vision of suffering as part of the historic mission of the people of Israel – this people which bears the sins of others and will help to bring all nations to the worship of God.

Though the Old Testament teaching had reached these lofty heights, a

different mood makes its appearance in the later Judaism, as though the
sufferings of this people had become too heavy, too galling. The finest
expression of this outlook comes in the time of Christ and a little while later,
when Jerusalem itself was destroyed again. It is felt that the tale of disaster
has been too long and consistent. Israel may have been the sinner in the
time of Jeremiah, but she now regards herself as a nation faithful to Yahweh
yet still harassed by persecution. It is not merely a case of God making an
ad hoc use of a heathen power to chasten His own people. All men sin sometimes, but what nation has kept God's precepts in the way that Israel has
kept them? There never was a time when the Gentiles had recognised
Yahweh; they had always been impious and wicked, yet each new generation sees them flourishing more and more. The religion of Yahweh is bound
to be brought into derision if its enemies are always allowed to be at the
top of the world. In the fourth book of Ezra, the complaint is extended
through a longer stretch of time and the final reward of the righteous
delayed. The attack is extended against the Creation itself. God formed
men and minds out of the dust of the earth. It had been better that the dust
had never existed if it was to be put to such a use. Clearly some of the old
assumptions were being shaken; the trouble now was that it was so difficult
to see judgement or justice in history. It was partly this very deep anguish
that caused the concentration on the eschatological hope, the vindication
that was to come for Israel at the end of history.

All these ideas represented important changes in the religious outlook
of the ancient Jews, and they sprang in a recognisable way from the
reflections of that people on its historic experience. They amount to a
considerable transformation in the Jewish attitude to history. Yet the writing
and the reading of more ordinary, mundane history did not cease. The Books
of the Maccabees, appearing a century or so before the birth of Christ, are
most interesting to the modern technical historian. The author of the Second
Book of the Maccabees tells of 'the infinite number' of people who wanted
to read the narrative of the Maccabean War, but could only be catered for
by the production of an abridged version. In any case the nation adhered to
the ancient Scriptures, and so could hardly have avoided an awareness of
history.

In this Jewish world, amongst the various parties and sects that arose in
the country and developed various aspects of Old Testament teaching,
Christianity began.

2 CHRISTIAN ACCOUNTS OF JESUS

Before Christianity presided over the rise of Western culture, even the
secular student of history cannot overlook the tremendous importance for
that culture of what happened in the Holy Land in the years (and indeed in

the weeks, no doubt in the few days) after the Crucifixion. That event found the disciples in disarray, apparently stunned by their appalling loss, still not clear in their ideas of Jesus, and a frightened Peter even denying any connection with him. The description of their shortcomings must have come from the confessions of the disciples themselves, for the authors of the Gospels could hardly have had any motive for inventing such things if they had not been known to be true, even though these pictures of human frailty do add realism to the narrative, and it might be argued that they served a purpose, bringing into greater relief the transformation that took place in the disciples immediately afterwards. The Christian religion, based on the belief in the risen Christ, emerged now, acquiring its familiar general shape with a rapidity that must be staggering to any historian. This might be more easy to explain if Jesus during his lifetime had adumbrated more of the faith than he did to the disciples – disciples who remained uncomprehending until, shortly after the Crucifixion, some sudden illumination enabled them to click everything into place.

From this time, they embarked on the greatest missionary undertaking of all time; and, though they had doctrines to preach, everything hung on their remembrance of what they had witnessed; everything depended on their words carrying conviction at precisely this point. Jesus had left no written works, and though Eusebius at a later date thought that he had tracked down a letter of His it turned out of course that he had been deceived. In relation to Jesus, therefore, we meet again a form of history that depends at the crucial point on what I call reporting, and on modes of oral transmission; and historical scholarship must suffer a considerable loss because, even on this basis, the earliest Christians were so little interested in recording mundane history just for its own sake. I am not convinced that religion suffers any loss for this reason; for I am not convinced that any scientific methods that are now open to historiography could alter the fact that we today are in a position curiously analogous to that of the people who heard the very early preaching – receiving the evidence of the disciples, very often at second-hand, and then having to decide what to make of it. In any case, we always have to remember that if a handful of us were to see with our own eyes and to touch and even to converse and exchange memories with a man whom we could absolutely attest to have died and been buried a week before, the task of communicating our certainty to other people who had not been actual witnesses would produce the same situation, the same problem, as it did for the disciples.

One gathers that in the early days of the Church many people believed in the preaching that they heard because of certain sanctions, certain external guarantees, that accompanied it. For the disciples themselves, who were undoubtedly convinced that they had seen the Risen Christ, the Resurrection itself was no doubt the ultimate sanction, the unanswerable guarantee, for the Christian religion; but it could operate in this way only for those who already believed in it. One gathers that many people believed in the preaching because of the miracles that accompanied it; but miracles again, unless one experiences them oneself, seem to require as much of a guarantee as they ever confer. For a present-day historian there are certain sanctions, external things which at least give some additional weight to the oral evidence that has been transmitted to us. These are: the transformation that took place in the disciples, the spiritual power acquired by a handful of comparatively humble men, and the amazing development of a movement led by these people, who braved the power of governments, prevailed against religions long entrenched, and defied the threat of imminent martyrdom. It is possible that many of those who heard the first missionaries did not put the microscope on any single historical event, even the Resurrection, but accepted the whole of the preaching as a package deal. They may have done so partly perhaps because it introduced them to a higher conception of God; partly perhaps because it corresponded to their experience of the whole human predicament; or partly because they were moved by the call to repentance in any case. Once they had adopted Christianity as a complete new outlook, they might well find the Resurrection less of a problem in itself. Or the momentum of the whole compound preaching might carry them over the hurdle. Furthermore, once they had thrown themselves into the new religion, they had the conviction that it ratified itself in their own inner life, that indeed they had found contact with a living Christ.

When we are trying to discover the relation of history to belief, it is necessary to put on the thinking-cap of the purely technical historian, who sees the life of Jesus and his impact on his followers as one of the pivotal epochs of world-history and asks what can be scientifically established — established in such a coercive manner that even the non-Christian can hardly deny it. In other words, how far does the tangible concrete evidence take us? And what is the nature of the evidence, what is the character of the early Christian historiography? It seems to be the case, even in regions that never developed any regard for 'history' as such, or any desire to see the centuries of the past in sequence, that men are interested in stories about other human beings — interested in the past as far back as the tales of a grandfather. Christianity, even where it has been otherworldly in many of its aspects, has seemed generally to foster this interest in people for their own sakes. It would be difficult to imagine the disciples failing to talk to one another, and to other men, about Jesus as a human being, and I cannot be convinced that those who heard for the first time about somebody who had risen from the dead, would not want to know something about the man himself, and engage in cross-questioning which would never appear in the more formal records. I am always reminded of the stories which are told about Winston Churchill and the hundreds of sayings of his which have come into general currency during the last quarter of a century. We may read these things in newspapers and books, but I wonder if we realise how often they appear to depend ultimately on a verbal report given by a single man. I am not sure of the truth of any one of the Churchillian anecdotes that has come to us by this particular route. I notice that even academic historians who are utterly reliable in their field of study find it hard to retail a story at dinner-time without adding something to round it off or to make it more piquant. So it would not be easy to establish in a watertight manner the truth of a great many of the single stories about Winston Churchill. Yet I have a hunch that many of them are true (though I cannot do the distinguishing), and that in any case the whole corpus of them shows us Churchill the man in quite an effective manner. Even a Churchillian story that ultimately proved to be apocryphal might well be more true in a sense, more typical of the man, than another which could be established as absolutely correct. The person who invents such a story, or rounds it off in order to give it the Churchillian ring, is just the one who struggles to produce what contemporaries will accept as typical. It might even be true that the anecdotes in the mass can bring us nearer to the man than an historical work which absolutely restricted itself to the things that can be documentarily demonstrated. At the first level of analysis the historian is in a somewhat analogous position in respect to the man Jesus. It is more possible for us to form a general picture of him than to distinguish which of the detailed anecdotes are authentic.

The stories and sayings of Jesus, however, went through a considerable amount of screening which in some ways assists the historian, though in others makes the problem more complicated. It permits a certain grading of the material which has come down to us, for it helps us to judge rather better what things are more likely to have come from the disciples and even perhaps to have a hunch about the kind of twist that they gave to their evidence. Some of the things in the Gospels (the Crucifixion and the Resurrection, for example) must have been firmly established from the very start in the early teaching of the Church, and I think that any historian would have to say both that the disciples were responsible for proclaiming these things to the world and that their belief was not merely genuine but overpowering. From the state of the available documents, it looks as though the developing tradition paid particular attention at first to the Passion of our Lord, the stages which led to the Crucifixion. Here, as one can see from the Gospels, there developed at an early stage the most detailed, most consecutive and most consistent piece of narrative about Christ that got into the transmission-process. And it has been pointed out that one or two incidents in this chapter of the story are included for no discoverable religious purpose, no propaganda reason, except possibly to call attention to certain outside people who had been identified as eye-witnesses. On the other hand, it is impressive to see how reticent in general the Gospels are about the manner of the Resurrection, where the imagination might have run riot. The sayings of Jesus were obviously an important matter from the start, and collections of them must have begun to appear very early. Some of the stories most likely to have come from the disciples themselves undoubtedly appeared in sermons and thereby began to acquire a semi-official kind of currency. It seems clear, and it would be the obvious thing in any case, that the disciples – who had actually known Jesus – would be regarded as the best authorities for either the stories or the sayings; and, after them, a special hearing would be given to their immediate successors, the men who had been intimate with them and had been taught by them. That this principle was firmly adopted is one of the earliest things that we know about primitive Christianity, and its importance was so much emphasised that it became the basis of the very peculiar conception of authority worked out by the Church in the succeeding centuries. The Gospels must have gathered together the things that had gone through the screening process and been accepted by the Church, at any rate in important centres; and only for such a reason could those writings have established themselves as canonical. From what is known of apocryphal stories and sayings of Jesus, the Church showed a good deal of discrimination in respect of this matter at various periods.

It would seem likely that the recognised tradition concerning Jesus reached its familiar general shape within about twenty years of the Crucifixion, while many eye-witnesses would presumably still be alive and obvious falsities would have to reckon with possible challenge. But the critical student cannot avoid the question of how far the disciples, whether consciously or unconsciously, may have given a twist at the very start to the evidence that they had to offer. The historian has to bear in mind that the best of men sometimes fail even to remember things properly. They reconstruct when they imagine that they are only remembering. Often they do not realise how the shape of their recollections may have been altered by events that occurred in the after-period. When their minds happen to be preoccupied with doctrine or dogma, this itself is sometimes capable of distorting the memory enormously. Nor can we today entirely rely on the virtue and sincerity of good men to prevent misreporting and the transmission of error. Virtue and sincerity are not by any means irrelevant and they ought to deter scholars from theories which too easily take for granted that there was a conscious kind of fraudulence. But the innocent are not always sufficiently critical, particularly in respect of what they hear and retail at second-hand. They are not sufficiently suspicious of their fellow-men.

In any case such evidence as exists has come down to us largely through the Gospels, which probably belong to the second half of the first century A.D. and perhaps a little later. The authors of the Gospels do not treat the life of Jesus simply in terms of what the disciples actually remembered; they tend to interpret His earlier years in the light of what happened after His death. And the Gospels do not represent what we should call straight-forward history. They tell the story of Jesus with the object of communicat-ing a particular view of Him. In this they do not differ from a great deal of other historical writing and literary material that the historian has to handle. Beyond this, however, they are, of course, governed by a strongly dynamic religious purpose and this in itself always tends to operate with a powerful transforming effect on the materials at its disposal. The writings in question are not – and in those days they could not have been – biographies in the modern sense of the word, close studies of the environment, the education, the early influences, the intellectual development and the all-round person-ality of a man. Much of their character depends on the fact that they were constructed, by the necessities of the case, out of oral evidence. Their ulti-mate basis consisted of those stories and sayings of Jesus which existed in the first place as unconnected anecdotes, though the author of St Luke's Gospel might try to give a chronological order to some of the stories and put them into a probable historical context, while the author of St Matthew might string many of the sayings together and present them as a continuous piece of preaching. The fact that the stories and sayings would find currency and achieve recognition through sermons, or in relation with some of the rites of the Church, meant that, in their telling, they sometimes came to be connected to some religious purpose. And, apart from the fact that this may help to explain the selection of the tradition – the reason why some things rather than others would be told and remembered – the religious preoccupa-tion would mean that the anecdotes themselves were liable to acquire a slant that might have to be taken into account. Some critics have actually said that we must be chary of stories and sayings of Jesus which support the teaching of the earliest Church; they may have been concocted or twisted for the very purpose of supporting that teaching. It has been similarly argued that we must be chary of stories and sayings that chime in with the Judaism of the time of Jesus. If there are stories or sayings that neither support the early Church nor chime in with Judaism, then, on the same argument, we can feel more sure of our ground, more sure that the anecdote was not produced to serve a polemical purpose. There is perhaps just the shadow of a useful hint in all this, but nothing more. With evidence of this sort, a general picture may be true (as in the case of Winston Churchill) while one has to accept the fact that any particular story is incapable of water-tight establish-ment. For the history that consists of anecdotes and depends on mere report-ing always tends to be in this position, even in recent time. And if it is taken that one item, one anecdote, is more probable than another for reasons so subtle as those that are alleged, we are faced with the fact that in history it is often the thing more inherently improbable that actually happens — history has this element of surprise.

In trying to understand how the early Christians recorded the life of their Lord on earth, therefore, we must remember that today we sometimes underestimate the tenacity with which the men of ancient times would cling to something that had come down from the past. We also underestimate sometimes the machinery that was available to oral tradition — available to the early Church, for example — for sifting the stories, even though the ones that passed the test might be used for propaganda purposes and some that survived the test may have done so because of their utility as propaganda for the faith. Stories of miracles by Jesus, and others that may seem to us improbable, were not handed down and received by early Christians in any spirit of dishonesty, but rather with a humility of mind. The authority accorded in the early Church to the accounts of witnesses had its roots in the idea of faithfully conserving what had been handed down. It derived from the need which the successors of Jesus's contemporaries felt to keep the evidence of the actual witnesses alive and pure.

3 THE RELATION TO THE OLD TESTAMENT

Second only to the faithful handing down of the inherited testimony about the life of Jesus, one of the most momentous of the many things which were ultimately to involve the Christian religion so profoundly with history — though we might almost say that the early Christians did their best to defeat the objective — was the decision to keep a connection with the past, to tie the new faith in a sense to ancient Judaism by accepting the Old Testament as Holy Scripture. It was hardly a conscious decision, for the simple fact was that, for the disciples as well as for Jesus, the Old Testament simply stood there; it had always been their sacred book. Thus the question of the actual nature of the relations between the Old Testament religion and Christianity was itself bound to raise issues of the profoundest kind, issues that were unmistakably historical. Christians were compelled to think of the new faith as a thing that had antecedents. And it is an important moment for historiography when people begin to see that an historical phenomenon is to be connected with its antecedents, and that this connection is liable to be a fertile one. Whether they liked it or not, they found themselves committed to making statements about the relations between the present and the past, statements which involved putting Judaism into its historical place. Above all, as soon as they began taking the Gospel to the pagan world, they not only had to persuade the Gentiles to believe in Christ, they had to induce them to accept the Old Testament too, to accept the traditions of this hitherto rather despised Jewish people. Clearly some explanation was going to be necessary from the very start. This explanation could not help taking the form of a résumé of Jewish history over a very long period and an exposition of its relevance. To make things more complicated, the Christians had to explain not only the continuity with Judaism but also the discontinuity. They had to show why, while accepting the Jewish Scriptures, they had broken with the Jewish faith. On top of this special need for historical explanation, it was true in any case that most of the Old Testament itself was history, and much of it, indeed, straight historical narrating. In the long run, the pull of the Old Testament was bound to draw Christians to history and to a recognition of the importance of history.

Yet the early Christians found the most interesting technique ever devised for evading the historical issue and for ensuring that their connection with the past should not make them historically minded. If the Jews after the Exile tried to turn everything in the Old Testament into Law, the early Christians went to the opposite extreme: they rejected the Law and tried to turn everything into Prophecy. They identified Christ with a concept of the Messiah which had long been a powerful feature of the Jewish tradition, but they also found much in the Old Testament which they regarded as applicable to Him and which deepened their appreciation of His rôle, including things which the Jews always swore had never had anything to do with any Messiah.

Once the early Christians conceived of Christ as the Messiah, they were bound to become closely involved with the Old Testament prophets, and in normal circumstances it would be very hard to believe that a man who had been crucified could be the Messiah of Hebrew prophecy. The curiously prophetic picture of the Suffering Servant in the fifty-third chapter of Isaiah had to be combined with the grander and more glorious concept of the Messiah before a crucified Christ could quite be made to fit the teaching of the older Scriptures. Indeed, the real problem of a crucified Messiah could only arise after the Crucifixion, and the Crucifixion would not have found the early Christians so bewildered if they had already been convinced that Christ was the Suffering Servant of Isaiah. And if Jesus had given them some indications at an earlier date, they were unlikely to have understood them. Here is an important clue to the almost incredible transformation that took place in the disciples so quickly after the Resurrection. And it must have been quick, for their preaching that Christ had risen after only three days would have been seriously damaged if the announcement and the new Gospel had been long delayed.

Once the disciples had arrived at their new understanding of Jesus – their identification of the Suffering Servant with the Messiah – their revised concept of Him was clearly greatly influenced by this; and even the portrait of Him in the Gospels was affected by the attention they paid to the analogies and the care which they took to call attention to them. Some scholars claim that the whole operation worked in reverse, suggesting that because certain things were prophesied, the early Christians presumed that they happened too. There are one or two points in the Passion story where there is a plausible case for saying that possibly the prophecy produced the anecdote of the event. This cannot be true in any large sense, however, for the disciples were certainly struck by the way in which the actual Jesus corresponded with prophecy; and some of the analogies between Jesus and prophecy were so far-fetched that nobody could have thought of creating the event to fit the prophecy. The first Christians must have been faced by the event and then been determined to find a prophecy for it somewhere, even if the connection was not entirely plausible. They were rather cavalier in their attitude to history, and to the Old Testament too. Soon collections of prophetic passages were in circulation, and it was curious that some of the prophecies which the Christians found and distributed were not in the accepted Hebrew text of the Old Testament. Strikingly, however, the prophecy came to be regarded as evidential proof of the factuality of a given event. Amongst early Christians there seems to have been a habit of demonstrating the actuality of the event by showing the prophecy, and the prophecy proved to them that things must have happened in this way. It may have been a linguistic usage, but we even read sometimes that a certain thing happened in order that prophecy should be fulfilled. At a later date, St Augustine produced the disturbing argument that the Old Testament must be accurate in its history because its prophecies had come true. If the Old Testament was able to foretell the future, it must *a fortiori* be right when it was engaged in the much easier and more pedestrian task of recounting what had happened in the past.

Over and above all this there was the fact that the *whole* of the Old Testament was now taken to be a prophecy of Christ and a preparation for Him, and this in itself produced many analogies that we might regard as far-fetched. Even the historical narrative ceased to maintain its importance as an historical record. For the early Christians it was evident that inspiration would not have been given to the writers of Holy Scripture merely to recapitulate what had happened. Everything in the Scriptures – Abraham and Moses and the Song of Solomon – now had an extra dimension; it provided types or analogies or pointers which now found their meaning in Christ. The narrative parts ceased to derive their real importance from the fact that they were an account of God's dealings with man. A twentieth-century historian might like to trace development in the Bible, to see how the high places in the Old Testament indicated, for example, a progress toward New Testament teaching. It is almost impossible for a twentieth-century person to realise how the mind had to work in days when these instinctive evolutionary notions were unthinkable. The modern historian handles the connections between the Old and the New Testaments very differently from the early Christians, therefore. But where they rightly recognised the connection, they did not see causes or antecedents, they only saw prophecy. They discerned the similarity of pattern in certain places – the correspondence between Christ and the Suffering Servant for example – and they further assumed that the whole of the Old Testament contains such patterns. Having little enough regard for the history as history, they concentrated on this new dimension that they found in the Scriptures. In the first century or two of Christianity there are works in which we should expect to find a long discourse on history and antecedents, and a mere glance over hundreds of pages would suggest that all the materials for it have been assembled. But what the reader actually discovers is a store and a kind of codification of countless detailed prophecies.

By attaching themselves to the Old Testament, however, the early Christians were committing themselves unawares. They were binding themselves to face in the future the question of the relations between Judaism and Christianity, the relation of the Old Testament to the New. The exposition of that relationship was calculated to produce interesting ideas about the march of history, the processes of time, the way in which the past prepares for the future. Furthermore, the whole attitude of the early Christians to this subject involved them in a significant notion, already partially adumbrated in later Judaism and very interesting to the historians. This was the idea that Christ had come 'in the fullness of time', that previous ages had been only preparatory, pointing to some culmination. If we set this concept of preparation and fullness in time against the views of history that prevailed in the ancient world, even among the Greeks, we can see that the idea was bound to have major significance for a Christian historiography.

Before long the early Christians also became involved with history in various minor ways, almost without themselves being aware of it. Two in particular are significant for our enquiry.

First, the apocalyptic belief of the earliest Christians that they were living in the fullness of time, and that the Last Trump would shortly sound announcing the end of the world, continued as an article of faith for a long period and engendered their lack of concern for the merely mundane aspect of events. But, as time passed and the expected end of the world did not come, the claims of history did begin to assert themselves. Christians looked back to the early apostles, they became interested in the earliest history of the Church itself, the fabulous extension of Christianity provided a great story, and there was a whole saga of St Paul's missionary journeys. Once it appears that the end had not really arrived, the spread of the Gospel became a real historical subject for Christians, and one of the greatest interest to them.

Secondly, the fact that the original disciples were the source of real authority in the Church meant that even the first Christians did have to look back to the past; and when the disciples were dead, their followers tried to maintain contact with this direct witness through their closest pupils. Once things were on this footing, the actual business of running the Church entailed a continual resort to the past. The followers of the original Apostles had to refer, for example, to decisions made by the Founders of the Church at an early date in Jerusalem. The earliest piece of Christian historical narrating that has survived in writing – earlier than the production of the written Gospels – is connected with this kind of harking back. It is in St Paul's Epistle to the Galatians, and it further illustrates the fact that controversies about the beliefs of the primitive Church (the controversies about the relations between Jewish and Gentile Christians, for example) necessitated the reference to precedent: in other words, the appeal to history. Indeed the very structure of the Church, or at least the structure of authority in the Church, was bound to carry this implication whether people intended it or not.

The Acts of the Apostles, which may have appeared before the end of the first century, was an answer to the desire of the faithful to have authoritatively on record the story of the original Church, the epic of the earliest missionaries, the account of the spread of Christianity. And though the work may suffer from some of the disadvantages of the Gospels from the technical historian's point of view, it is like the other work that is associated with the name of St Luke in that it shows a certain aspiration to see the past as history. It has a narrative which overlaps the one by St Paul in the Epistle to the Galatians, and the discrepancies between the two have caused much difficulty for the faithful and much controversy amongst scholars. St Paul's is the earlier account and comes from an eye-witness; at the same time it is written in a more obviously polemical mood. But the Book of the Acts contains part of a diary by a man who accompanied St Paul on some missionary travels.

4 THE ESTABLISHMENT OF A CHRISTIAN INTERPRETATION OF WORLD HISTORY

The fact that the faith was attached to Christ may have meant that in the long run Christians were bound to be committed to history, and, as time proceeded, men could hardly help seeing Him as connected with a particular date, having a place in the time-series. In the theological conflicts that arose after Christian communities had become widely scattered through the eastern part of the Roman Empire, the teachers who clung to the idea of the humanity of Jesus – the school of Antioch as against the school of Alexandria, for example – could not help vindicating the idea of the Jesus of History, Jesus the man who had lived at a certain time and in a definite place. Here their religion was fastened to the hard earth, though their spiritual preoccupations, their continuing concern about the possible imminent end of the world, and their contact with Greek philosophy all helped play down this aspect of the matter. Often they seemed more anxious to calculate the date of the Second Coming than to establish the picture of the past. Very considerable writings in the second century A.D., for example, which if written today would doubtless have taken the form of dense and detailed studies of the antecedents of Jesus and the developments in the pre-Christian era, were produced in a very different form, raking the Scriptures and the history of the ancient Hebrews for pre-existing types and patterns, turning everything into prophecy. Even when the Bible itself inspired men to think for a moment of the whole history of mankind from the Creation, as is the case with Chapters VII to IX of St Paul's Epistle to the Romans, early Christians would come out with the thought that Adam was in a way the prototype of Christ (each summing up the whole human race – very much a theologian's rather than an historian's idea).

But when Christianity had moved into the Roman Empire, and, still more, when the Roman Empire had become the effective seat of the religion, certain practical needs helped to bring men's minds closer to the earth. It became necessary, for example, to meet the charge that Christianity was a recent innovation. This made it more important than ever to insist on the continuity with the faith of the Old Testament – a thing which came to be strongly stressed in spite of the fact that their hostility to the Jews had mounted in quite a phenomenal way. If it was necessary to defend the continuity with the Old Testament, it was equally necessary to explain why in such a case one wanted to break with the Jews, why, if the Old Testament was right, one should not be satisfied with Judaism. And history was necessary both to explain to the Gentile world why the Hebrews had been important and to justify the charges whether against the contemporary Jews or against Judaism. In reality, both the continuity and the breach with the older faith were reconciled through a great change in the interpretation of the older Scriptures.

The case against the pagans of the Roman Empire was proved capable of a remarkable extension. It proved possible to show that the religion of the Christians was earlier than the wisdom of the Greeks. The earliest philosophers and Homer himself were nothing like as old as Moses. Pythagoras and Plato were later than some of the greater prophets of Israel. Plato, whose thought was so greatly valued and awakened many sympathies in learned Christians, had actually acquired his deeper wisdom from the Jews, though he, like the men of other nations, had perverted and misunderstood what he had received. The Christians, like the Jewish historian Josephus, said it was the Greeks who had been born only recently; and the Hebrews, who had so long been neglected, were presented as the oldest people of all, the key to the history of culture, the source of such wisdom as had spread into the nations of the world.

All this had the effect of giving something of a shape to universal history itself; and the mere fact of bridging the Gentile and the Jewish worlds forced the Christians to have conceptions about the mundane history of all mankind. The Scriptures themselves contributed in a powerful manner to such a view, starting with the Creation, telling about the primitive beginnings of the human race, and then describing the division into nations and languages. In fact the book of Genesis, besides inspiring Christians with the notion of a global history, set the pattern for the early chapters of universal histories until the eighteenth or nineteenth centuries. It has generally been the case – and has substantially remained so – that the men who write political history tell the story of their own state, their own city, their own nation. It is from religious or from what we must call quasi-religious ideas (as in the case of the Stoics) that the notion arises of a universal human history, and Christianity was to give a great impetus to this notion.

Even so, this came by a curious route. It was necessary to prove that Moses came earlier than Greek philosophy, that the famous prophets preceded Plato. This seems to have been the point at which Christians became conscious of the fact that ordinary, mundane history gave them the pull as against their pagan rivals. But it required reflections on chronology, as so many people – so many separate cities even – had had their own ways of dating events, and it was difficult to correlate one with another. Quite early, the priority of Moses had been established (and he had been placed long before the Trojan War) but such questions could not be settled by merely doing mathematics with a calendar. Events that were known to synchronise with one another and monarchs who lived in different countries at the same time had to be considered. The Christians developed in a remarkable way the attempt to find a universal chronology, but even the working out of this involved them in the events of universal history. Some time around A.D. 221, Julius Africanus elaborated a whole chronology of world history; he was skilful in his arithmetic and precise for those days, realising that he was slightly wrong in accepting the popular view that a year was equivalent to 365 days. It is not surprising that he produced also a synopsis of world history. By this time, Christian scholars were doing detective work on the Sacred Scriptures themselves, and Julius Africanus produced an attack on the view that Daniel wrote the book which is described by his name. There was also particular controversy about the actual authorship and authority of the Book of Revelation. It looks as though the passage of time was bringing the Christians down to earth.

The attitude of the Christians to the sacred history – the connection with the Old Testament – proved also to have interesting possibilities of development and led to the generation of new and important ideas. It had the effect of binding the present to the past, and it came to involve a dynamic relationship between the past and the present. The actual hostility to Judaism, and the condemnations of the Jewish people in the writings of the prophets, brought rather quickly a new notion of Hebrew history as a whole. There were biblical texts which supported the idea that circumcision and the Law of Moses represented a purely local and temporary dispensation – a particularly tough prescription necessitated by a special hardness of heart in the people of Israel. In the long period before Moses, in the time of Abraham, in the age of Noah, a purer kind of religion had flourished, without the need of the Law. Christianity was a return to something like this. However, the general view that the Old Testament itself represented only a provisional dispensation was calculated to affect the general attitude of men to the processes of time. Time itself played a part in human destiny and became a generative factor in the story; there were things that could only happen in the fullness of time. What came earlier must by necessity have been imperfect, and time was needed for its completion. The Old Testament was in a certain sense only provisional, and existed in a way only on a lower plane of reality. Time carries it further, carries it even higher; it enters into our judgements and valuations and becomes the framework for the dispensation of God, the whole plan of salvation. By about the year A.D. 180, these ideas are becoming apparent in the work of St Irenaeus 'Against the Heresies', attacking the Gnostics. In his view, the fault of the Jews lay in being anachronistic by failing to keep up with the development of God's plan.

One of the characteristics of Judaism in the period immediately before the Christian era had been the tendency to periodise history, to divide it into epochs, each of which had its character because it was dominated by certain forces. It was a practice stimulated particularly by the eschatological speculation, the description of the successive stages in the working-out of the Last Things, perhaps a division of events that were to be in a certain sense outside history but still an effective division of time. To the people of Israel, the rise of colossal neighbouring empires which had begun to make political life almost impossible for them and had led to the exile, had appeared to be a tremendous judgement of God; and as one vast empire succeeded another, bringing frustration and repeated disasters for them, the Israelites began to count these colossal empires as the prelude to the end. They caught from abroad the theory of the Four Monarchies, the Four World Empires, which makes its appearance in the book of Daniel. And the Christians took over the idea. By this time, Rome tended to be thought of as the last of the Four, and it therefore stood as the final Empire before the End. In the Judaism of the first century A.D., and in Christianity rather later, it is explicitly held that the continuance of the Roman Empire is the only thing that is holding back the end of the world. Tertullian in the third century A.D. says that Christians want to defer the End and support the Roman Empire partly for this reason. This Four-Empire system became the accepted way of periodising world history in Christian Europe; it received a new lease of life at the Reformation and it continued to be used into the seventeenth and even the eighteenth century.

But even after Christians had ceased to be holding themselves tense, in the expectation of the absolutely imminent end of the world, they continued to speculate about the possible date of the end, in spite of the fact that Christ was reported as saying that it was not for them to know the times and seasons. And these speculations for a long time interested them more than actual history seems to have done. Eschatological ideas may even have been the stimulus behind the historical work of Julius Africanus. In the Epistle of Barnabas it was argued that the Creation took six days, that according to the Second Epistle of Peter, 'one day is as a thousand years with God', and that the end of the world would come 6,000 years after the Creation. Christian writers accepted the Bible chronology and swept out of court the Babylonian and Egyptian teaching that the world was already much older than 6,000 years. It was sometimes estimated that the birth of Christ took place 5,500 years after the Creation. The end of the world was not too remote even on this calculation, and what we call millenarian speculation ran riot. On the same theory the whole of history was divided into six periods, based on the genealogical tables at the beginning of the Gospels of St Matthew and St Luke.

5 THE CONVERSION OF CONSTANTINE: EUSEBIUS

People in the first centuries after Christ envisaged a remarkably small world, with the stars overhead as part of the scenic background, and the sun specially created to be of service to men. Amongst the Jews, one finds the saying that Jerusalem was the centre of the world, that God created Jerusalem first and then the rest of the world around it. Dante was to have a similar idea of the extent of the land on the globe, and he, too, saw Jerusalem at its very centre. It was easy to insert a sort of symbolism into a geographical point like this, and indeed into certain things in history itself. There is a similar symbolism in Aristotelian physics where the noblest things – fire and air – rose to the top and the heavenly bodies themselves were made of an ethereal kind of matter. The time-scale was small – 5,500 years between the Creation and Crucifixion, it was thought – and now the world was coming to an end. Jewish writings of the first century A.D. say that it was getting old, that nature herself was becoming exhausted. It was all a small affair and the earth was the scene of a small-scale human drama, of which the final act was now supposed to have begun. For both Christians and non-Christians the air was full of active spirits, some of them wicked demons. Not until the seventeenth century did science free man from the necessity of regarding spirits as the source of some of the motions, some of the activities, of the physical universe. As time went on and masses of people had come to be converted to Christianity, there appeared many who were sincere enough in their religion, but held it in somewhat the way they had held their pagan beliefs, regarding the Christian God as the one who worked the successful magic.

The moment had now arrived when historical consciousness had developed, and it found expression in a leading personage who had no use for millenarian speculations; he had a mind for more concrete things, the things that had actually happened. Moreover, Christians, looking back, could now take stock of their whole enterprise, assessing their history as though it were a chapter of a completed story. Perhaps it was a deceptive moment for churchmen to choose for taking their bearings and working out an interpretation of history; but one of the reasons why they became history-conscious at this time was the fact that they themselves saw events reach a great climax. They could feel that a tremendous kind of history-making was going on around them. By this time the Church comprised a very considerable section of every province in the Roman Empire. It suffered the worst and most bitter of the persecutions, but it surmounted these, and through the conversion of Constantine it captured the Roman Government. At this point there emerges Eusebius, developing his ideas in a number of learned works in the decades before and after the year A.D. 300.

In general, Eusebius set out to meet the charge that Christianity appealed only to the feelings of ignorant men and that it was a newly invented faith. He tried to show how it had recovered the natural religion of primeval man, and how it had collected into itself the best that ever existed in either pagan or Hebrew history. In his view, the Hebrews were the real source of culture, the first ever to study the material universe, the only people who from the first devoted its mind to rational speculation. He followed Josephus in taunting the Greeks as being mere children; they had plagiarized all their philosophical lore, he said, and had added nothing of their own, except force and elegance of language. In the revised system of chronology that he produced, Moses was not as anterior to Greek philosophy as the Christians had once imagined; but he could afford to make concessions on this point because his results still put Moses 400 instead of 700 years before the Trojan War. And in his judgement Plato too declined from wisdom insofar as he parted from his Old Testament antecedents.

Christianity owed its chief debt to the Hebrews, but from the Old Testament it took over the Prophecy, not the Law. In this connection, Eusebius maintained that the prophecies contained hidden secrets, 'disguised', he said, because the Jews would have destroyed the writings if the predictions of their doom had been written plain. Moses was not so important to the Christians. After the free religious life of the primeval ages, he had established a polity and a law to curb the unruly spirit of the

Jews. All was only of local and temporary importance, limited entirely to
the Jewish people, not practicable even for the Jews of the Dispersion –
not practicable for anybody who did not live in the Holy Land. Even in this,
the Jews were better than the other peoples of the world, who were given
over to wicked demons who posed as gods and established polytheism. The
system of Moses was a narrow and interim affair, says Eusebius. It was like
having a doctor to heal the illness, the demoralisation that set in, after the
Jews had been contaminated by contact with the Egyptians. The Law was
'like a nurse and governess of childish and imperfect souls'. There is almost
a hint of progress in this view, a glimpse of the idea one catches in Irenaeus,
the idea of the 'pedagogic' function of time. It is perhaps significant that
Eusebius, writing on this subject, calls his work 'The preparation for the
Gospel'.

It is when Christ appears that mundane history in the writings of Eusebius
seems to take an almost magical turn. It is not sufficient that Christ comes
in the fullness of time. He comes just at the moment when the Jews have
no king of their own line. In *Genesis* (XLIX, 10) it was said : 'There shall
not be wanting a king from Judah or a leader from his loins until he come
for whom it is reserved.' Here is a reference to the Incarnation which occurs
when the Roman Emperor Augustus has imposed on the Jews a foreign
monarch, Herod. But Christ coincided also with the establishment of the
Roman Empire, comprising the bulk of mankind, which produced peace
and facilitated communications over a wide area – a providential arrange-
ment for the preaching of Christianity. Furthermore, soon after the Crucifixion, the Jews rebelled against the Roman Empire. Jerusalem and the
Temple were destroyed and the Jews suffered a final dispersion, a final
punishment for their rejection of Christ. And there were other remarkable
happenings. From the time of Christ there was an improvement in the
habits and customs of even the pagan world. From just this moment the
oracles ceased to function, and human sacrifice finally disappeared. Above
all, Christ had had a victory on the cosmic level. He had thwarted the evil
demons and if they fought desperately still, it was because they realised
their doom. This meant that there was a general drift in the world at large
away from polytheism. This drift helped the establishment of peace, for the
multitude of the gods had been connected with the multiplicity of the
nations, and so had been responsible for the repeated wars.

From this point in the story, Eusebius becomes virtually the founder of
what we call 'ecclesiastical history'. In this aspect of his work, one of his
objectives was to establish the succession of bishops in the important sees,
a momentous matter since authority had to be traced back to the original
disciples. He also desired to commemorate the martyrs – a theme to which
he was particularly attached – and to leave a record of what they had suffered
during his own lifetime. Then, again, he wanted to give an account of the

successive heresies, though here he failed to enter into the historical point
of view and explain the case for the other party or the reason why the
troubles arose, since he too was convinced that heresies were the work of
wicked demons. On the other hand, when he comes to his own time, he
uses very strong language about the evils that had arisen in the Church in
a time of considerable prosperity. He regards the persecution as, in part, a
chastening permitted by God for this reason.

It was the culmination of the story which was so remarkable. The policy
of persecution had to be abandoned. The most successful Emperor of the
time, the famous Constantine, was a convert to Christianity. By his own
account the Emperor achieved military victory through a miracle, and found
that the Christian God was the one who succeeded in battle. Also by his own
account he received direct messages from Christ; and Eusebius tells us how,
by divine means, he learned the devices of his enemies in advance, gained
the foreknowledge of future events, found the expedients to employ in
times of extremity, and even reached some of his military dispositions. The
Roman Empire had been a glorious thing to Eusebius, but now it was to be
a Christian Empire too. Now it was drawn together again by Constantine,
the eastern half united with the western half. Constantine 'alone of all
rulers' had pursued an unbroken career of conquest. He had gained authority
over more nations than anybody before him. And he was the first Emperor
since Augustus to reign for over thirty years. And Eusebius, who, if he
liked to record the sufferings of the martyrs, liked also to note the early and
violent deaths of persecutors, was able to point out that Constantine, unlike
many recent emperors, was allowed to live to a good ripe age.

From the beginning of time there unfolds, therefore, a grand design of
Providence, and everything is beautifully patterned and symmetrical, the
past containing symbols and prophecies which pointed to the glorious
future, now an actuality. And the story was coming towards its consummation : there were only a few nations outside the system to be gathered in.
In a sense it was a glorification of sheer success, success which indeed might
have a certain spiritual aspect, but was also of a very tangible mundane kind.
And Eusebius jeers at the ancient gods, who are going into decline, and are
proving so incapable of doing anything to stop the rot. He jeers at the
oracles that failed to give warning of the catastrophe – warning of the
advent of Christ, who was to put them out of business. For Constantine
himself, the Christian God is often the most effective of the wonder-workers
and magicians. He is really the one who sees that His followers prevail in
actual battle. And Eusebius sometimes produces the same kind of impression when he tells Constantine to impute his successes, especially his military
victories, to God and to connect Christ with them. Eusebius, even when he
is producing a congratulatory oration in the presence of Constantine, will
talk in fact much more about Christ than about the Emperor. In his admira-

tion for the Roman Empire, especially after its government had become Christian, he produces a kind of political theology; and even secular history seems to become sacred history in his hands. The *rapprochement* with religion seems over-crude. There are subtle ways in which the affairs of the spirit can become entangled with the affairs of the world, but Eusebius, who in any case would overlook the paradox of the wicked emperors who were allowed to enjoy a long life, sometimes allowed his assessments to be based on externals. He would have had to present a different picture of the ways of Providence if he had been taking his bearings at the present day.

6 AUGUSTINE

Eusebius belonged to a time when Christians could hardly help feeling that human history had come to another tremendous climax. Had not persecution been surmounted, and the mighty Roman Empire come under Christian leadership with the conversion of one of the greatest of the emperors, Constantine? St Augustine, a century later, confronted a different kind of scene and brought to the examination of history a different kind of experience. He had seen something of the evils that could exist when the world was under Christian rulers. In his day, that Roman Empire which many had deemed eternal was being overrun by barbarian peoples. In A.D. 410, the city of Rome itself was for a short time in the hands of these barbarians, and he had to answer the charge that the disasters were due to the neglect of the ancient gods and the triumph of the Christian faith. It is quite a thrilling thing that we possess some of the literature in which the last controversies between pagan polytheism and the Christian faith were fought out; and the intensity of the colossal feud explains why so much of Augustine's writing concerned itself with topics not quite relevant to us, and somewhat alien to our mentality.

Augustine met his particular problem by producing at a lofty level a significant kind of historical study, a very ambitious analysis of the whole drama of human life in time. He wrote as a believing Christian and he regarded the inspired Scriptures as containing the most accurate historical writing in existence. And he vindicated his view by saying that the prophecies had been fulfilled, and a work which so successfully predicted the future could be relied upon to discharge the easier task of merely recounting the past. Unlike Eusebius, Augustine did not love the collection of mere facts, the hunt for sources or the recording of contemporary events for the sake of the future. He accepted the date provided in the stock classical histories or in the Old Testament, though he resorted to some ingenious criticism when faced by a glaring anomaly. He was even perfunctory when he had to do any narrating – any mere recapitulating of monarchs or wars or famous occurrences. It was part of his plan to show that Rome had suffered no end of disasters before the Christian religion had even appeared; but he had not the patience for such a work of enumeration, and he handed that part of the task to a disciple of his, Crosius, who worked the matter out in a book of his own.

Augustine was not primarily concerned, therefore, with what we today would call straight history. He is forever turning aside to discuss the fundamental questions of human destiny: Why and how did the world begin? What existed before it? What is the nature of time itself? Is the human race merely the prisoner of a kind of fatality? How are we to deal with the problem of human suffering? Some of his questions, however, come closer to being historical in our sense of the word: Why are primeval men recorded as having had longer life and greater stature than we should have thought possible? Those men who lived for hundreds of years — at what age would they begin producing children? Where did civilisation take its rise? How ancient is the wisdom of the Greeks? Why were the primitive Romans so successful and how did their successors come to establish an empire so extensive, so enduring? He had a remarkable way of handling the problem cases, for example, the discrepancies between the Hebrew Scriptures and the ancient Greek translation of them, the Septuagint. Taken all together his book must remain, outside the ancient Scriptures, the supreme example for study if one is interested in the connection between history and belief. Indeed, Augustine is one of the very greatest minds that ever set out to discuss the human condition, and so to tackle history at a really fundamental level. The work of his which concerns us, 'The City of God', presents us with a paradox. He seems much nearer heaven, much more spiritually profound, than Eusebius, but to a twentieth-century historian he is also nearer to the earth, with a very much better idea of the way in which history works.

His superiority, especially in relation to Eusebius, is shown almost at the start in the way in which he grapples with the problem of God's judgements in history. It is as though he were trying consciously to reverse a good deal of Eusebius and do a little demythologising of his own. He insists that God sends the sunshine, the rain, and the blessings of the world on the good and the wicked indifferently. And this applies, he says, to the acquisition of thrones and empires and to success in war — matters in which divine Providence is most emphatically involved. It applies even to the gift of long life: he would have nothing to do with the view hitherto current that God gives the Christian kings lengthy reigns but sends the persecuting monarchs to a quick and terrible death. If God rewarded the Christians with mundane happiness, they would think too much of worldly prosperity and regard it as a sign of spiritual grace. Men would become Christians for the wrong reasons. The good differ from the wicked in the way that they take, the way that they use, misfortune. They regard it as part of the discipline of mun-

dane life, as something which tests their virtues and corrects their imper-
fections. Christians will accept even in itself a judgement or a chastening or
a reminder of their own shortcomings. For they know that they too have
their part in man's universal sin; the best of them will have some lurking
infirmity, perhaps pride in his own righteousness or anxiety about his repute
in the world.

Yet this same God, according to Augustine, does actually give mundane
rewards to men − rewards even for pagan virtues. Augustine sets out to
examine the secret of purely worldly success; and the crucial example for
him is the rise of ancient Rome. He will not admit that the heathen deities
gave their assistance here; it was a matter only within the Providence of the
Christian God. And he writes : 'Let us consider what were the virtues which
the true God, in whose power are also the kingdoms of the earth, chose to
assist, in order to produce the Roman Empire.' In that primitive city of
Rome there were pagans who were ready to sacrifice their private fortunes
for the good of the state; they were prepared to brave death rather than
sacrifice liberty. And if, even after winning their own struggle for freedom,
they went on to seek domination over others, they did this for the love of
glory, which, says Augustine, was better than living for wine, women and
song. These men were 'good in their own way', he says; they were 'laudable
doubtless and glorious according to human judgement'. They knew what
they wanted, namely, power in the mundane sphere, and they disciplined
themselves, they sacrificed their private comforts to secure it. They were so
faithful to the earthly city that they ought to stand as an example to those
who are members of the heavenly city. They could not be candidates for
Heaven, of course, but, says St Augustine, if God had also withheld terrestrial success from them they would not have received the reward for
their virtues, the terrestrial reward that was due to them. His argument
culminates in the quotation : 'Verily, they have their reward.'

In spite of his overwhelming preoccupation with the things of the spirit,
Augustine recognises the existence of profane history, and almost concedes
to it a certain autonomy. He can insert mundane ideas about causation; and
he says that recent despoiling of Rome after the irruption of the barbarians was the result of the customs of war. He accepts the earlier, pagan
view that the destruction of Carthage − elimination of the one thing that
Rome had to fear − by ridding the citizens of anxiety, produced a relaxation
of discipline and morals, a decline of public spirit. When the expanding
republic came to be harassed by social and civil wars, he did not say that
this was a judgement of God, though his doctrines might well have allowed
him to do so. He said that Roman conquests had become too vast, and that
the empire was breaking under its own weight. So far as the field of profane
history was concerned, he had a more flexible view of the workings of
Providence than Eusebius, though in regard to sacred history, salvation

history – in regard to the Incarnation, for example – he would have seen events taking place according to God's prearranged plan. But the God who gave vast empire to the great Augustus, gave it also to the cruel Nero, because that was the government which the people of the time deserved. Augustine is not so ready to see the Roman Empire installed by a kind of magic, to coincide with the coming of Christ. Because he recognises that the Empire united many nations and created a great area of peace in the world, what he stresses is the fact that Christians share in the blessings of peace that the secular state provides; they owe something to the body politic which enables them to have the material necessities of life. Judges in the terrestrial city have to torture innocent people, and cannot be sure that they may not have condemned an innocent man to death. Still the office is important, and the wise men ought not to reject the responsibility of it. The true Christian would realise that he could never be happy in office; he would never long for it, but would, rather, pray that he would not have to drink this cup. This is the spirit in which he should accept an office, if he felt he ought to do so at all. And the same would be true with the greatest office, that of the Emperor : the Christian would accept it only as a means of service.

All this Augustine concedes to profane society and discusses almost in the terms of a secular historian. Yet he must have had a deep hostility to Rome, which he also covers with vituperation and treats as the second Babylon. We find him a stage still more remote from the political theology of Eusebius – for example, that writer's sanctification of the Roman Empire – when he declares his preference for a world of little states, living in amity, rather as families live side by side in a city. He is aware of the human cupidities which make that ideal so difficult to achieve, however; and he seems to accept that it was the turbulence of the neighbouring states which goaded Rome into fighting them and conquering them. All the same, he has an exceptional hatred of war; and when people talk of the Pax Romana – the vast area that has been pacified by Rome – he always wants them to remind themselves of the terrible bloodshed through which that peace had been achieved.

The virtues of the profane world and the importance of profane history are anyway only relative to Augustine. Rome belongs to the earthly city, not the city of God; and the state is a combination of people for the procuring of mundane ends. On a spiritual view, even the relative virtues become vices, because the motive of that combination ought to be the love of the heavenly city. Yet the profane is not evil in itself, for God did not create anything evil, and even the devil is not evil by nature. Augustine almost says that evil itself is not absolutely evil; God would not have allowed it to exist if he had not foreseen some good that He would be able to achieve by it later. So the darker side of life is, for Augustine, like the shadows in a painting, with the contrast enhancing the beauty of the whole, though we who are entangled in life are not in a position to see it. He argues that things themselves are not evil and that even the love of profane things is not evil. The sin occurs when men devote to the lower things the love that they should give to the higher. In other words evil, when it occurs, lies not in things themselves, but in the will of man. Here, in the actions and choices of the will (things not determined by God), lies the real evil, evil *par excellence*. For this reason, when Augustine is wearing one thinking cap, when he is speaking as a profane historian, he can talk of the virtues of the ancient pagans. When he is wearing another thinking cap, those virtues are themselves described as vices. In this way he gives profane history a place, though its virtues are only relative.

But Augustine differs from his former Greek philosophic teachers in that he recognises the Christian's commitment to history. In his 'City of God', he argues his way out of the Greek cyclic view of the process of things in time, even the extreme version of it which asserted that all history goes on exactly repeating itself throughout endless ages, everything happening over again in the same way. He saw that any form of the cyclic view of the time-process robs history of all significance, turning it into aimless revolvings and pointless repetitions. He said that the idea of Christ returning to be crucified again in another repetition of the cycle would turn the whole salvation story into a kind of cosmic puppet show. The eternal bliss that was to be granted to the saints was utterly inconsistent with the idea of everybody having to return and to relive the miseries of this mortal life. It has been plausibly suggested that his attitude was affected by the pull of the Old Testament, which he regarded not merely as prophecy and symbol but as actual history. He certainly picked up the Old Testament view that history is at least pointing to an end which will occur when the number of the elect, determined by God, is reached. This was what, in Augustine's eyes, gave some meaning to history, and in a certain sense 'The City of God' is an attempt to work out this meaning.

CHAPTER SEVEN

The Development of Historical Criticism

1 PRE-CRITICAL SCEPTICS IN EUROPE

The project of recovering the remoter past, if once the memory had been lost, must have been almost inconceivable at first, but if in a given age somebody had produced a record of contemporary events, and this had survived, future generations would cling to it rather superstitiously, cling even to its exact words – any historian of a future age would have to draw upon it. It is virtually true to say that this is the first really broad formula for the writing of history – a scissors-and-paste method – you simply followed whoever it was who had written a history of his own times or an account of something that had happened in his own day. And you were lucky to have even that – you would often have nothing to check against it; in other words, there was not much of an opening for criticism. What you had to do was to keep to the original record; and on this view it was understandable that Josephus should claim virtue for Jewish history on the ground that it had been handed down for so many centuries quite unchanged.

It would be useful if we could know a little more about the machinery of oral transmission in the earlier stages of the story. There were always liable to be cases where for some particular reason there was a special need, an urgent need, to know exactly what happened in the past. For example, the whole ordering of society seems to have made genealogy a matter of real importance even in days before there was any serious interest in history as such. The matter must have required peculiar care even in the days of purely oral transmissions. An African scholar, Dr Dike, formerly Professor of History and then Vice-Chancellor at Ibadan, tells me of his work with an African people who still keep thirty remembrancers at court, to preserve the oral record of the past and the present. The employment of thirty remembrancers should provide a fairly serious safeguard against aberrations. R. G. Collingwood, in his *Idea of History*, tells us that the Greeks made one important contribution to historical method – the cross-examination of witnesses – one of the things that must be behind the success of both Herodotus and Thucydides. We all know the limitations of those who speak as eye-witnesses or give evidence in a court, or write personal memoirs. Men cannot see properly – they catch a glimpse of half a thing and piece out the rest in their imagination. They cannot even remember properly – they reconstruct when they think they are only remembering – their later reminiscences of the past will be distorted by things that have happened in the meantime. And all this can happen unconsciously before any question arises of a deliberate desire to prevaricate or a determination to mislead the world. It is quite a momentous thing, therefore, if you learn that you must heckle and cross-examine the eye-witness or the memoir-writer – press him if one part of his evidence does not square with another part or with what other people have said. After Sir Edward Grey had published memoirs covering the origin of the war of 1914, Professor Temperley and Dr Gooch met him and debated with him and drove him into a corner – it is a good thing that we have a written account of this conversation. Of course the ancient Greeks were weak on the distant past and took history most seriously where it was a case of writing about recent affairs – and this is a realm in which the cross-examination of eye-witnesses is particularly relevant. And until comparatively recently it was the writer about contemporary affairs who for the most part was the creative historian – it was understood that he could do far better work than anybody else. He would also be the writer whom everybody in the future would have to follow. The rest of the historical writers would use a scissors-and-paste method, copying those who in ancient days had written the history of their own times. For this reason, what we call the contemporary historian had an important contribution to make to the development of historical method.

In eleventh-century Europe, there emerged what one might not expect to find so far back in the Middle Ages – a really impressive interest in what we should regard as mundane history. And in accordance with what we see from very early times down to our own generation, this interest was provoked by stirring events in the world at that time – events that made people history-conscious – the Norman Conquest of England, the beginning of the Crusades, the tremendous reform of the Church in the eleventh century, and the rise of the Investiture Contest, the epic conflict between Popes and Emperors. A certain monk of the time, Ordericus Vitalis, concerned himself with something like contemporary history and had interesting ideas about the way in which it should be written. He went to archives; he studied burial inscriptions; he bewailed the destruction of manuscripts by the

Vikings; he complained that monasteries did not take better care of their papers. He visited monasteries abroad in order to read their local records; he consulted the great men of the time; he collected oral tradition; he made a practice of talking to peasants who have a way of keeping things in memory. When he wrote about important events, he tried to attach them to their causes – when he dealt with the Norman Conquest of England, he tried to treat it genetically. For centuries it remained true that the writer of contemporary history had to be original – he had nobody to copy; and when an important statesman or noble undertook the task (especially if it was a case of writing about events in which he had taken part), he would have access to the official papers – he was the man who would think of going to such records. There was a remarkable example of this at the Renaissance, the famous Italian historian, Guicciardini, who had been an important diplomat and then produced a history of his own times.

The history of the past as distinguished from the present was on a shaky footing even at the Renaissance; and many people were probably content to tell stories without quite giving their souls to them. After all, if you started to enquire into their accuracy or their origin you would simply end by having no story to tell. The exception to this would be that there was a peculiar confidence in the superiority of the ancient classical writers, and biblical history, of course, was under a special divine guarantee. And this explains what has mystified scholars sometimes – the low place given to history in the hierarchy of knowledge, the tendency to regard it as a branch of rhetoric or a section of *belles lettres*. The Renaissance awakened a tremendous passion for classical antiquity, of course, but men in those days did not really reconstruct ancient history for themselves – they read the well-known writers of Greece and Rome, almost treating them as historians of their own times. Some of them criticised and distrusted Herodotus, and the controversy on this point is one of the things that helped the development of a critical technique in the early modern period; but even that distrust of Herodotus had been taken over from ancient Greece itself, where he had acquired a bad name. They were copying the ancient world even in this act of criticism. The Renaissance served the cause of history by developments in the editing of ancient literary works and in what we might call textual studies; and it is associated with a significant achievement in the field of criticism – one which is often regarded as the real beginning of the modern story. This was the demonstration by Laurentius Valla in 1440 of the spurious character of the Donation of Constantine, a document which, amongst other things, was supposed to have conveyed the Western half of the Roman Empire to the Pope.

The genuineness of this Donation of Constantine had been challenged – challenged by vested interests – before 1440, and Valla himself is an example of the fact that perhaps some spur was needed to drive men to the effort of historical criticism – the stimulus of a vested interest. When Laurentius Valla exposed this forgery, he happened to be secretary to an Aragonese King who was in conflict with the Papacy – his treatise was avowedly part of a publicistic campaign against the Pope. But his handling of the Donation of Constantine shows what was possible even in those days, once there existed the drive, the impulse, to criticise a document; and it is just sufficient to make one wonder why the general practice of criticism developed so slowly in the following centuries. First of all, Valla makes resort to common sense. No Emperor would treat his family, his heirs, so shabbily, nor would the Roman Senate have allowed anything so unconstitutional to take place. The Roman people would have asked who was to defend them against the barbarians if the government was to go to a pious bishop. Secondly, he looked at the context in Roman history – there was no evidence of a ceremonial transfer of government or the appointment of new magistrates by the Pope. On the contrary, the sons of Constantine can be seen exercising the effective rule after his death. Finally, Valla examines the document itself. It does not exist amongst the decretals of Gratian, and whoever invented it at a later date failed to put it in its proper place in the series. It is not mentioned in other contemporary sources, and, in fact, there are innumerable decretals that are inconsistent with it. In any case, it contains contradictions and absurdities: Constantine, only just converted to Christianity, pretends to be giving the Bishop of Rome the power to ordain priests – a thing he had been doing already. The document even purports to establish Constantinople as one of the four patriarchal sees, yet it claims to date from a time when the Emperor had not yet even thought of founding the city. It talks of making the Roman clergy 'patricians', but, though they might have been made 'senators', nobody could be a 'patrician' except by birth. The forger of this document was even ignorant, and he did not understand the technical terms he used. Even his latin phraseology was sometimes barbarous. He clearly belonged to a later and more corrupt age. These are just a few examples of Valla's objections, which run to the size of a little treatise.

The history of criticism tends to bunch itself round certain controversies and these controversies often relate to some conflict between vested interests. But there was a great controversy in the sixteenth century which was not provoked by any vested interests – indeed, those who took up the critical endeavour knew that they could reap nothing but trouble for their pains, since the truth for which they were struggling went against national desires and general sentiment. It is astonishing to see how many nations in those days (including Britain) took pride in the fact that they were descended from Trojans, who, after the fall of Troy, were supposed to have fled westwards into Europe. Sometimes a foreign historian would pour cold water on the story – as the Italian Polydore Vergil did in the case of Britain, causing further offence to Englishmen by his doubts about the legends of King Arthur. Serious historians set out to demolish the myth in the sixteenth century. But the fullest critical treatment that I have seen is a very considerable one, written by a Frenchman to discredit the story of the French or the Frankish descent from the Trojans. It is a work by a man called La Popelinière, and it appeared in 1599.

Like Valla, he begins with arguments from common sense and general experience, showing how, after the fall of Troy there could not have been a mass exodus of the defeated, sufficient to be the progenitors of new nations. He speaks as a man who has had experience of war, and he says that historians often have no idea of war, except as they have seen it in battle paintings. He refers to sieges which he has actually known in France and insists that the survivors of a fallen city would never be allowed to get away *en masse* in the manner that the story assumed. And if they had got away, these Trojans would not have been allowed to move into foreign countries as a people – even Christian states of our own day would not tolerate such an immigration, says La Popelinière – and he adds that no military operation is more easy than resistance to invasion by sea. Then, again, like Valla, he sets out to show that the whole legend does not square with the rest of what we know about the history of Europe in the period in question. It does not even square with itself, he says. Then, finally, he discusses the evidence. The most ancient writers, he says, give no hint of any migration of the Trojans after the fall of the city. The Franks, the ancestors of the French, claim to trace their origin to a certain hero, Francion, supposed to be the son of Hector. However, Homer mentions no legitimate son of Hector except Astianax. In any case these ancient stories are always doubtful, says this critic – in fact the oldest and most reliable of the historians tells us that Helen never went to Troy. The Homeric epic itself springs only from popular songs, and in any case, the Greeks, who were thieves and rogues, would alter Homer to suit their purposes. Some people attached importance to the fact that France had a city called 'Troyes', but La Popelinière showed that in ancient times this city had had a different name, one which was connected with a different 'trois' – the number three. Some said that Paris had been called after the son of Priam – but, again, La Popelinière says that this was a comparatively modern name for that city. Then he moved the whole argument a stage further – he did what historical criticism ought always to try to do if it wants to complete its task – granted that a story or a document is untrue, the argument should be crowned by showing how the error or the legend arose. He points out how at an early date, the Romans, the Gauls and the Venetians had claimed the refugees from fallen Troy as their ancestors. The Franks, a barbarian people, came conquering into France, and, in the flush of success, they wanted to find for themselves an equally honourable origin. In that period of Barbarian invasions there was considerable moving and mixing of peoples and all kinds of legends did arise – those about King Arthur, says La Popelinière, were a case in point. In particular, the warrior-leaders always tried to claim that they sprang from heroic ancestors. The story of the descent from the Trojans was a late one and when it first appears in Gregory of Tours this writer does not assert that it is true – he merely gives it as something that the Franks believe. All this was very foolish, says La Popelinière, for the Germanic origin of the Franks was far more honourable than any descent from the lascivious, thieving Trojans, who were even worse than the Greeks.

These works of Valla and La Popelinière show that there existed sufficient ingenuity for a critical endeavour, and the use of it could be stimulated by some challenging problem; but what these men produced was a kind of *tour de force* – we must not imagine that these established or put into currency critical spirit or a critical code that came to be generally recognised. We are still faced with the question: why did historical criticism develop so slowly? Certainly if controversy helped to stimulate the right kind of ingenuity there can be no doubt that the momentous controversy that was to be important in the general development of history was the Reformation, and this is the supreme example of the way in which passionate partiality could work paradoxically for the promotion of a judicious kind of historical science. Looking at the whole story, not excluding the experience of the present day, there appears a kind of indolence of mind which suspends criticism and produces a mood of acceptance, unless a powerful motive makes it an urgent matter either to get at the truth or to denounce a current version of it. The very issues of the Reformation involved history – including the whole question of whether the Papacy had usurped its powers; and the Protestants were not by any means always right. They needed to reverse a good deal of ecclesiastical history, as it had come down under Catholicism, and much general history as it had appeared in monkish chronicles. They set out to reverse everything that did not suit them. Two of the great reversals that took place in English history were the bitter attack on St Thomas à Becket because he had been unpatriotic, and the adoration of King John because he had been victimised by a Pope. In the course of the sixteenth century both the religious parties came to see that, if they made wild statements, the enemy was there, ready to catch them out. They learned to be more careful and to find support for their statements – the conflict kept each side on its toes, making both more scientifically critical. The resort to archives, the use of manuscript sources, was greatly promoted by the writers of contemporary history, but in the development of actual criticism of sources, the leadership lay in the fields of Theology and Classics, amongst students of the remoter past. They developed the techniques which were ultimately to be consciously taken over – transposed and adapted – for historical writing in the modern field.

There is one aspect of the story, however, which our minds may not have been prepared to expect. The emergence of a more critical temper, at a time when men did not have the resources which the twentieth century possesses for the reconstruction of the past out of raw materials, had a very upsetting effect, especially in the field of ancient history, and it led before the end of the seventeenth century to a curious phenomenon – what we call 'historical Pyrrhonism' – a scepticism about the very possibility of history. This was carried to an extreme in the eighteenth century when the Père Hardouin claimed that the bulk of the ancient classics were forgeries, perpetrated in the later Middle Ages. If you decide too early that you cannot believe what has been handed down to you – if you decide this before you have yet acquired either the materials or the techniques for discovering the positive truth by detective work, you are thrown into Pyrrhonism – this scepticism about all history. As late as the 1720s there occurred in the *Académie des Inscriptions* in Paris some discussions of the problem of criticism which show how shaky were the foundations of the history of the remoter past. At this time it was assumed that the accuracy of history depended on the authority of the historians, of the writers of books in older times. It was necessary to check the reliability of the author. This is very different from what we should want today – we should want to establish facts independent of the reliability of the man reporting them. If two different authors of the past gave two different versions of a story, it was sometimes explicitly recommended that a narrative should be produced embracing both, though sometimes the reconciliation was rather lengthy. Only where this process failed would arise the necessity of deciding between the two authorities. It was coming to be felt in the eighteenth century that the ancient writer ought to be fairly contemporary with the events he is describing if he is to be accepted as authoritative, though before 1700 it had been asserted that he could be regarded as virtually contemporary if he came only two or three hundred years later. If he was nearly contemporary he ought to be believed unless there was a special reason for distrusting him – the burden was on the criticiser to demonstrate that he was unreliable. But when the historians were of great reputation they could be accepted though they lived much later than the events they narrated. Livy must be reliable – he was accepted in his own day when men were in a much better position to assess his work than we are. For the early periods, he must have used older sources now lost. Moses must have used records going back to Adam, but now lost, and these must have been in writing, because details so precise could never have been communicated orally.

Authority was allowed to things that had come down in tradition, though there were rules about this. A tradition could be believed if it was about a great simple event like the Flood, but it was not to be depended upon for the precise details of a complicated story. It could only be reliable for the kind of events which were of public notoriety at the time when they happened – so that one could expect the story to have been contradicted, throttled at birth, if it had been wrong. The tradition must for the same reason go back to the time of the events themselves; and it must be shown that nobody would have had any special interest in inventing untruths about the point in question. The tradition, in order to be valid, must also have been widespread, and it must not be contradicted by other known facts of history.

All these criteria – which would be very unsatisfactory today – had to be accepted because if more severe ones were adopted there could not have been any history at all, except comparatively recent history. Amongst those who wished to be more severe – even amongst those who accepted most of the criteria I have mentioned – there came to be grave doubts about the first five centuries of Roman history, doubts about Livy's account, doubts about the possibility of history.

All this belongs to the pre-critical period. Roughly speaking it went as far as the Chinese ever got in what we call historical criticism, though they became very skilful in literary criticism, textual criticism. The rest represents a development that was peculiar to the West.

2 THE CRITICAL RECONSTRUCTION OF THE PAST

Already, however – and particularly in the seventeenth century – there had begun the movement which was to raise the whole status of history and establish it with its own technique. Important things happened now in the field of medieval history; and they were assisted by the lawyers, who, like the historians, were interested in historical documents, concerned with the interpretation of the past, but intent on institutions and technical matters rather than the chronicles of wars and courts. The common law of England in particular involved a close relationship between the present and the past, and its practitioners first established that Whig interpretation of history which implied that the British constitution – House of Commons; trial by jury; British liberty – went back to time immemorial, and that *Magna Carta* had guaranteed liberty for everybody. This interpretation of history underlay the ideology of the seventeenth-century civil war, but the reaction against it, chiefly after 1660, produced a more profoundly historical point of view – one which insisted on construing *Magna Carta* as a feudal document, interpreting it in terms of the society which produced it, and remembering that words change their meaning in the course of time – that the word 'free-man' in 1215 might not mean the same as in the seventeenth century. All this – that a document must be interpreted in terms of the social context from which it sprang – involved quite a sensational change in the treatment of England's medieval history, and was an important contribution to the interpretation of historical documents and the reconstruction of the past, although it did not pass into general practice straight away.

In the same later decades of the seventeenth century another very significant step was taken – one which made it clear that some things in history could be established in a more positive manner than had hitherto been realised – established independently of any mere reporting even by eye-witnesses. Here again, the lawyers had a certain part to play, and the development was not unconnected with the needs and the operations of the practical world. It concerned ancient charters, which had long been important for the establishment of property rights, constitutional franchises and monastic privileges. Fraudulent ones existed, however, and they had been easy to forge, so the lawyers had had to find ways of testing them. The charters were important, for historians too, who in the latter part of the seventeenth century were using them particularly for monastic histories; and in France a Jesuit, Papebroch, tried to collect a code of rules for establishing their genuineness. His attempt did not quite come off, however, for while his tests enabled him to detect some things which were forgeries, they had the effect also of condemning others which in fact were genuine. Amongst those which suffered from the unjust verdict were some famous Benedictine documents at the abbey of St Denis, and the Benedictines, taking this as a provocation, set their most brilliant scholar, Mabillon, to produce a counter-blast. Mabillon did his work so beautifully that the other side collapsed, Papebroch becoming his admiring friend. Indeed, almost by a single stroke, Mabillon established the auxilliary science of what we call 'diplomatic'. In the treatment of charters, the idea was to examine the parchment, the writing materials, the form of the seals, the description of the dignitaries mentioned in the document, the way of describing the date, the conventional formulas for beginning and ending the document, the technical terms employed, the kind of Latin that was used, etc. These things enabled the 'placing' of the document. Historical scholarship had to reach a fairly advanced stage before it could make use of the method – identify the date of the handwriting or the Latin usages, for example – but it became possible to identify the kind of charter that belonged to a given locality and a given date, and to demonstrate its genuineness with moral certainty. Here, at least, there was a firm foothold for the historian.

Even now, development was taking place very slowly, especially when compared with the natural sciences, which had moved to a modern basis, establishing a technique of discovery which received its vindication in Sir Isaac Newton before the end of the seventeenth century. The slowness of history is all the more remarkable in that, ever since the Renaissance, men had been busily collecting the actual remains of the past – the archaeological survivals, the inscriptions, the coins, the manuscripts. The movement had kept on growing, partly indeed by a kind of collector's mania – in the latter part of the seventeenth century, the same man might collect both coins and shells. Historical documents were being collected in the same way, and large volumes of them were published often from official archives, a movement very remarkable in the early decades of the eighteenth century, for example. Sometimes a writer would patch some of them into his narrative, though documentary criticism was still at an elementary stage. The period 1660 to 1720 has been described as the grand age of scholarly and anti-quarian research, but the antiquarians often stood on one side while the general writers of history stood on the other. This was particularly the case in the age of Voltaire, the age of the French *philosophe* movement. The literary men wrote a literary man's kind of history. They would talk about criticism, but this too often meant merely inverting the previous Catholic tradition, and it could often be as wrong-headed as the Protestants had been.

The radical development in criticism was really taking place not in the ordinary fields of historical study – not in history departments in univer-sities – but amongst the classical scholars and theologians. Here is a further paradox in the story, for the real detective work – the kind that transformed historical study – was developed in classical studies, in ecclesiastical history and in the biblical field, and the procedures only came later to be trans-formed to the historiography of more recent times, reaching the field of modern history last of all. One famous example illustrates so well the kind of procedures that became important to historians. It concerns the Penta-teuch, the early books of the Bible, and the Fathers of the Church, who belonged to an advanced civilisation, had themselves begun the criticism of these. Some of the early Fathers realised that the Bible, as they possessed it, had suffered from the carelessness of transcribers, and that the verses and chapters had got out of order because the scrolls had not been properly attached to one another. Criticism began to be interesting again in the seven-teenth century when, for example, Thomas Hobbes showed that Moses could not have written the whole of the Pentateuch, which carries a verse saying that nobody knew where his sepulchre was. In 1695 a French writer, Richard Simon, picked up the problem, saying that he was only continuing the criticism begun by the Fathers of the Church. He said that Moses must have used detailed chronicles of a much earlier date, but that a good deal of inspired editing must have been done after his time. In the middle of the eighteenth century, however, some interesting detective work was done by a French physician called Jean Astruc. He took the line that when Moses was quoting God he explicitly said so, but when he was writing history he quoted previous annals, just as any other writer of history would. He seized on a point which some of the early Fathers had noted – namely that there were long sections of *Genesis* where God was called by one name, other sections where He was called by another. He assumed that two different historical accounts had previously existed and then had been cut up and mixed together, forming the terrible jumble that *Genesis* now is. Using the different names for God as the original clue, he separated out the pieces belonging to the two accounts, and tried to join each of them up in its original continuity. In this way he was able to produce a better narrative than the *Genesis* that we possess, because the mixing of the two had resulted in stories getting out of order, stories being repeated, the narrative becoming confused. He found other documents behind *Genesis* too, and his technique has been very much refined and elaborated since; but he gave a signal example of the way in which it is possible to get behind a piece of historical writing and not merely detect the lost sources of it but actually reconstitute those sources.

Such work as this, as well as similar work in the field of classics (including the development of the technique of handling literary texts), bore its fruit in our own field in the later decades of the eighteenth century when what we call 'academic history' was founded in the famous university of Göttingen. Now criteria were established for historical scholarship which would come into general currency, because they were accepted at the university level, they were set by the academic profession. Göttingen was in Hanover and had a freer intellectual atmosphere than found elsewhere in Germany because its patron was at the same time King of England. The connection enabled it to concern itself with political matters and it became a school of statesmanship for well-born young men all over Germany. For this reason it made a great development on the historical side, creating the first historical seminar, and the first learned journal in the subject. Here the scholarliness of the antiquarians became combined with the breadth of view that we associate with the general literary writers of history in the age of the *philosophes*. Here, in the early 1780s also, Professor Eichhorn produced a profounder form of the analysis of *Genesis* than Astruc had put forward, going much further than Astruc had done. The most brilliant of the Göttingen professors on the history side was a man called Schlözer, whose most significant work was an edition of a medieval chronicle, a Russian chronicle, called the 'Chronicle of Nestor'. It was intended to be – and in a sense it proved to be – the example and the model for the publishing of all Germany's medieval chronicles. He declares that he found his own models in the realm of biblical scholarship, and amongst other things he did with the 'Chronicle of Nestor' something of what Astruc and Eichhorn had done with *Genesis* – he found a lost source on which it was based, and set out to reconstitute that source.

What was important was the fact that criticism was no longer merely negative, merely a case of rejecting one writer as unreliable and copying another writer regarded as reliable. Detective work enabled discoveries to be made which led to constructive results. Much work had been done in this direction in the field of classics (on Homer, for example) – even legends could be used as clues, leading to discoveries of an unexpected sort. The lies themselves could be used in order to get at the truth. The early books of Livy might be legendary, but that did not mean that they should be discounted. Another historian, Niebuhr, was still able to use them, helped in his interpretation by his experience in an agrarian world which offered analogies with the ancient world. The whole of this movement represents the most important revolution that ever occurred in the historian's attitude to his evidence.

Modern history was also affected. Lord Acton once pointed out that, down to this time, the writing of modern history had been too easy. It became an established commonplace amongst historians that the era of modern criticism began in 1824 when the famous German historian, Ranke (then a very young man), published his first book on the *Latin and Teutonic Nations 1494–1514*. He appended to it his famous *Criticism of Modern Historical Writing*, a study of those writers who in the period he had been writing about – the age of the Renaissance – had written the history of their own times. His object was to show that it was inadmissible to base the writing of history on those contemporary authors who had produced histories of their own times. It was a great reversal of the assumption on which historical writing had been based from the very earliest civilisations. His particular target was the Renaissance historian Guicciardini, and in regard to this man we now know that Ranke made many mistakes. As the nineteenth century proceeded, it was shown how often Guicciardini had in fact been right. In the twentieth century his actual working papers came to light and revealed to what a degree he had gone to manuscript sources (which Ranke himself had not done in his own book) and how carefully he used them. Some of the things which Ranke had challenged as baseless have since been found in Guicciardini's sources. He used diplomatic correspondence no longer available in any archives. In some respects a great man could anticipate much future development – and the world did not know it because Guicciardini did not provide any footnotes. Of course, Guicciardini had been a writer of contemporary history, and the contemporary historian had long been in advance of the rest in the use of manuscript sources. Yet fundamentally Ranke made out his essential case and henceforward it was recognised that these writers of contemporary history, these historians of their own times, should no longer be accepted as first-class sources. It meant also that it was no longer legitimate to write history on the basis of the memoirs of soldiers, statesmen, etc.

From this curious beginning, Ranke advanced with the nineteenth century, and indeed, so far as the modern field is concerned, he became the leader of the advance. He began as a critic of the historians who had preceded him, and he submitted them to the kind of analysis which biblical history had received. His next book was based on archival sources; and very soon he was saying that modern history ought to be torn to pieces and entirely re-written from manuscript sources. At first he did not quite realise that an historical document needed to be criticised just as much as an actual work of historical narration. He had compared Guicciardini's History with the letters written by the same man at the time when the events were actually happening and he had assumed that, where they differed, the letters would be right and the History wrong. There were occasions on which this assumption led him astray. He developed very greatly, however, and the art of reading between the lines of a document would be regarded as an important aspect of his genius. Very important was the fact that the public archives now became open to scholars – partially in the 1830s, much more widely and completely in the 1860s. Without this, history could never have made its remarkable advance in the nineteenth century; and those who had the first dip into the archives were luckier than their successors could expect to be – with remarkable speed they were revolutionising the main stories in century after century. Now, at last, men really felt that they could study history. They were not dependent on the copying of earlier historians, or on mere reporting even by memoir-writers and eye-witnesses. And the most important thing of all was that they could study the transactions of governments, churches, universities – anything else – by examining the very papers in which business was carried on.

CHAPTER EIGHT

The Great Secularisation

1 THE HAND OF GOD

We must now turn our attention to the secularisation of the Christian outlook, and in particular the Christian attitude to the course of history.

It is a subject with many complications. Those who talk about the secularisation of thought with reference to its effects in the realm of historiography must be prepared to use a certain amount of discrimination. History happens to be concerned with mundane events, and in some of its aspects tries to be a re-presentation, tries perhaps to be no more than a transcript, of events as they might have been observed by eye-witnesses. In all ages and under various kinds of creed, a piece of narrative may be set out in a purely secular manner. There is historical writing that gives the mundane story so effectively, not only without mythological interferences but in such a way as to provide in itself an historical explanation, that the commentator is easily tempted to say that the spirit is secular. Yet I have doubts about adopting this interpretation without further evidence of the writer's outlook, for I feel fairly certain that the pious man can have a clear eye for the world of concrete things, and can have his feet close to earth, without losing his spiritual outlook. I have sometimes wondered whether Christianity does not give men a clearer vision of the facts and the factual setting than the pagan beliefs of either the past or the present often have. In other words, only through Christianity can one acquire a healthy kind of worldly-mindedness. And Christianity will not produce such a thing if it is itself too concerned to mix the spiritual with the mundane and to see spiritual things with worldly eyes. There is a kind of history which uses religion as a means of producing a schematisation of historical events which in fact is too mixed with earth. And those who have no religion tend to produce schematisations of a different sort. Those who make gods of sticks and stones or forces in nature or abstract nouns can insert considerable confusion into both science and history. The Christian is – or he ought to be – trained to distinguish very clearly between the Jesus who is a historical figure and the Christ who belongs to the realm of the spirit. A Christian like the seventeenth-century Frenchman, Mabillon, for example, or David Knowles in our own day, can have a very steady eye for the concrete in history. There may be something in the view that connects our modern science and our modern historiography with Christianity. It may not be an accident, therefore, that these and other features of our Western civilisation developed out of Christian soil.

It was quite a significant fact, thousands of years ago, that men in Mesopotamia and Egypt, for example, would on occasion forget the real purpose of their literary work because they simply lost themselves in the telling of an interesting human story. In the case of the Hittites, whose historical writing was quite remarkable for its stress on the activities of the gods – something unparalleled until the emergence of the Old Testament writings – there are some pieces of narrative which are remarkable in a further sense: they are so constructed that the story is at the same time the historical explanation, accounting at the ordinary human level for the turn which events had taken at a particular time. And it is important to note that this aptitude for the ordinary human explanation of events can exist in works which (as in the case of the Hittite writings) show also the most extravagant belief in divine intervention. Even in the Old Testament one finds interesting passages in which a piece of history is allowed to unfold as an ordinary human story. An example of this is the story of the succession to King David in the early chapters of the first Book of Kings. In ancient Judah and in the neighbouring nations there existed what is usually called the 'Wisdom School'. Though this School had a genuine conception of God, its members tended to produce history of the more worldly type. In Jerusalem it would seem to have been connected with the palace rather than the temple, and certainly it directed particular attention not to the policies of God but to the concrete affairs of the practical world. It showed a more precise concern with the procedures that are necessary for a successful life or for the conduct of government. However, it cannot be argued that a purely secular, non-religious attitude was achieved. Behind this writing there is a faith in God. The sheer technique of keeping records at the palace may have led to a great concentration in the events themselves, the mundane story. In any case the kind of annals which were produced in the palace at Jerusalem would naturally be more secular in character than those which issued from the region of the temple. For obvious reasons it was the religious interpretation of the history – the account of the acts of God – which survived all the destructions, survived as a body of sacred writings. But there can be no doubt that, under the ancient Jewish monarchy, more factual kinds of history were produced. In the case of the Book of Maccabees there is ample evidence of the faith, of actual religious fervour, even of belief that the hand of God can decide battles. But the hand of God does not actually appear in a mystical manner. And there is an excellent eye for history — not merely the concrete recording of events, item by item, but a capacity to give the gist of the matter, to insert a general survey of a body of historical happening. The account of what happened at the death of Alexander and the unexpected chapter which gives a 'nutshell description' of the historical position of the Roman Empire are cases in point. But the summaries of campaigns are similar achievements of general narrative, not merely pieces of factual reporting but attempts to extract the essential gist of what happened. Between diaries of events as they occurred day by day and the narrative here produced we can see the generalising presence of an historian of real discrimination.

One factor in the secularisation of historical writing must arise, therefore, out of the technique itself, and does not need the intervention of any outside influences. After all, the thing that the outward eyes of men actually see is the succession of mundane events. Sometimes one might feel that the introduction of God, or the hand of God, or Providence, is the thing which is really the afterthought, the result of an attempt to find an explanation of what happened. The introduction of God into the story is what needs to be explained. It might come at remarkable moments, for instance when people feel that they have been saved by a miracle from some dreadful disaster, or when a tyrant, who from a mundane point of view had seemed impregnable, is brought low in a manner that nobody could have expected. It might come when men have prayed and the result comes like an answer to their prayer, or when virtue has seemed to be rewarded and the wicked have been struck down. Whenever the causes seemed incommensurate with the results or the mundane explanation seemed inadequate, whenever chance or a curious conjuncture produced something that conflicted with expectations, whenever extraneous factors not normally brought into the reckoning (such as a disease that ruins an invading army) give the narrative a surprising twist, in all these cases one would thank God and believe that He had intervened.

This recourse to divine intervention to explain the unexpected illustrates the importance of contingency in history; the inability at early stages in the development to see all the connections between events; the cataclysmic character of many of the happenings; the fact that great consequences can proceed out of little causes; the fears that men have in a world, the proceedings of which they do not understand; the feeling men have that history is a thing that happens to them rather than something that they are making; the feeling of dependence which they would doubtless have when they

were unable to understand or master the operations of nature; the mystery
of natural happenings such as the awfulness of thunder that broke like the
anger of heaven; all these would lead men to feel in life that much depended
on the gods and that the gods were really active amongst them. Above all,
even amongst the Greeks when scepticism had developed greatly and many
superstitions had been thrown overboard, there remained the belief that
hybris was a challenge to the gods and a provocation that would lead to
overthrow. Perhaps this (or something like it) was the first and remained
the last basis for a general belief in divine intervention in history. In all
these cases the divine intervention might be felt to be a casual thing – an
occasional interruption of life – and there may even have been a time when
the gods were presumed to act out of pure caprice. It would need much
reflection to conceive of God as the guiding hand in history, as embracing
the whole world in His survey, and as having a plan, a notion of what He
was going to do ultimately with the human race.

It is interesting to note the important part played by war in the rise of
the notion that God has a part in history. Indeed, it is one of the surprises
of history to learn for how long, and over how wide an area, war was a
sacred thing, and was particularly associated with the action of gods. The
Old Testament writings are no exception, for in them war is a matter that
particularly concerns Jehovah, particularly involves his active intervention.
Next to prayers for the harvest, prayers for victory in war must have had
the priority in the petitioning of the ancient world, and must surely also
have it in that of the modern. For in war everything – the welfare of the
state and also the future of any individual – hangs to an unusual degree on
fate. And the result, particularly in ancient days, was peculiarly unpre-
dictable. Great distances might have to be covered, at a time when intelligence services were elementary, and except when a colonial power was
overrunning a very small one, there was no certainty as to what would be
met. Indeed sometimes it would appear that very large armies fell before
very small ones for one reason or another. Who in May 1940 really
expected the downfall of France? It would appear that even in those days
France knew too little about herself, too little about her enemy. The actual
catastrophe came like a bolt from the blue, like the crashing of a doom
from heaven. For most people it was so little related to what had gone
before that it seemed like a stroke from God. Indeed it was interpreted by
many as a moral judgment. For them it was not the victory of one kind of
strategy over another, of an imaginative leader over unimaginative ones,
but the reaction of the cosmos against the moral unworthiness of a degene-
rate people.

In the ancient days a monarch, when he went to war, would feel that he
was commissioned by the gods to undertake the enterprise. By appeals to
the oracle or by various kinds of divination, he would seek to know the will

of the gods, taking action only at their command or when he was sure that he had their favour. It was the god who won the victory, sometimes to the discomfiture of another god. Or if the god brought about defeat, it was as a reaction against neglect or disobedience. The god could win the victory without any superiority of forces. The Old Testament shows God more than once demanding the depletion of the army, in order to show that he was not dependent on numbers. The human leader who relied on the numbers of his men rather than on the hand of God might even be punished for his lack of faith. In this sacred kind of war the booty would be reserved for the god, and any individual who secretly took part of it for himself, or took part of what had been reserved for the god would, if caught, meet with unusually severe punishment. The ups-and-downs of states depended very much on the issue of wars. This issue was the real throw of the dice, the real test of one's destiny, the moment for the most drastic of divine judgments. When the Elizabethans defeated the Armada, they said that God blew the winds and the enemy was scattered. When the allies won the war of 1914, they attributed the victory to God. The writings of the Hittites make it clear that sometimes the resort to war was regarded as an appeal to the judgment of God. The conflict in such a case was a kind of trial in which heaven was the adjudicator. Often these views retain their power when there is no suggestion that the god makes an actual mythological appearance or is physically present during a battle. The god may act just by mysteriously depriving an army of its courage or wasting it by disease. We might bear in mind the use that the ancient Israelites made of the ark in time of battle. Also, there are some remarkable battlesongs in the Old Testament. War, and particularly battles, have occupied an exceptional position in the development of historical awareness and historical explanation. On the one hand, from the very beginning down to the twentieth century, war has been a more powerful stimulus to historical writing, and a more powerful factor in awaking historical interest than almost anything else. On the other hand, it has consistently been regarded as particularly connected with the gods or God. In ancient days victory was probably ascribed so clearly to the gods because winning a battle was so chancy an affair that it was difficult to know what happened. Primitive historians are greatly concerned with wars, but rarely enable us to see why one side defeated the other. Though they may describe in great detail what led up to a battle, in the most mundane way and with the most matter-of-fact explanations, they collapse when they come to the battle itself, resorting to poetry and mythology.

The first attempts to see regularities in history, and therefore to discover general laws, may have been due to the fact that a certain degree of rationality was ascribed to the gods themselves. The first such is the thesis that public misfortune came as the punishment for some neglect of the gods. It can only have been from reflection on observed facts that men came to a significant modification of this view: namely, the theory that, since the real culprit was sometimes allowed to live out a happy and successful life, the punishment might be postponed – the sins might be visited on the man's successors, to the third and fourth generation. Even in the days of superstition we see men exercising their rational faculties but directing them to the wrong objects. Believing that the stars were closely connected with human events, men concentrated attention upon the heavenly bodies and tried to discover what type of happening on earth accompanied a particular conjuncture in the skies. The Babylonians so identified a particular kind of omen with a given kind of event. They performed their quasi-scientific operations on the analysis of the omens rather than of the events themselves. Furthermore, having produced a kind of law, they could use it to carry them further than anything they had actually experienced. If two lambs born from a single sheep happened to precede a serious misfortune, and three preceded something equally or even more serious, the conclusion was that nine lambs born all at once (a thing they could never have observed) must mean the worst catastrophe of all – the extinction of the reigning dynasty. Those who believed that disaster came through an act of a god might still interest themselves in the secondary causes, as in the case of the Hittite monarch Murshilish II who accepted the plague as a judgement of a god and a punishment for sin, yet discovered also that it had been brought by prisoners taken in a war with Egypt. In Europe in the Middle Ages men could ascribe a disease to God, but still enquire into its more immediate mundane causes. In seventeenth-century Europe, Christian rationalists set out to show how the physical universe worked according to law, and why this must be the case, even though, as yet, they lacked the data for demonstrating the point. They decided in advance that the universe must be like a piece of clockwork, for otherwise the Creation itself would have been imperfect. They claimed that precisely by the methods of science, they could demonstrate the rationality of God. In most civilisations the belief in the rationality of God or the gods appears to be anterior to the belief in the rationality of the universe. Thus, once the historian interested himself in the telling of the human story or in the production of a narrative that contained its own explanation, the area of the episode that was amenable to rationalisation (capable, for example, of being reduced to the ordinary mundane operation of cause and effect) would expand as more of human affairs, and more of the connections between events, became understandable. After all, statesmen have to consider the consequences of action, and indeed the remoter consequences as well as the more immediate ones, whether they believe in God or Providence or not. They cannot choose their policies or decide their actions in a world in which arbitrary caprices of gods constantly make nonsense of the simplest calculation. And something of the attitude of the statesman must pass into the mind of the historian when he is dealing with politics and war, along with something of the attitude of the observer of the phenomena of nature who is trying to discover the laws of the physical universe.

Apart from this, men at an early stage began to confront history with questions. They wanted to know why mankind had been divided into nations, why there had arisen the confusion of tongues, how agriculture and the arts of civilisation had arisen, how certain places and people had got their names, and why certain mountains and rivers were sacred. At first they could only think that some man or god had willed the result, that some actions of men had resulted in the rise of separate peoples, or the confusion of tongues or the development of an industrial art. Some story must explain how a tribe acquired its name or why a river had become sacred. And similarly in these early rationalisations wars were usually the result of quarrels between individuals. Often, as in the case of the Trojan War, they would spring from a dispute over a woman. Even in modern times wars are sometimes ascribed simply to the wilful action of bad men. It has required a much more advanced science of historiography to realise that there might have been profounder causes — great economic movements, for example — behind an ancient war. Even today we can often answer this question of causes at different levels for different classes of people. Some might attribute the war of 1914 simply to the aggressiveness of Kaiser Wilhelm II, while others might see that an international deadlock gradually built itself up over the course of the forty previous years. There have been people who simply blamed wicked men for the Industrial Revolution! Today most of us dig more profoundly for impersonal causes. In regard to both the 1914 war and the Industrial Revolution, we examine the history-making that goes on over men's heads. But our remoter ancestors, who knew nothing of these interconnections between events, would interpret any history-making of this kind, if they were aware of it at all, as something with no apparent rational cause — the results of the wills of men and of the inscrutable gods.

2 THE MUNDANE APPROACH

We saw in Chapter IV the tremendous contribution of the Greeks to the development of historical writing. They came to the subject when something like a scientific mentality had already begun to emerge in other fields, disentangling itself from other things, changing the vision of the external world. In a way, history in Greece emerged from a more scientific background, coming almost as a by-product of geographical and ethnographical studies. The narrative could not simply be copied from older writers: history presented itself from the first as something requiring investigation.

The eye was turned to neighbouring nations and peoples, to other civilisations whose ways and traditions called for elucidation and comparison. And the Greeks went much further than any of their predecessors in pursuing the mundane explanations and in eliminating the gods from the argument. They used their experiences in city-states to help them to find out how consequences proceed out of causes in politics. They tried to discover the laws which govern the succession of events and the rise and fall of states. They even elaborated political science into an independent field of study. They could talk about the effects of climate on human character, for example; they could envisage a constitutional development as almost a self-explanatory succession of causes and effects; they could ponder on the long-term processes of time. They focused so much of their minds on concrete events and the connections which existed between them that, granted the general constitution of human nature, the course of events largely explained itself. In this way they accustomed the world to thinking that a good deal of human history, as well as of nature, was amenable to rationalisation. But as we have seen, they had to leave something to chance; they did not exclude the intervention of the gods, so they did not quite eliminate the mystery from history. But their approach was clearly a case of picking up a different end of the stick, looking at the story from the mundane side.

The greater prophets of Israel also did something to bring the course of history under the jurisdiction of reason. Some of these men surveyed the position of many nations and predicted, sometimes with extraordinary shrewdness, the next step of their story, such as the subjection of Babylon, or the results of Israel's unwise policies, like her tendency to rely on Egypt. They went on to predict the next stage but one, the destruction of Babylon herself, in spite of her current victories. It would appear that these judgments involved something of an insight into events themselves as well as a number of assumptions or insights in respect of the nature of God. In a sense it seemed to the Israeli prophets that history was being laid out as a plan that existed in the mind of God. And because God himself was conceived as being rational, the course of history too had a rationale.

Perhaps the Greeks were able to achieve their more sophisticated and more scientific approach to history while the Jews remained locked in a more religious mould because of the inadequacy of Greek religion to explain the unfolding of events in the world. How did Aeschylus differ from the Old Testament writers in his view of history and human destiny and the judgment of heaven? In the *Oresteia* there is an outlook much more grim and pessimistic, much more harassed by fear. The two views (regarded as world-views) might in general be fundamentally the same, except that allowance must be made for the fact that the Jews were not like the rest of the world because they had a special relationship with God, having the advantage of the Promise. But in Aeschylus there is something hard and mechanical in the conception of fate – something which seems to bind gods as well as men. Peoples were in a difficult position if they held anything like that view of life but did not believe in a single god who was really omnipotent. Part of the gloom that hangs around the plays and part of the darkness of the outlook are due to the machine-like remorselessness – the way in which the family of Athens looks as if it will be doomed from generation to generation. The fundamental difference between this and the Old Testament lies in the fact that the gods are not open to persuasion and there is no forgiveness of sin. Crime goes on begetting more crime because it is necessary that revenge should be taken. And though the revenge takes place through human instruments, it is part of the system of things – for which either the gods or fate have the ultimate responsibility. Aeschylus gets out of the difficulty in the *Oresteia* because the god Apollo actually orders Orestes to avenge his father by killing his mother. Even so it is through an appeal to the Athenian Areopagus that Orestes is exonerated; though it was Athena who saved him by giving him her casting vote. Indeed it is the rescue of Orestes – the cutting off at that point of the tragedy that came down through successive generations – which seems to be the least plausible part of the theory. Aeschylus seems to believe that the gods set out to punish men for their sins and are not moved simply by jealousy of their prosperity or happiness. Some of the things that are said in his plays suggest the latter view, but at a crucial moment in *The Agamemnon* he seems to decide definitely in favour of the former. Also, he seems to hold that the postponement of the penalty is likely to involve a severer punishment.

One curious point is that Yahweh insists on the obedience of Israel, and indeed on a sort of continuous obedience, so that he keeps his eyes on all that men do. In Aeschylus it looks as if Fate intervenes when some special kind of offence has triggered off its action. And the concern of the gods is more spasmodic. Although relationships are established with gods – for instance, between Orestes and Apollo – they only seem to extend to the particular matter that is on the agenda at the moment. There is not a continuing and developing personal relationship, such as became curiously spiritual in character amongst the children of Israel even before the deity had been conceived as spiritual. Such spasmodic divine intervention was not enough to satisfy the enquiring Greek mind.

The early Christians went further than the ancient Greeks and Jews, not only in rationalising history but also in discarding secular interpretations arising out of the nature of events. By developing the ideas of the Hebrew prophets, they were able to reduce mundane history to a kind of diagram which represented a piece of actual planning by God, various stages leading to an appointed end. The Fall, the election of Israel, the work of the prophets, the Exile, the Incarnation, Crucifixion and Resurrection and also the rise of the Greek philosophers, the establishment of the Roman Empire and the conversion of Constantine were all points in the great plan. Some of them were supramundane in their reference. Christ, for example, had destroyed the power of demons and produced a reconciliation between God and man. But also the establishment of the Roman Empire was part of the preparation of the Gospel, part of God's unfolding plan. The conversion of Constantine had its place in the economy of Providence. So, even human history itself showed the marks of the divine hand. Not only did God direct the events of the world, but his intervention (and its underlying purpose) was for the early Christians the only thing that gave any meaning to history. Furthermore, Christians believed that they knew what was the essence of history, the central movement to which everything else was subordinated. Indeed, for them, the real purpose of history had already been fulfilled, and nothing that might happen in the future could really matter because the issue was already decided. In contrast to the Greeks especially, they held that the meaning of history was not anything that could be abstracted from the facts themselves. Indeed it was not from history as such that one could learn the meaning of history. At least, in their view, unless one believed that Christ was the Son of God or accepted this as a part of history, one sensed no meaning in history. The meaning was brought to it extraneously; it came from religion. In the Christian view of those days, however, Christ, his divinity, his resurrection, and his saving power were demonstrated by history. In other words, the history and the divinity were intermixed.

While the Christian attitude to history followed the course described in Chapter VI, the more sophisticated and more scientific methods of the classical Greeks were taken up within Islamic civilisation, and produced results there which were not achieved in the West until much later. Many centuries before the Italian Renaissance the Mohammedans had arrived at ideas about history which we associate with that period or even with the eighteenth century.

Islam was another historical religion, centred on events which happened to men at specific times and places. It drew on Jewish and Christian sources, and continued to have contacts with those traditions, particularly the orthodox Christianity of the Byzantine Empire, which encouraged the development of a historical sense. Muslim scholars were familiar with the work of Eusebius and Orosius. But they do not seem to have discovered the great historians of classical Greece, in contrast with their great interest in Greek science and philosophy. The Prophet Mohammed showed and taught a profound interest in history. Since the life of the Prophet was for Muslims the central dividing line of history, the need to know more about him and the men around him, and to elucidate the many difficult historical references in the Qur'an, also greatly stimulated Muslim research. It is therefore not surprising that an exceptionally large proportion of the literature of the Islamic peoples is involved in some way with history. Islam carried this attitude with it as it spread. Some countries and civilisations, of which India is the most important, did not previously have what we should today call a historiography. The accounts compiled by Muslim historians after the coming of Islam, of which the most remarkable is that of the Persian Ferishta (*circa* 1600), had no counterpart on the Hindu side, and their historical narratives must be amplified and balanced by reference to Hindu inscriptions and other archaeological evidence.

Islamic historical writing in the eighth century developed the traditional Semitic descriptions of a great event followed by a song (which we also find in the Old Testament) into literary pieces dealing with a single person or event. Greek and Byzantine influences stimulated the threading together of such pieces into annals, which also included unusual natural occurrences and, more significantly for the use of generalisation and abstraction and as techniques in the writing of history, accounts of cultural developments which were not tied to specific events. In the tenth century men of wide culture but little experience of the workings of history came to the fore, and greatly developed the study of the past. At this time a number of world-histories were produced, which correspond to the diagrammatic world-histories of the early Christians. The Muslim world-histories of that time have considerable literary merit; but they did not devote the same attention to the remoter past, or seriously try to establish a pre-Islamic chronology. The most influential and most culturally sensitive Muslim world-history was that of the famous al-Tabari at the beginning of the century, which set a pattern for others. In the same way Muslim documentary studies were impressive but limited in their range of interest, and did not consult archives for more systematic knowledge of pre-Islamic times. What the annalist wrote about his own times was regarded as authoritative, and was reproduced without alteration by subsequent historians, much as happened in Europe. Much of this palace chronicle history was produced by official historians who were employed to write the life of a ruler; and they did indeed write with authority because they were usually men of practical experience in politics who also held high office, knew what had happened and had access to the documents. The commissioned biographies, combined with the abiding interest in the lives of the Prophet, his associates and immediate successors, resulted in an enormous output of biographical history, which became a major genre of Muslim historiography. Under the ever-present but inscrutable hand of Allah, the course of politics was seen as determined by human wills, by the personal character and motives of individual actors. Akin to the biographies, but allowing for more poetic and literary art, were great numbers of historical novels, which put still greater emphasis on human motives and emotions. At the other end of the spectrum of Islamic historical writing were learned research treatises which compared events in a given category, such as the incidence and impact of plagues and epidemics, or 'the Rulers of Islam who received the Oath of Allegiance before reaching Puberty'.

Yet many Muslim theologians were jealous of history. It remained a minor branch of study, without any place in higher education, and never became the stimulus behind a great intellectual movement. The West in the Middle Ages seized on Muslim science, but largely ignored Muslim historical work. By the time of the Renaissance it may be questioned whether Muslim history would have contributed to the development which was in fact taken by European historiography anything like the contribution made by Muslim philosophy and natural science.

In the particular fields in which Muslim history was concentrated, it was more sophisticated than any which had been written in the world up to that time. The most outstanding of all Muslim historians, and the one writer who might have exercised a considerable influence on the West had his works been known there, was ibn Khaldun (1332–1406). He developed the tradition of world-history and cultural awareness, and the political history of the biographers, into a scientific treatise written with great literary skill on the formation of states, the rise and fall of dynasties, the nature of law and what was necessary for the maintenance of the fabric of civilisation. He may have learnt from the Greeks to relate people to their environment, and was particularly concerned with an abiding problem of Islam from its very origins – the relation between urban and desert societies. He seems to stand alone among Muslim writers in his attempt to connect history with the study of statecraft and political science on the one hand and with forms of sociological enquiry on the other. Though he believed in divine intervention, his History accords it only an exceptional role, which does not interfere with the study of processes in history. He did not introduce the idea of progress, but held to a cyclical view of the fate of dynasties and states. When the Europeans belatedly discovered him, they were astonished that Islam had produced anything so mundane and 'enlightened', anything so comparable to the writings of Vico and Montesquieu and the French *philosophes* generally.

For Europe it is the Renaissance that is important. From that time there was a great division in historical writing between the sacred and the secular. Some of the Florentine writers, like Machiavelli and Guicciardini, took over not merely the methods of the ancient classical writers, but the results of their work – the laws or generalisations or maxims produced by Aristotle, for example. This meant studying the laws that govern the movements which take place in politics rather in the way that the student of mechanics dealt with motion in physics. It meant examining the processes that take place over very long periods – finding a scientific explanation for the rise and fall of empires instead of merely attributing these events to a divine decree. And all this was bound to be worked into the narration and the exposition of history – bound to alter the texture of ordinary historical writing. There was a tremendous emphasis on political history. History was promoted as an education in statesmanship, and an attempt was made to use historical data in a scientific manner so as to arrive at maxims of statecraft and political analysis. This proved an enduring feature: henceforward many who have proclaimed the importance of history have stressed its value as a guide to political action.

In Renaissance Italy, as in ancient Greece, however, there was one important factor in the case which seemed to escape all the efforts of the rationalisers. Those who have tried to turn history into a self-explanatory system have often found that there are pieces left over, things not quite assimilated into their system. They solve their problems, not by moving to a wider synthesis, a higher order of thought, but by attributing a great deal in history to chance and contingency. The historical thought of the Renaissance, like Greek thought, ascribed a decisive importance to Fortune. It regarded chance and contingency as involving something that was irreducible; it was almost like bringing the gods into the story, bringing them in again by a back door. Nevertheless the whole Renaissance outlook was eminently secular – a fact to be attributed not merely to classical influence but also to developments that had been taking place in the city-states of fifteenth-century Italy. It took a long time for European thought in general to reach the same kind of sceptical worldly-mindedness again.

The great features of the sixteenth century were the Reformation and the Counter-Reformation. They brought about a tremendous awakening in the Christian world, but they also introduced a period of religious obsession, religious passion, religious war. Apart from the concern of the Protestants to attack the traditional Catholic view of ecclesiastical history, Luther, and still more, Melanchthon, attached some importance to history as a part of education, though they emphasised its utility as an instrument of moral teaching, and subordinated the subject very severely to theology. They are significant in this connection because they revived the early Christian interest in universal history, the overall history of mankind; and they established an enduring teaching-tradition in this subject, which was to have great importance in the latter part of the eighteenth century. The emphasis which the Reformers placed on the whole Bible had the effect of raising the Old Testament to greater importance than had been given to it in medieval times, and the results of this in one area after another – including political and constitutional theory and also historiography – now form a variegated and interesting field of study. The Book of *Genesis* retains its old importance as the starting-point for the history of the whole human race; and the theory of the Four World-Empires, as drawn from the Book of *Daniel*, now had quite a revival as the basis for the periodisation of universal history. Those who try to see the whole story of mankind as a unity and to encompass the whole history of civilisation in a single survey (as in their different ways the Jews, the early Christians and the Muslims all attempted to do) have to do considerable abridging, selecting and interpreting. They tend both to choose and to interpret their facts according to a theory – at first a religious theory. In sixteenth-century Europe the two traditions of sacred and secular history continued to exist side by side. And it is easy to understand why the conflict between the religious and secular writers came to its climax in the discussion of universal history, and not in the more detailed narratives, the more local, short-period studies.

So, if the belief in divine intervention and the hand of God is the first thing that has to be accounted for in historiography, the universality of this view and its long endurance and recurrence make it necessary to explain in the second place how men finally found their way out of such a system of ideas, and how they came to see history as a system that should be entirely self-explanatory.

3 THE IDEA OF PROGRESS

If we are envisaging the history of European thought in general, we shall find that the really important transition – the really radical stage in the process of secularisation – is the one which occurs at the end of the seventeenth and in the course of the eighteenth century, a change affecting the entire human outlook. In so far as it involves religious scepticism, it still comes at a slower pace than students of history often realize, and it must be identified with a restricted class, what we call the intelligentsia. We are sometimes inclined to forget how widespread the Christian religion still was in Britain in the early years of the twentieth century. An important factor in the intellectual revolution of the seventeenth and eighteenth centuries was a change in men's attitude to time, to the whole process of things in time and to the providential order itself. It was a change calculated to have a transforming effect on the study and the writing of history. Behind it was the emergence of the idea of Progress and the remarkable development that was given to that idea.

In the very ancient times it had sometimes been realised that man had made an advance since the really primeval period. It was held that there were certain gods or certain men who had introduced the various arts and crafts. It was realised on occasion that the passage of time brought an increase in knowledge, and that knowledge was a thing which grew by sheer accumulation. The ancient Greeks were aware that there had been an advance in the arts of civilisation, but they also recognised the possibility of a corresponding decadence, and they tended to believe that, owing to recurring catastrophes of a colossal kind, the human race had repeatedly to start the process at the beginning again. Oddly enough, it is in the spiritual realm that one meets some of the interesting analogues to the idea of progress. In the Old Testament the notion of God's Promise to His people comes to be carried to a higher plane, and we find the recurring suggestion that the future is going to be better than the past. We also find the belief that God did not exhaust his creative powers when He first made the universe, and is able to produce absolutely new things in the course of history. We saw that the early Christians also had a diagrammatic idea of progress. They regarded the religion of the Old Testament and the philosophy of the Greeks as a 'preparation' for the Gospel – a Gospel which was to appear only in the fullness of time. They held that the Mosaic system was fitted only for an imperfect and immature state of the world, and that the passage of centuries had educated and would continue to educate all mankind up to something higher.

There seemed always to exist a contrary tendency, however, which may correspond to something rather curious in human nature. A few decades ago I traced back almost to the year 1600 the controversy which had occurred every half-century in Great Britain on the question of why the weather in this country had got worse in the last fifty years. The obsession on this subject had persisted throughout the very period when men were supposed to be so credulous about the idea that the world was getting better and better in every way. It may be the case that, no matter what epoch may be in question, men are only too conscious of the fact that there is something wrong with the world. It may be that, compared with the expectations that we had as little children, we always feel that life has turned out to be rather a let-down. But, for one reason or another, even the optimists will betray that they have the secret superstition that at a certain point the world took the wrong turn, after which things could never be the same again. The Protestants might say it was the conversion of Constantine; the Catholics seem to think that it was the Reformation. Both are liable to forget that the Fall of Man was much earlier still. In any case, the view that the best days were far away in the past – the Golden Age, the Heroic Age, the time of primitive Teutonic freedom – is one of the most ancient of all notions about the course of things in time. In our seventeenth-century civil wars the anti-royalist ideology was based on the view that the British constitution and British liberty went back to a happy era, indeed to time immemorial. The supporters of the Revolution of 1688 claimed to be restoring to its original principles a system of free government which had long been in decline, and the official historiography of that period supported the view.

The men of the Renaissance believed that they were on the point of recovering all the splendours of the ancient classical civilisation; but in their view there had been a thousand years of decline since the fall of

Rome, and, even now, they did not believe in a future of broadening horizons and expanding progress. They believed that a period of good fortune, the advent of a great genius, or some high endeavour by a gifted people, might bring about a great advance in society and culture, but once the special effort was relaxed, the world would be released to the natural processes of decline. An apple rots if it is left to the ordinary activities of nature; and in the field of the natural sciences it was held that organic substances, compound bodies, tended to disintegrate in this way. In the political and historical realm, institutions were regarded as compound bodies in this sense and subject, therefore, to corruption. At the very beginning of the Christian era, there had been Jewish writers who said that the world was getting old and that nature was becoming exhausted. And this astonishing idea can be traced still further back. At the end of the seventeenth century also, men were saying the same thing, saying that nature, in its present jaded state, could no longer produce men, or even trees, as large and vigorous as in ancient times. It was possible to believe that knowledge advanced with the passage of time by sheer accumulation, while still holding that institutions had a propensity to decline. Partial views could be held without any commitment to any idea of an overall advance or decline taking place in history. Many people seem in general to have envisaged all ages as very much the same, as differing only in accidental matters – differing because in one age one country came to the top, and in another age another country. The world itself was regarded as fairly static, with everything looking much the same one century after another.

What drew attention to the question of the general advance or decline of the human race was the famous controversy between the Ancients and the Moderns, a controversy which goes back to the Renaissance. Those who asserted the superiority of the Moderns found their most popular argument in the fact that the compass, gunpowder and the art of printing had been unknown in classical antiquity. It was easy to show also that the present had the advantage of the astronomical observations recorded in antiquity, those that had been made in the meantime, and those that could now be added. The controversy between the Ancients and the Moderns came to new life again towards the end of the seventeenth century, when some people argued that the literature of the reign of Louis XIV excelled that which had been produced in classical antiquity. Even this did not necessarily involve the idea of progress, however, for those who claimed that everything had come to a new peak in the reign of Louis XIV could still entertain the idea that another relapse was likely to take place in the subsequent period. Perhaps more important was the fact that in those days the victory of the Scientific Revolution, the achievements of Sir Isaac Newton and the overthrow of Aristotelian physics, struck a tremendous blow at the authority hitherto enjoyed by both the Middle Ages and classical antiquity. The tangible successes of the natural sciences, the advance of technology, and the general improvements in city life helped to carry the day for the Moderns, and opened the way for the idea of progress. In any case, it came to be seen that society itself was no longer static – change was taking place so quickly that it was visible to the naked eye. In addition, the writings of travellers in newly-discovered parts of the world helped to provide vivid pictures of more primitive states of society. There was, therefore, a consciousness of a general progress of the human race – progress as an all-embracing principle.

In so far as it was a verdict on the tendencies of the past, it was the result of reflection on empirical observation, but in so far as it was a hope reaching out into the future, progress represented something more like an act of faith. It was almost like a secularisation of the ancient Jewish belief in history as based on the Promise. Some of the patterns of the Old Testament did tend to imprint themselves upon the minds of men even in modern times. The notion of being God's 'chosen people' – chosen to fulfil a special mission – has been a feature of modern nationalism and is visible in Puritan England in the seventeenth century. Modern political messianism has many of the features of ancient Jewish messianism; but in all cases the idea was secularised – and this happened in the case of the notion that history is based on the Promise. The idea of progress had tremendous implications, some of which are visible in the works of Sir Francis Bacon early in the seventeenth century. He had firm ideas about the past and the future progress of science, but he struggled for new scientific methods, struggled as a man who saw the need for something like an intellectual revolution. Bacon's account of what would happen to the world once science was placed on a proper footing must be regarded as one of the most wonderful of all attempts to prophesy the future. But he planned to bring about the kind of future which he prophesied, and seldom have the apostles of a great revolution managed to achieve so completely the result that they had intended. It was a case of man taking over the control of his own destiny, not just leaving the development of the world to Providence. In the era that was now opening, man was beginning much more to play Providence for himself.

The idea of Progress was bound to have important repercussions on the study of the past and on the general conceptions that men had concerning history. Here at last was something which made it possible for men to give shape and structure to the whole course of the ages. It was no longer a case of one generation succeeding another on the same unchanging stage, all living out their lives on very much the same terms, though good fortune and ill fortune might be redistributed periodically, as between one country and another. What was more, here was an idea that seemed to give meaning to the course of history. Progress gave some purpose to the time-succession, the system of one century perpetually succeeding another. A Jewish writer of the first century A.D. had reproached God Himself for creating the succession of ages. If only He had put the whole of the human race on earth together, to live out its life at the same time (instead of one generation succeeding another) the misery could have been gone through much more quickly, he said. With the idea of Progress, however, it comes to be accepted that the long train of centuries has a meaning, because it is producing something. The passage of time implies change of a fruitful character, the gradual introduction of things that are radically novel. Time itself is in fact a generative thing. Without going outside the sphere of mundane events – without looking, for example, to a final act of intervention of God – there appeared a purpose, and an objective in the world's history. The future itself had become a thing to live for. The verdict of posterity on a man or a nation or a generation superseded the notion of the Last Judgment. For centuries men had seemed to have their eyes turned towards the past, and perhaps it was understandable therefore that they should be interested in history. But now that all eyes came to be turned to the future, the surprising thing happened. Men seemed to become more interested in history than ever before, because they felt that it had acquired meaning and direction and shape. The eighteenth century became particularly interested in long surveys, and in studying the way in which mankind, from a primitive beginning, had come to reach its present high state of culture.

This new outlook became so much a part of men's mentality that even the people engaged in the natural sciences began to envisage the universe historically. The study of geology and the interest in fossils helped to provide material for such an attitude. The eighteenth century saw much speculation about the history of the earth, the history of the animal kingdom, the history of the solar system. Already the idea of progress had come to be seen as only a special case in a larger scheme of evolution which comprised the development of the universe itself. It seemed that the final goal of science was the laying-out of the history of the entire cosmos.

4 PHILOSOPHIES OF HISTORY

The secular and the religious views of history tended to diverge from one another most radically not when telling a detailed story (such as the narrative of the execution of Charles I) but when covering a whole succession of centuries in a bird's-eye view. The issue between them became most clear, therefore, when men were dealing with the whole stretch of universal history, and perhaps that is why, for a century and a half, the production of large-scale universal histories became a significant feature of Western European literature. For a long time the term 'philosophy of history' was used to describe the kind of all-embracing work which, while recounting the whole story of man, purported to give a final explanation of the whole meaning of the human drama. And the use of that very term was itself a sign of the secularisation that had taken place.

The modern story really begins with Bossuet, whose famous *Discourse on Universal History* appeared in 1681. Apart from being a magnificent expression of the spirit which informed literary work in the France of Louis XIV, it is quite imposing as an outline of history and an example of seventeenth-century scholarship. It is thoroughly religious, thoroughly Catholic, in outlook; yet it is not based on the cruder ideas of Eusebius and Orosius but on the more imposing example of St Augustine, who was ready to give due place to the operation of secondary causes, though he regarded the system of causation itself as part of the providential order. In a sense the work is an advance on St Augustine, whose doctrine of the heavenly city almost suggested that the conflict between good and evil was a conflict between two organisations. He had also engaged the good angels and the evil demons so closely in the conflict that he gave the warfare a cosmic character and produced too harsh a dualism. Bossuet sees an ultimate ordaining power behind history, turning men's actions to surprising results that they never intended. He followed to a certain degree the theory of the Four World-Empires, based on the Book of *Daniel*, and he saw each of these empires consciously working to carry out its own purposes, but, in that very act, serving unconsciously a divine purpose too. That of the Assyrians and Babylonians was used for the chastisement of the Hebrew people. That of the Persians was used to bring about their restoration and the re-establishment of their religion. Bossuet was accused of assuming that these vast empires had been brought into existence purely in order to carry out God's purposes with the Jews. Even the Roman Empire was ordained for the destruction of that people as the retribution for their rejection and crucifixion of Christ, though it fulfilled a further divine object by facilitating the spread and the triumph of Christianity. Yet in Bossuet the divine ends are often achieved through secondary causes. When he is treating of the great empires, he gives a preliminary brief sketch of God's purpose in allowing them to arise. Then he gives long accounts of the empires themselves, and here he seems to be writing in terms of ordinary, mundane history, and the course of the whole story is repeatedly decided by the fact that men and nations are what they are. Thus God, who operates all the time through human history, achieves His object chiefly through His control over the human heart. Now He puts a bridle on human beings and they are disciplined, they keep in the path of virtue. Now, however, He releases His control, and leaves them to be the prey of their passions. He turns the heads of the Egyptians, for example, and, as a result of this, that people come into a state of decadence. Oddly enough, therefore, the key to human history is the spirit of men, 'l'esprit des hommes', though, by a kind of determinism God can control that spirit. And this is very interesting, because the divine determinism had only to be knocked out, and what was left was a self-consistent system of a secular kind, the Voltairean view that history depends on the spirit of men.

For after Bossuet, who represents a high spot in the history of modern Catholicism, and who turned the Christian view of world-history into a literary masterpiece, came the Age of Voltaire, the *philosophe* movement of eighteenth-century France, and the reaction against everything ecclesiastical. This reaction involved the elimination of theological dogmas, the negation of otherworldliness and the removal of the element of the supernatural; and what resulted was the phenomenon of the 'lapsed Christian', the man who lets everything spiritual evaporate away, but in the realm of mundane affairs still holds to the ideals and the values which had hitherto developed under the wing of Christianity.

Historians have never sufficiently brought out the importance of the 'lapsed Christians' in the development of the modern world. Their rôle is analogous to that played by the nonconformists at a preceding stage in the story – the part played by nonconformists in England, indeed, until a comparatively recent period. They fought on behalf of beneficent reforms against the 'Establishment', when the 'Establishment' was a combination of both Church and State; and they struggled for just those things which differentiate our system from that of the Communists, those freedoms and values which we today often regard as Christian, though they are comparatively recent even in the West, only established since 1700, only possible after the Church had lost its dominance in society. Because the lapsed Christians hated established churches, which they saw as the great obstruction to their mundane ideals, they did not recognise how much Christianity had shaped their minds, how much their secular ideals went back to the first principles of the Christian religion. They cherished a doctrine of 'individualism' but forgot how much of the basis of this had rested on the belief in the spiritual nature of man, the teaching that every person, as a soul born for eternity, had a value incommensurate with anything else in the created universe. Some of them moved to doctrines of egalitarianism, not realising that the religious nonconformists who had first preached this doctrine had taken it from the Bible – from the teaching in it that all men are equal in the sight of God. Sometimes the lapsed Christians seem to have half-realised that they themselves had sprung from Christianity, for they claimed that they were better Christians than the Churchmen themselves, because they attached themselves to the principle of charity rather than to rites and ceremonies and superstitions. And it is a serious criticism of historical Christianity that these people, by leaving the Church, seemed able to throw off the shackles of custom and mere convention, and were freed for a wider exercise of charity than the ecclesiastical systems of the time could tolerate. And sometimes they seemed like the representatives of what we should call an ethical religion. For instance, a man who would never have gone to Church could say how good it was for people to hear an ethical discourse once a week. Indeed, prizes were awarded for excellence in moral conduct and public spirit.

When the lapsed Christians came to the writing of history, they behaved in very much the same way. They were determined to cut out the theological dogmas, the otherworldliness and the element of the supernatural. The story had to proceed without miracles, without divine interferences; everything had to be explicable by the laws of nature and of history. And if, like Bossuet, they were to take the line that the spirit of men was the important factor in the story – the key to the rise and fall of states – they would not agree that a sort of divine determination was responsible for producing vigorous people in one region and a decadent mood in another. To analyse the matter further, it would be said that the climate of a country or the form of the government helped to decide the character of a people. Very often, as in the case of the writings of St Augustine, the key points in the examination of the processes of history would be the places where the writers expounded the rise and fall of Rome. This was a continually recurring theme in the literature of the times, and is well illustrated by the example of Montaigne's *Grandeur and Decadence of Rome*.

At the same time, these writers unconsciously mimicked the Christians, producing universal histories which were intended to lay out the meaning of the whole human drama. They provided an alternative meaning, an alternative view of the whole purpose to be fulfilled by man on the earth. And, like the Christians, they did not draw the meaning out of the historical narrative itself, out of the historical data as such; they simply ran their views of life into their history, and moulded the story so that it stood as an expression of those views. In a similar way in the twentieth century, H. G. Wells produced his *Outline of History* which stood as the comprehensive expression of the H. G. Wells view of life – really the view of a man whose mind had been shaped by the natural sciences at a certain date. Just as the Christians had tended to produce what might be called a theology of history, the lapsed Christians too ran their philosophy into their narratives and expositions, and for a century or so they would call their surveys of world-history 'the philosophy of history'. Instead of the Creation passages in the Book of *Genesis*, the works would begin with a scientific study of the globe, or a history of the earth, or an account of the operation of natural conditions. These people would complain that the Christian writers had confined themselves to the Greek and Jewish antecedents of Christianity; and they extended the horizon of the historian by including India, China and the Islamic world. Sometimes they regarded it as a feather in their cap if they found a new country to include, for example, Tibet.

By their works, the lapsed Christians did much to encourage the treatment of history as the story of civilisation. They are important in the technical development of historiography because they were not content to narrate a mere story of one thing happening after another. They set themselves problems, they turned history into exposition, they developed the art of historical explanation. But what interested them was their providential plan, their alternative to the Christian interpretations of history. They had their eye on that kind of history-making which goes on over men's heads, carrying out a purpose which is not realised by the people who are acting in the drama, turning men's actions to results that were never intended. For the lapsed Christians there was still an over-riding purpose, but it was one that was to be achieved in this present world — the advance of human society, the perfecting of man himself, or the general unfolding of human reason. And that is why the idea of Progress was so important to the writers of this class. It enabled them to feel that the wheels of this universe were not merely revolving and grinding to no purpose: they were busy manufacturing something that was higher than the individual purposes of living men. Sometimes there was no God to play a part in the story. Or if man had to fulfil some purpose for which God created the world, he would do it by becoming more rational. This was the new way of saving the soul. But sometimes Reason itself would be seen as a kind of immanent god, working as the very soul of history. Reason was pictured as struggling through all the centuries to achieve itself, struggling to realise its potentialities. It was almost as though the wheels of the universe were turning and grinding to create God, or to secure his ultimate liberation. In this way the idea of progress became a fundamental article of faith and came to be turned into a kind of mystique. It reached its most imposing expression when it was made the basis for an interpretation of universal history.

Even Christians were affected by the movement, now writing universal history in a similar way. And since there was often a tendency to put the case in a religious language, it is not always easy to tell whether the writer of a universal history is speaking as a Christian or a deist. (But there was also criticism from the Christian point of view. Schlegel, for instance, could not reconcile himself to the view that all the generations of men, through century after century, had lived tragic lives, all for the sake of a generation that would enjoy the fruits of their suffering at the finish.) Voltaire's *Esprit des Moeurs* is an important representative of the eighteenth-century type of universal history. Another outstanding example is Herder's *Outline of a Philosophy of History of Man*. The whole movement culminated in Hegel's *Philosophy of History*, first delivered as lectures in the early 1820s.

When what we call academic history began to develop, particularly in Göttingen, in the later decades of the eighteenth century, it set itself against this movement. The Göttingen historians were opposed to universal history as understood by the philosophers of history. To them it was history selected to support a theory. It was a case of generalisations produced too much out of the air, not from a massive knowledge of detail. Too much of the philosophy of history merely meant arguing from an armchair about what *must* have happened (always a great danger – always so very different from doing research to find out what actually did happen). As the nineteenth century proceeded, the giant historian Ranke set himself against the giant philosopher Hegel. Yet even Ranke, all his life, had the dream of producing his own vast universal history, the crown of all his work. For him it was to be the cream of all his studies, the final harvest after ploughing in detail into one field after another. The philosophers thought they could use history to discover the meaning of life, or, rather, to illustrate their view of the meaning of life. Ranke insisted that history sets out, using tremendous engines of research, just to discover what actually did happen – what observable things can be demonstrated to have happened.

Appendix

A CHINESE HISTORIAN – SSŬ-MA CH'IEN

It was perhaps appropriate, and certainly it proved strategically important, that the time of the Former Han dynasty also produced one of the most famous of Chinese historians, the most influential of all of them, and a leading figure in the global history of our subject. He was Ssŭ-ma Ch'ien, and he lived from 145 to 87 B.C., succeeding his father as astrologer-archivist at the imperial court in 110 B.C. – a contemporary, therefore, of Polybius. He believed that his ancestors had been chroniclers and keepers of records. In his official capacity he had to devote part of his time to the reform of the calendar. It was his father, Ssŭ-ma T'au, who conceived the design of a general history of things from the very beginning, first setting himself to the task and then handing it down to his son. The object was to attain a kind of glory which would prevent death from involving the fall into oblivion. Ssŭ-ma Ch'ien himself seems to have given offence to the Emperor Wu in the course of his official duties and was punished by castration. He explains at some length why he did not take what was apparently the expected course, and commit suicide rather than endure the shame. Summing the matter up, he says:

> But the reason I have not refused to bear these ills and have continued to live, dwelling in vileness and disgrace without taking my leave, is that I grieve that I have things in my heart that I have not been able to express fully, and I am ashamed by the thought that after I am gone my writings will not be known to posterity. . . .
> Before I had finished my rough notes I had met with this calamity. It is because I regretted that it had not been completed that I submitted to

the extreme penalty without rancour. When I have truly completed this work, I shall deposit it in the Famous Mountain archives. If it may be handed down to men who will appreciate it, and comes to penetrate to the villages and great cities, then, though I should suffer a thousand mutilations, what regret would I have?

Both he and his father would have learned all that the ancient historians had to say, and the early part of their great work, the *Shih Chi* or 'Historical Memoirs', gives a mythical history of mythical times, repeating older writers at length, no doubt, though making use also of inscriptions on monuments. The work becomes more detailed, more personal, more precise a piece of narrative, from the middle of the third century B.C. when a ruler of Ch'in, a principality on the north-western frontier, put an end to the 'feudal' anarchy, united the country, and as Shih Huang Ti gave himself the title of 'First Emperor'. After the account of his remarkable reign, there is a full and picturesque story of the insurrections and wars which between 209 and 202 B.C. led to the downfall of the family of Ch'in and the firm establishment of the Han dynasty on the throne. Then Ssŭ-ma Ch'ien, using official records, but supplementing this by his own personal experiences and by the cross-questioning of eye-witnesses, gives a full history of the Han dynasty down to the Emperor Wu.

The account of the revolts against the Ch'in dynasty and the conflicts which brought the Han dynasty to the top is an impressive piece of work in which we can see something of the methods of Ssŭ-ma Ch'ien but also something of his reflections on history. The narrative induces him to turn his mind back for a moment to the earlier history of China, and at this point we meet with the notion that virtue itself may be connected with a kindred vice, and may carry its own kind of danger – an idea which easily develops into a cyclic view of history:

The government of the Hsia dynasty was marked by good faith which in time had deteriorated until mean men had turned it into rusticity. Therefore the men of Shang who succeeded to the Hsia reformed this defect through the virtue of piety. But piety had degenerated until mean men had made it into a superstitious concern for the spirits. Therefore the men of Chou who followed corrected this fault through refinement and order. But refinement again deteriorated until it became in the hands of the mean a mere hollow show. Therefore what was needed to reform the hollow show was a return to good faith, for the way of the Three Dynasties of old is like a cycle which, when it ends, must begin over again.

But the Ch'in dynasty, which unified the empire in the middle of the third century B.C., did not correct the deterioration of the previous period

— the later Chou — but 'added instead its own harsh punishments and laws. Was this not a grave error?' Elsewhere he says: 'Ch'in failed in goodness and great leaders rose to vex it.' The situation induces him to reflect on the past again:

In ancient times, when Shun and Yü became rulers, they had first to accumulate goodness and merit for twenty or thirty years, impress the people with their virtue, prove that they could in practice handle the affairs of government and meet the approval of Heaven before they were able to ascend the throne. Again, when Kings T'ang and Wu founded the Shang and Chou dynasties, they had behind them ten generations of ancestors, stretching back to Hsieh and Hou Chi respectively, who had been distinguished for their just and virtuous conduct. Yet, though eight hundred nobles appeared unsummoned to aid King Wu at the Meng Ford, he still did not venture to move; it was only later that he assassinated the tyrant Chou, and only after similar cautious delay that King T'ang banished the tyrant Chieh. [The principality of] Ch'in first rose to prominence under Duke Hsiang and achieved eminence under Dukes Wên and Mu. From the reigns of Dukes Hsieh and Hsiao on, it gradually swallowed up the Six States until, after a hundred years or so, the 'First Emperor' was able to bring all the noblemen under his power. Thus, even with the virtue of Shun, Yü, T'ang and Wu, or the might of the 'First Emperor' it is, as one can see, an extremely difficult task to unite the empire in one ruler.

After the Ch'in ruler had assumed the title of emperor, he was fearful lest warfare should continue because of the presence of the feudal lords. Therefore, he refused to grant so much as a foot of land in fief, but instead destroyed the fortifications of the principal cities, melted down the lance and arrow points, and ruthlessly wiped out the brave men of the world, hoping thus to ensure the safety of his dynasty for countless generations.

In another place he quotes an account of the Ch'in 'First Emperor' from an essay which a famous poet, Chiu I, had written on 'The Faults of Ch'in'.

The 'First Emperor' cracked his long whip and drove the universe before him, swallowed up the Eastern and Western Chou, and overthrew the feudal lords. He ascended the throne of honour and ruled the six directions, scourging the world with his rod, and his might shook the four seas. . . . [He built the Great Wall] . . . so that the barbarians no longer ventured to come south to pasture their horses. . . .

Thereupon he discarded the ways of former kings and burned the books of the hundred schools of philosophy in order to make the people ignorant. He destroyed the walls of the great cities, assassinated the powerful leaders, and collected all the arms of the empire. . . . He garrisoned the strategic points. . . . When he had thus pacified the empire the 'First Emperor' believed in his heart that, with the strength of his capital within the Pass, and his walls of metal extending a thousand miles, he had established a rule that would be enjoyed by his sons and grandsons for ten thousand generations.

Ssŭ-ma Ch'ien has his own comment to make on an emperor who relies on the impregnability of a military position:

It is by the lay of the land and its strategic fastnesses that one's position is made secure, and by the force of arms and law that one executes its rule. And yet these alone cannot be relied upon. The kings of antiquity made humanity and righteousness the root of their rule, and considered strategic power, laws and regulations as no more than its branches. Was not this a just view?

These, then, are the kinds of general reflection which Ssŭ-ma Ch'ien would make on a great chapter of catastrophic history. His actual account of the upheavals which led to the change of dynasty is peculiar in form, for the story has to be repeated in different ways as he deals with the leading characters in turn, and addresses himself to the events that hang around each. The reader of any single account will feel that he is missing some of the continuity and some of the explanation, and not until he has covered all of them, and done some dove-tailing, will he feel able to command the whole scene. It was as though Ssŭ-ma Ch'ien was at ease with a linear series of events but was not sure of his ordaining power in respect of the whole network. He takes, for example, the case of Ch'en She, the poor man who, summoned to join the army, was delayed, along with others, by heavy rain, and, since he realised that he was punishable by death in any case, decided to raise a revolt. Ssŭ-ma Ch'ien writes: 'The lords sprang to revolt like a great wind rising, like clouds that cover the sky, until the house of Ch'in at last crumbled.' He described how Ch'en She succeeded, becoming a King 'all in all . . . for six months', at the end of which time he was murdered by his carriage-driver. The views of the poet Chiu I are presented:

Now the empire of Ch'in at this time was by no means small or feeble. Its base in Yung-Chou, its stronghold within the Pass, were the same as before. The position of Ch'en She could not compare in dignity with the lords of Ch'i, Ch'un, Yen, Chao, Hann, Wei, Sung, Wei and Chung-shan. The weapons which he improvised from hoes and tree branches could not match the sharpness of spears and battle pikes; his band of garrison conscripts was nothing beside the armies of the Nine States. In deep plotting and far-reaching stratagems, in methods of warfare, he was far inferior to the men of earlier times. And yet Ch'en She succeeded in his undertaking where they had failed, though in ability, size, power and strength his forces could in no way compare to those of the states east of the mountains that had formerly opposed Ch'in. Ch'in beginning with an insignificant amount of territory, reached the power of a great kingdom, and for a hundred years made the ancient eight provinces pay homage at its court. Yet, after it had become master of the six directions and established its palaces within the Pass, a single commoner opposed it and its seven ancestral temples toppled, its ruler died by the hands of men, and it became the laughing-stock of the world. Why? Because it failed to rule with humanity and righteousness and did not realise that the power to attack and the power to retain what one has thereby won are not the same.

Ssŭ-ma Ch'ien has his own comment to make on the fall of the unpretentious hero of this story:

Ch'en She appointed Chu Fang as Rectifier and Hu Wu as Director of Faults, putting them in charge of his other ministers and officials. . . . If it appeared that [these] had not carried out their orders exactly, these two officials bound them like animals and subjected them to the severest examination to determine their loyalty. . . . Ch'en She entrusted everything to these two men . . . and for this reason his generals felt no personal attachment to him. This is why he failed. Although Ch'en She himself died very early, the various rulers and commanders whom he set up and despatched on various expeditions succeeded in overthrowing the Ch'in. . . . Down to the present day he has continued to enjoy the blood and flesh of sacrifices.

The story of the revolt is taken up from the point of view of another leader, the adventurer Hsiang Yü, who, working with his uncle in the region of Wu, learned of the action of Ch'en She and, at this signal, cut off the head of a city-governor and assumed the local command. He conquered Ch'u, where he set up the grandson of a former monarch to act as a puppet-king; he became 'supreme commander of the leaders of the various states', but, after a long conflict, he fell before a rival amongst the rebels. Ssŭ-ma Ch'ien quotes him as saying before his death:

It has been eight years since I first led my army forth. In that time I have fought over seventy battles. Every enemy I feared was destroyed, everyone I attacked submitted. Never once did I suffer defeat until at last I became dictator of the world. But now suddenly I am driven to this desperate position. It is because Heaven would destroy me, not because I have committed any fault in battle.

Ssŭ-ma Ch'ien's judgement is rather different. He will not allow that the man's fall was due to the judgment of Heaven rather than to his own mistakes:

How sudden was his rise to power! When the rule of Ch'in floundered and Ch'en She led his revolt, local heroes and leaders arose like bees, struggling with each other for power in numbers too great to be counted. Hsiang Yü did not have so much as an inch of territory to begin with, but by taking advantage of the times he raised himself in the space of three years from a commoner in the fields to the position of commander of five armies of feudal lords. He overthrew Ch'in, divided the empire, and parcelled it out in fiefs to the various kings and magnates; but all power of government proceeded from Hsiang Yü and he was hailed as dictator King. He was not able to hold this position to his death, but from ancient times to the present there has never before been such a thing.

But when he went so far as to turn his back on the Pass and return to his native Ch'u, banishing the Righteous Emperor and setting himself up in his place, it was hardly surprising that the feudal lords revolted against him. He boasted and made a show of his own achievements. He was obstinate in his own opinions and did not abide by the ancient ways. He thought to make himself a dictator, hoping to attack and rule the empire by force. Yet within five years he was dead and his kingdom lost. He met his death at Tung-ch'eng but even at that time he did not wake to or accept responsibility for his errors. 'It is heaven,' he declared, 'which has destroyed me, and no fault of mine in the use of arms!' Was he not deluded?

The man who destroyed Hsiang Yü and came out as the hero of the whole story was Kao-tsu. At the beginning of the rebellion he was raised to the governorship of P'ei against his will; he was the first to subdue the formidable region of the Pass; he became King of Han, and finally Emperor – the founder of the Han dynasty. Ssŭ-ma Ch'ien suggests a miraculous birth for him and speaks of supernatural portents, but makes the judgment: 'Hsiang Yü was violent and tyrannical while the King of Han practised goodness and virtue.' Much of the story receives its explanation in the account of Kao-tsu, and an encounter of this man with Hsiang Yü throws further light on the reasons for the fall of the latter:

The King of Han and Hsiang Yü faced each other across the ravine of Kuang-wu and talked back and forth. Hsiang Yü challenged the King of Han to meet him in single combat, but the King berated Hsiang Yü saying: 'When you and I bowed together before the command of King Huai [brought to the throne of Ch'u by Hsiang Yü himself], we agreed that whoever should enter the Pass the first and conquer the land [should hold it]. But you went back on this agreement, making me King of Shu and Han instead. This was your first crime. Feigning orders from King Huai, you murdered His Lordship Sung I, the commander of the army, and elevated yourself to this position. This was your second crime. After you had gone to rescue Chao, it was proper that you should have returned and made your report to King Huai, but instead you wantonly seized the troops of the other leaders and entered the Pass. This was your third crime. King Huai promised that whoever entered the Pass would commit no violence or theft. Yet you fired the palaces of Ch'in, desecrated the grave of the 'First Emperor' and appropriated the wealth and goods of Ch'in, for your private use. This was your fourth crime. You inflicted violent death upon Tzu-yiu, the King of Ch'in, who had already surrendered; this was your fifth crime. At Hsinan you butchered 200,000 of the sons of Ch'in whom you had tricked into surrender, and you made their general, Chang Han, a King; this was your sixth crime. You enfeoffed all your generals as kings in the best lands and transferred or exiled the former kings, setting their subjects to strife and rebellion. This was your seventh crime. You drove the Righteous Emperor from P'eng-ch'eng and set up your own capital there, seized the territory of the King of Han and made yourself ruler of the combined areas of Liang and Ch'u, appropriating all for yourself. This was your eighth crime. You sent a man in secret to assassinate the Righteous Emperor at Chiang-nan. This was your ninth crime. As a subject you have assassinated your sovereign, you have murdered those who had already surrendered, administered your rule unjustly and broken faith with the agreement that you made. . . . [You have committed] such heinous treason as the world cannot forgive. This is your tenth crime. . . . I have plenty of criminals and ex-convicts that I can send to attack and kill you. Why should I go to the trouble of engaging in combat with you myself?

In another place, Ssŭ-ma Ch'ien describes how Kao-tsu on one occasion put the question: 'Why is it that I won possession of the world and Hsiang Yü lost?' He received the reply:

Your Majesty is arrogant and insulting to others while Hsiang Yü was kind and loving. But when you send someone to attack a city or seize a region, you award him the spoils of victory, sharing your gains with the whole world. Hsiang Yü was jealous of worth and merit, hating those who had achieved most and suspecting anyone who displayed his wisdom. . . . He gave his men no reward . . . never shared the spoils.

Kao-tsu replied:

You have understood the first reason but you do not know the second.

When it comes to sitting within the tents of command and devising stratagems that will assure us victory a thousand miles away, I am no match for Chang Liang. In ordering the state and caring for the people, in providing rations for the troops and seeing to it that the lines of supply are not cut off, I cannot compare myself to Hsaio Ho. In leading an army of a million men, achieving success in every battle and victory with every attack, I cannot come up to Han Hsin. These three are all men of extraordinary ability and it is because I was able to make use of them that I gained possession of the world. Hsiang Yü had his one Fan Tseng but he did not know how to use him and he thus ended as my prisoner.

For further details of the civil wars and the victory of the Han dynasty, we have to see Ssŭ-ma Ch'ien's biographies of the people with whom Kao-tsu was comparing himself. Hsiao Ho, who had been his helper since the humble days of his youth, became something like Prime Minister. Han Hsin, the brilliant general, was also of humble origin – once 'unable to make a living as a merchant and therefore constantly dependent on others for his meals'. At a crucial moment, when Kao-tsu wished to march eastward, out of the Pass and away from his kingdom of Ch'in, in order to challenge the formidable Hsiang Yü, he asked Han Hsin's advice, while confessing for his own part that Hsiang Yü excelled him in fierceness of courage and depth of kindness. Han Hsin's reply provides a further analysis of the situation :

I once served Hsiang Yü. I would like to tell you what sort of a person he is. When Hsiang Yü rages and bellows it is enough to make a thousand men fall down in terror. But since he is incapable of employing wise generals all of it amounts to no more than the daring of an ordinary man.

When Hsiang Yü meets people he is courteous and thoughtful; his manner of speaking is gentle; and if someone is ill or in distress he will weep over him and give him his own food and drink. But when someone he has sent upon a mission has achieved merit . . . he will fiddle with the seal of investiture until it crumbles in his hand before he can bring himself to present it to a man. . . .

Now although Hsiang Yü has made himself dictator of the world and subjugated the other nobles to his rule, he has not taken up his residence in the area within the Pass but has made his residence at P'eng Ch'eng. He has gone against the agreement made with the Righteous Emperor and instead given out kingdoms to the nobles on the basis of his own likes and preferences, which has resulted in much injustice. The nobles, seeing that Hsiang Yü has banished the Righteous Emperor and sent him to reside in Chiang-nan, when they return to their own territories in like manner drive out their own sovereigns and make themselves rulers of the choicest lands. Hsiang Yü has left death and destruction everywhere he has passed. Much of the world hates him. The common people do not submit to him out of affection but in truth he has lost the hearts of the world. Therefore I say that his might can easily be weakened.

Now if you could only pursue the opposite policy and make use of the brave men of the world, what enemy would not fall before you? If you were to enfeoff your worthy followers . . . who would not submit?

. . . When you entered the Wu Pass you inflicted not a particle of harm but repealed the harsh laws of Ch'in. . . . There was none of the people of Ch'in who did not wish to make you their king. According to the agreement . . . you ought to have been made king of the area within the Pass, and the people of the area all know this. . . . Now if you will raise your army and march eastward you can win over the three kingdoms of Ch'in simply by proclamation.

On these materials we can form some impression of Ssŭ-ma Ch'ien as a historian, and see both his methods and his underlying ideas. He is dealing with a cataclysm that overwhelmed an empire, and the successive passages show how he considers the rise and fall of empires. On the one hand he seems prepared to see a judgment of Heaven. On the other hand he will not allow the decree of Heaven to supersede the responsibility of individuals. The doom falls because of the action of men themselves, and is the result of some defect in them. But what the historian surveys is the interplay of the leading men. He does not explain the story by examining society, and when he does comment on society, he speaks in a vague and moralistic way. There is a sense in which the narrative does not progress or unfold itself — one thing simply happens after another, and each emerges almost as an anomaly. The actual story of the conflict leaves the reader puzzled : it is a story of war but we see only vaguely what is happening; the author is not concerned about problems of strategy; we do not know why battles are won or lost. Rather we are provided with anecdotes about them — particularly tales of confrontations between one leading person and another. It reminds one of the accounts of a battle that will be given by eye-witnesses, who have known what happened here and there but have had no idea of the character of the engagement, the strategy of the campaign. It is history as it exists for those people who look only for an account of events, an account that has not yet risen to the need for connections, developments, causes — all the things that make the narrative more organic. And no doubt in these early days of historiography, Ssŭ-ma Ch'ien saw the panorama in this way. Only the collapse of an empire or the fall of a war-hero called for reflection that was almost a kind of moralising. And we must wonder whether Ssŭ-ma Ch'ien does not put some of his analysis or his moralising into the mouths of the personages whose speeches he relays to us. These can hardly have been based on documents, even if they may correspond with some reports that have been handed down. Indeed, Ssŭ-ma Ch'ien's war-history does not seem to be of the type that would have been produced from a study of military documents. He collected stories and sometimes one wonders about the stories. They have the charm of Chinese anecdotes, and they hold an important place because they have a beautiful pointedness.

Ssŭ-ma Ch'ien was under the strong conviction that history was a guide to the actual practice of government. It is interesting to note that, according to him, the Emperor in the time of his father regarded it as a toy for the amusement of children, and supported the historiographer as he would a singer or a jester. It is not clear that he was capable of judging statesmanship or military affairs in a profound way, though this would not mean that his history was of no use in the education of a statesman. He may indeed have been a good judge of contemporary affairs – he was a bitter opponent of the policies of the Emperor Wu – and the imperfection would lie in the notion of history, the necessarily imperfect state of historical analysis at the early stage in the story. He seems to have shared with the rulers, officials and scholars of his time a belief in the significance of portents. It is only very slowly that a world starting from such presuppositions can reach the modern ways of historical analysis and historical assessment. Ssŭ-ma Ch'ien had one idea that is worth noting, and it is interesting that we should see it put forward in China. He writes: 'Why must one learn only from ancient times? . . . Take for your model the kings of later ages, for they are near to us and the forms of their customs are like ours.'

He provided a model that the future was to follow, and is important for the great influence that he had. His work consisted of an historical record of imperial history, chronological tables, monographs, annals of vassal princes, and biographies – including lives of individuals belonging to certain groups, for example, scholars. The monographs included studies of music, the state of the calendar, hydrography, political economy. In this type of production – as in the study of administrative institutions – Chinese histiography was to be of great use to the public officials.

Bibliography

1 BOOKS

von Albertini, Rudolf, *Das florentinische Staatsbewusstsein im Übergang von der Republik zum Principat* (Bern, 1955).

Aron, Raymond, *La Philosophie Critique de l'Histoire* (Paris, 1950).

Babinger, F., *Die Geschichtsschreiber der Osmanen* (Leipzig, 1927).

Baeyers, Herman, *Begrip en Probleem van de Renaissance* (Louvain, 1952).

Baron, Hans, *The Crisis of the Early Italian Renaissance* (Princeton, N. J., 1955).

de Beaufort, Louis, *Dissertation sur l'incertitude des cinq premiers siècles de l'histoire romaine* (Paris, 1738).

Becker, Carl, *The Heavenly City of the Eighteenth-Century Philosophers* (New Haven, Conn., 1932).

von Below, Georg, *Deutsche Geschichtsschreibung von den Befreiungskriegen bis zu unseren Tagen* (München und Berlin, 1924).

Behrheim, E., *Lehrbuch der historischen Methode und der Geschichtsphilosophie* (Leipzig, 1903).

Breasted, James H., *Ancient Records of Egypt, I-V* (Chicago, 1906–1907).

Bresslau, H., *Geschichte der Monumenta Germaniae Historica* (Hanover, 1921).

v. den Brincken, Anne-Dorothee, *Studien zur lateinischen Weltchronistik bis in das Zeitalter Ottos von Freising* (Düsseldorf, 1957).

Brumfitt, J. H., *Voltaire, Historian* (Oxford, 1958).

Bury, J. B., *The Ancient Greek Historians* (London, 1909).

——, *The Idea of Progress. An Inquiry into its Origins and Growth* (London, 1920).

——, *History and the Homeric Iliad* (California, 1976).

——, *The Homeric Odyssey* (London, 1977).

Butterfield, Herbert, *Christianity and History* (London, 1949).

——, *The Englishman and his History* (Cambridge, 1945).

——, *Man on his Past* (Cambridge, 1955).

——, *The Statecraft of Machiavelli* (London, 1940).

Callahan, John F., *Four Views of Time in ancient Philosophy* (Cambridge, Mass., 1948).

Caponigri, A. R., *History and Liberty: the historical writings of B. Croce* (London, 1955).

de Caprariis, Vittorio, *Francesco Guicciardini: dalla Politica alla Storia* (Bari, 1950).

Carpenter, Rhys, *Folk Tale, Fiction and Saga in Homeric Epics* (California, 1974).

Chadwick, Hector Munro, *The Heroic Age* (London, 1974).

Collingwood, R. G., *The Idea of History* (Oxford, 1946).

Creel, Henlee Glessner, *Studies in Early Chinese Culture, 1st Series* (London, 1938).

Croce, Benedetto, *Storia della storiografia italiana nel secolo decimonono* (Bari, 1921).

——, *La Storia come Pensiero e come Azione* (Bari, 1954).

——, *Teoria e storia della storiografia, 2nd ed.* (Bari, 1920).

Cullmann, Oscar, *Christus und die Zeit, Die urchristliche Zeit – und Geschichtsauffassung* (Zürich, 1946).

Denton, R. C. (ed.), *The Idea of History in the Ancient Near East* (New Haven, Conn., 1955).

Dilthey, W., *Das 18 Jahrhundert und die geschichtliche Welt,* Gesammelte Schriften III (Leipzig und Berlin, 1927).

Dockhorn, Klaus, *Der deutsche Historismus in England* (Göttingen, 1950).

Douglas, D. C., *English Scholars,* 2nd ed. (London, 1951).

Driver, T. F., *The Sense of History in Greek and Shakespearean Drama* (Columbia, 1960).

Engel-Janösi, Friedrich, *Four Studies in French Romantic Historical Writing* (Baltimore, 1953).

Evans, Joan, *A History of the Society of Antiquaries* (London, 1956).

Farnell, L. R., *Greek Hero Cults and Ideas of Immortality* (Oxford, 1921).

Ferguson, Wallace K., *The Renaissance in Historical Thought* (Cambridge, Mass., 1948).

Flint, Robert, *History of the Philosophy of History, Vol. I* (Edinburgh, 1893).

Forbes, Duncan, *The Liberal Anglican Idea of History* (Cambridge, 1952).

Franke, O., *Studien zur Geschichte des confuzianischen Dogmas und der chinesischen Staatsreligion: Das Problem des Tsch'un-ts'iu . . .* (Hamburg, 1920).

Fueter, Ed., *Geschichte der neueren Historiographie* (München und Berlin, 1911).

Galbraith, V. H., *Historical Research in Medieval England* (London, 1951).

Gardner, C. S., *Chinese Traditional Historiography* (Cambridge, Mass., 1938).

Gogarten, Friedrich, *Entmythologisierung und Kirche* (Stuttgart, 1953).

Gooch, G. P., *History and Historians in the Nineteenth Century* (London, 1913).

Gundolf, E., *Anfänge deutscher Geschichtsschreibung* (no source or date).

Gurney, O. R., *The Hittites* (London, 1975).

Hartung, Fritz, *Zur Entwicklung der Verfassungsgeschichtsschreibung in Deutschland* (Berlin, 1956).

Hölscher, G., *Die Anfänge der hebräischen Geschichtsschreibung* (Heidelberg, 1942).

Horawitz, A. H., *Zur Entwickelungsgeschichte der deutschen Historiographie* (Wien, 1865).

Hostenkamp, Heinrich, *Die mittelälterliche Kaiserpolitik in der deutschen Historiographie seit von Sybel und Ficker* (Berlin, 1934).

Hypollite, Jean, *Études sur Marx et Hegel* (Paris, 1955).

——, *Introduction à la Philosophie de l'Histoire de Hegel* (Paris, 1948).

Jodl, F., *Die Kulturgeschichtsschreibung, ihre Entwicklung und ihr Problem* (Halle, 1878).

Klibansky, R. and H. J. Paton (ed.), *Philosophy and History, Essays presented to Ernst Cassirer* (Oxford, 1936).

Kluback, William, *Wilhelm Dilthey's Philosophy of History* (New York, 1956).

Kohn, Hans, *German History: Some New German Views* (London, 1954).

Kraus, Michael, *A History of American History* (New York, 1937).

Lasch, B., *Das Erwachen und die Entwicklung der historischen Kritik im Mittelalter (vom VI-XIII Jahrhundert)* (Breslau, 1887).

Legge, James, *The Ch'un Ts'en with the Tso Chuen Chinese Classics, V* (Hong Kong, 1872).

Lhotsky, Alphons, *Geschichte des Instituts für österreichische Geschichtsforschung 1854–1954* (Köln-Graz, 1954).

Marron, H. I., *De la connaissance historique* (Paris, 1954).

Meinecke, Friedrich, *Die Entstehung des Historismus* (München, 1936).

——, *Vom Geschichtlichen Sinn und vom Sinn der Geschichte* (Leipzig, 1939).

Mellon, Stanley, *The Political Uses of History: A Study of Historians in the French Restoration* (Stanford, California, 1958).

Meyerhoff, H., *The Philosophy of History in our Time. An Anthology* (New York, 1959).

Momigliano, A., *Contributo alla storia degli studi classici* (Roma, 1955).

Murray, Gilbert, *History of Ancient Greek Literature* (New York, 1937).

——, *The Rise of the Greek Epic* (Oxford, 1949).

Niebuhr, Reinhold, *Faith and History: a Comparison of Christian and Modern Views of History* (London, 1949).

Nilsson, Martin P., *Homer and Mycenae* (London, 1933).

Nordholt, H. Schutte, *Het Beeld der Renaissance* (Amsterdam, 1948).

North, Christopher R., *The Old Testament Interpretation of World History* (London, 1946).

Olmstead, A. T., *Assyrian Historiography, A Source Study* (Columbia, Missouri, 1916).

Overbeck, F., *Über die Anfänge der Kirchengeschichtsschreibung* (Basle, 1892).

Page, Denys L., *Folk Tales in Homer's Odyssey* (Harvard, 1974).

Pearson, Lionel, *Early Ionian Historians* (Oxford, 1939).

Peter, Hermann, *Wahrheit und Kunst, Geschichtsschreibung und Plagiat im Klassischen Altertum* (Leipzig und Berlin, 1911).

Pocock, J. G. A., *The Ancient Constitution and the Feudal Law, English Historical Thought in the Seventeenth Century* (Cambridge, 1957).

de la Popelinière, Lancelot Voisin, *Histoire des Histoires, avec l'Idée de l'Histoire accomplie* (Paris, 1599).

Rickert, H., *Die Probleme der Geschichtsphilosophie* (Heidelberg, 1924).

Rosenmund, Richard, *Die Fortschritte der Diplomatik seit Mabillon vornehmlich in Deutschland-Oesterreich* (München und Leipzig, 1897).

Rosenthal, Erwin, *Ibn Khalduns Gedanken über den Staat* (München und Berlin, 1932).

Rosenthal, Franz, *A History of Muslim Historiography* (Leiden, 1952).

——, *Ibn Khaldun, The Muqaddimah, An Introduction to History, Vol. I* (London, 1958).

Rossi, Pietro, *Lo storicismo tedesco contemporaneo* (Giulio Einaudi editore, 1956).

Rouché, Max, *La Philosophie de l'Histoire de Herder* (Paris, 1940).

Rüffner, V., *Die Geschichtsphilosophie B. Vicos* (Bonn, 1943).

Sastri, K. A. N., *A History of South India* (Oxford, 1955).

Schargo, Nelly N., *History in the Encyclopaedia* (New York, 1947).

von Schlözer, A. L., *Nestor, Russische Annalen in ihrer Slavonischen Grundsprache verglichen, übersetzt, und erklärt* (Göttingen, 1802–1809).

Schmidt, Nathaniel, *Ibn Khaldun: Historian, Sociologist and Philosopher* (Columbia, 1930).

Schulz, Marie, *Die Lehre von der historischen Methode bei den Geschichtsschreibern des Mittelalters (VI-XIII Jahrhundert)* (Berlin und Leipzig, 1909).

Semler, J. S., *Versuch den Gebrauch der Quellen in der Staats- und Kirchengeschichte der mitleren Zeiten zu erleichtern* (Halle, 1761).

Shill, Roger L., *Christianity and the Problem of History* (New York, 1953).

Shotwell, J. T., *The History of History* (New York, 1939).

Sinor, Denis (ed.), *Orientalism and History* (Cambridge, 1954).

Solomon, Bernard S., *The Veritable Record of the T' and Emperor Shun-Tsung (Feb.-Aug. 805)* (Cambridge, Mass., 1955).

Soltau, Wilhelm, *Die Anfänge der römischen Geschichtsschreibung* (Leipzig, 1909).

Spengler, Oswald, *Der Untergang des Abendlandes, 2 Bde* (München, 1918–1922).

von Srbik, H. R., *Geist und Geschichte vom deutschen Humanismus bis zur Gegenwart* (München und Salzburg, 1950).

Stadler, Peter, *Geschichtsschreibung und historisches Denken in Frankreich (1789–1871)* (Zürich, 1958).

Stange, Hans O. H., *Die Monographie über Wang Mang* (Leipzig, 1939).

Teggart, F. J., *Rome and China, A Study of Correlations in Historical Events* (Berkeley, Calif., 1939).

——, *Theory and History* (New Haven, Conn., 1925).

Thompson, James Westfall, *A History of Historical Writing, 2 Vols.* (New York, 1942).

Toynbee, A. J., *Greek Historical Thought from Homer to the Age of Heraclius* (London, 1924).

Toynbee, A. J., *A Study of History* (Oxford, 1934).

Troeltsch, E., *Das Historismus und seine Probleme* (Tübingen, 1922).

Ts'ien (Ch'ien), Ssǔ-ma, *Mémoires Historiques* (trans. by E. Chavannes, 5 Vols.) (Paris, 1895–1905).

Uscatescu, Geo., *Juan Bautista Vico y el Mundo Histórico* (Madrid, 1956).

Varga, Lucie, *Der Schlagwort vom 'Finsteren Mittelalter'* (Baden, 1932).

Vyverberg, H., *Historical Pessimism in the French Enlightenment* (Cambridge, Mass., 1958).

Wagner, Fritz, *Geschichtswissenschaft* (München, 1951).

Watson, Adam, *The War of the Goldsmith's Daughter* (London, 1963).

von Wegele, F. X., *Geschichte der deutschen Historiographie seit dem Auftreten des Humanismus* (München und Leipzig, 1885).

Weis, Eberhard, *Geschichtsschreibung und Staatsauffassung in der französischen Enzyklopädie* (Wiesbaden, 1956).

Weiser, D. Artur, *Glaube und Geschichte im Alten Testament* (Stuttgart, 1931).

Welch, A. C., *The Work of the Chronicler: Its Purpose and its Date* (London, 1939).

Wessendonck, H., *Die Begründung der neueren deutschen Geschichteschreibung durch Gatterer und Schlözer* (Leipzig, 1876).

Wolter, Hans, S. J., *Ordericus Vitalis, Ein Beitrag zur Kluniazensischen Geschichtsschreibung* (Wiesbaden, 1955).

Wright, G. Ernest, *The Old Testament Against its Environment* (London, 1950).

Yushan, Han, *Elements of Chinese Historiography* (Hollywood, Calif., 1955).

2 ARTICLES, INTRODUCTIONS AND LECTURES

Acton, Lord, 'German Schools of History', *Historical Essays and Studies*, London, 1919, 344–392.

Alexander, S., 'Artistic Creation and Cosmic Creation', *Proceedings of the British Academy*, Vol. XIII, 1927?.

Atkinson, J. J. Boone, 'Taine on the French Revolution: A Study in Historiographic Controversy', *The Historian*, Vol. XV, No. 2, Spring 1953.

Aydelotte, W. O., 'Notes on the Problem of Historical Generalisation', Typescript, N. D.

Balázs, Etienne, 'Chinesische Geschichtswerke als Wegweiser zur Praxis der Bürokratie', *Saeculum*, Vol. VIII, 1957.

Barnes, Harry Elmer, 'Review of Burleigh Taylor Wilkens: *Carl Becker: A Biographical Study in American Intellectual History*', *Annals of the American Academy of Political and Social Science*, Vol. 338, Nov. 1961.

Barraclough, G., 'Metropolis and Macrocosm: Europe and the Wider World', *Past and Present*, N. D.

Barzun, Jacques, 'The Sense of History', *The Griffin*, Vol. 7, No. 5, May 1958.

Beale, Howard, 'The Professional Historian', *The Pacific Historical Review*, Vol. XII, No. 5, Aug. 1953.

Beckett, J. C., 'The Study of Irish History', Inaugural Lecture, Queen's University, Belfast, 1963.

Ben-Israel, Hedva, 'William Smyth, Historian of the French Revolution', *Journal of the History of Ideas*, Vol. XXI, No. 4, 1960.

Benz, Ernst, 'Weltgeschichte, Kirchengeschichte und Missionsgeschichte', *Historische Zeitschrift*, Heft 173/1, Feb. 1952.

Bergstraesser, Arnold, 'Religiöse Motive des universalgeschichtlichen Denkens', in *Deutschland und Europa, Festschrift für Hans Rothfels*, Berlin, 1951.

Beumann, Helmut, 'Die Historiographie des Mittelalters als Quelle für die Ideengeschichte des Königtums', *Historische Zeitschrift*, Vol. CLXXX, 1955.

Blount, Charles, 'The International Exchange and Review of History Textbooks', *Cambridge Journal*, Vol. V. No. 2, 1951.

Bromley, J. S., 'History and the Younger Generation', Inaugural Lecture, Southampton, 1961.

Brundage, Burr C., 'The Birth of Cleo' in *Teachers of History, Essays in Honour of L. B. Packard,* 1955.

Bryce, Rt. Hon. James, 'Presidential Address', to International Congress of Historical Studies, London, 1913.

Buchholz, G., 'Ursprung und Wesen der modernen Geschichtsauffassung', *Deutsche Zeitschrift für Geschichtswissenschaft,* Vol. II, 1889.

Butler, J. R. M., 'The Present Need for History', Inaugural Lecture, 1949.

Cam, H. M., 'Zachery Nugent Brooke, 1883–1946', *Proceedings of the British Academy,* Vol. XXXII, N. D.

Campbell, Lily B., 'Tudor Conceptions of History and Tragedy in "A Mirror for Magistrates" ', Faculty Research Lecture at University of California at Los Angeles, 1935. Berkeley, California, 1936.

Chambers, R. W., 'Bede', Annual Lecture on a Master Mind, Henriette Hertz Trust, 1936, *Proceedings of the British Academy,* Vol. XXII, N. D.

Clark, G. Kitson, 'G. M. Trevelyan as a Historian', *Durham University Journal,* Dec. 1962.

Clark, G. N., 'George Macaulay Trevelyan', *Proceedings of the British Academy,* Vol. XLIX, N. D.

Collingwood, R. C., 'Human Nature and Human History', *Proceedings of the British Academy,* Vol. XXII, May 1936.

Conze, Werner, 'Leibniz als Historiker', Leibniz zu seinem 300. Geburtstag 1646–1946, Berlin, 1951.

Conzemius, Victor, 'Zur Characteristik von Ignaz v. Döllinger', *Zeitschrift für Bayerische Landesgeschichte,* Band 22/Heft 1, 1959.

Coulton, G. G., 'Some Problems in Medieval Historiography', Raleigh Lecture, British Academy 1932, *Proceedings of the British Academy,* Vol. XVIII, N. D.

Creed, John Martin, 'The Slavonic Version of Josephus' History of the Jewish War', *Harvard Theological Review,* Vol. XXV, No. 4, Oct. 1932.

Croce, Benedetto, 'Recenti Controversie intorno all'unità della storia d'Italia', Annual Italian Lecture of the British Academy, 1936.

Danielou, Jean, 'Marxist History and Sacred History', *Review of Politics,* Vol. 13, No. 4, Oct. 1951.

Dawson, Christopher, 'Edward Gibbon', *Proceedings of the British Academy,* Vol. XX, 1934.

Delekat, Friedrich, 'Christentum und Geschichte', *Theologische Literaturzeitung,* Nr. 5, 1953.

Dockhorn, Klaus, 'Englands und Deutschlands Stellung in der Geistesgeschichte der Neuzeit', aus der Zeitschrift 'Die Sammlung', 3 Jahr.; 4 Heft, April 1948; 5 Heft, Mai 1948; 6 Heft, Juni 1948.

Douglas, David, 'The Norman Conquest and British Historians', David Murray Lecture, University of Glasgow, 20 Feb. 1946, Jackson Son & Co., Glasgow, N. D.

East, W, Gordon, 'The Political Division of Europe', Inaugural Lecture, Birkbeck College, May 1948.

Engel-Janosi, F., 'The Growth of German Historicism', *The Johns Hopkins University Studies in Historical and Political Science,* Series LXII, No. 2, 1944.

Erdmann, Karl D., 'Deutsch-Französiche Vereinbarung über Strittige Fragen Europäischer Geschichte', *Geschichte in Wissenschaft und Unterricht,* Heft 5, 1952.

——, 'Das Problem des Historismus in der Neueren Englischen Geschichtswissenschaft', *Historische Zeitung,* Heft 1/170, Juni 1950.

——, Themen der Euopäischen Geschichte', *Geschichte in Wissenschaft und Unterricht,* 1955.

——, 'Die Zukunft als Kategorie der Geschichte', *Historische Zeitung,* Heft 198/1, Feb. 1964.

Ernst, Fritz, 'Philippe de Commynes, Memoiren: Europa in der Krise Zwischen Mittelalter und Neuzeit', 1952.

——, 'Zeitgeschehen und Geschichtsschreibung', *Die Welt als Geschichte,* Heft 3/, 1957.

Farrington, Prof. Benjamin, 'Diodrus Siculus: Universal Historian', Inaugural Lecture, University College of Swansea, 1936.

Fastnacht, G. E., 'Lord Acton on Nationality and Socialism', two lectures at Oxford Summer School, August 1949, Oxford, 1949.

Fellowes, Sir Edward, 'Die Kontrolle der Executive durch das britische Unterhaus', *Arbeitsgemeinschaft für Forschung des Landes Nordrhein-Westfalen,* Heft 110, N. D.

Field, G. C., 'Some Problems of the Philosophy of History', Annual Philosophical Lecture, 1938, *Proceedings of the British Academy,* Vol. XXIV, N. D.

Finley, M. I., 'Introduction' to *The Greek Historians,* New York, 1959.

Firth, C. H., 'A Plea for the Historical Teaching of History', Inaugural Lecture, 9 Nov. 1904, Oxford Clarendon Press, 1904.

Fisher, H. A. L., 'The Whig Historians', Raleigh Lecture, British Academy, 1928, *Proceedings of the British Academy,* Vol. XIV, N. D.

Fitzsimmons, Matthew A., 'Politics and Men of Learning in England, 1540–1640', *Review of Politics,* Vol. 6, No. 4, Oct. 1944.

Franke, Herbert, 'Some Aspects of Chinese Private Historiography in the Thirteenth and Fourteenth Centuries', no source or date.

Fueter, Eduard, 'Geschichte der Gesamtschweizerischen Historischen Organisation', *Historische Zeitschrift,* Band 189, Dec. 1959.

Galbraith, V. H., 'Historical Study and the State', Inaugural Lecture, University of Oxford, 1948.

Gallie, W. B., 'Explanations in History and the Genetic Sciences', *Mind,* Vol. LXIV, No. 254, April 1955.

——, 'The Historical Understanding', *History and Theory,* Vol. III, No. 1, 1963.

Gerhard, Dietrich, 'Vergleichende Geschichtsbetrachtung und Zeitgeschichte', *Geschichte und Gegenwartsbewusstsein,* Festschrift für Hans Rothfels zum 70 Geburtstag, N. D.

Geyl, Pieter, 'The American Civil War and the Problem of Inevitability', *New England Quarterly,* Vol. XXIV, No. 2, June 1951.

——, 'From Ranke to Toynbee', Five Lectures on Historians and Historiographical Problems, *Smith College Studies in History,* Vol. XXXIX, Northampton, Mass., 1952.

——, 'Huizinga as Accuser of his Age', *History and Theory,* Vol. II, No. 3, 1963.

Glover, Willis B., A Historian's Approach to Theology', *Church History,* Vol. XXV, No. 4, Dec. 1956.

Goldinger, Walter, 'Die österreichischen Archive und die Geschichtswissenschaft', *Mitteilungen des österreichischen Staatsarchiv,* Vol. VII, 1954.

Gooch, G. P., 'Lord Acton: Apostle of Liberty', *Foreign Affairs,* July 1947.

——, 'Recent Historical Studies', Offprint from revised edition of *History and Historians in the Nineteenth Century.*

von Grunebaum, G. E., 'Studies in Islamic Cultural History', *The American Anthropologist,* Comparative Studies of Cultures and Civilisations, No. 2, Vol. 56, No. 2 Part 2 Memoir No. 76, April 1954.

Haenische, E., 'Das Ethos der chinesischen Geschichtsschreibung', *Saeculum,* Vol. I, 1950.

Harbison, E. Harris, 'Religious Perspectives of College Teaching in History', no source or date.

Hassow, Peter, 'Der Historiker und Seine Gegenwart', Verlag Hermann Rinn, Munich, 1948.

Heimpel, Hermann, 'Über Geschichte und Geschichtswissenschaft in unserer Zeit', *Vortragsreihe der Niedersächsischen Landesregierung zur Förderung der Wissenschaftlichen Forschung in Niedersachsen,* Heft 13, N.D.

——, 'Über Organizationsformen Historischer Forschung in Deutschland', *Historische Zeitschrift,* Band 189, Dec. 1959.

Holborn, Hojo, 'Greek and Modern Conceptions of History', *Journal of the History of Ideas,* Vol. X, 1949.

Holtzmann, Walther, 'Paul Fridolin Kehr', *Deutsches Archiv für Erforschung des Mittelalters 8 Jahrgang,* Heft 1, 1950.

Horn, D. B., 'The University of Edinburgh and the Teaching of History', Inaugural Lecture, 1954, *University of Edinburgh Journal,* Autumn 1954.

Hughes, H. Stuart, 'The Historian and the Social Scientist', *American Historical Review,* Vol. LXVI, No. 1, Oct. 1960.

Humphreys, R. A., 'William Robertson and his "History of America" ', lecture delivered at Canning House, 11 June 1954.

Iggers, Georg G., 'The Image of Ranke in American and German Historical Thought', *History and Theory,* Vol. II, No. 1, 1962.

Izard, Georges, 'La Marche Révolutionnaire de l'Histoire', *La Nef,* N. D.

Jackson, J. Hampden, 'What is History?' Bureau of Current Affairs, 1949.

Jover, Prof. Dr. José María, 'Panorama of Current Spanish Historiography', *Journal of World History,* Vol. VI, No. 4, 1961.

Joynt, Carey B. and Nicholas Rescher, 'Evidence in History and the Law', *Journal of Philosophy,* Vol. LVI, No. 13, 1959.

——, 'On Explanation in History', *Mind,* Vol. LXVIII, No. 271, July 1959.

——, 'The Problem of Uniqueness in History', *History and Theory,* Vol. I, No. 2, 1961.

Kammenhuber, Annelies, 'Die hethitische Geschichtsschreibung', *Saeculum,* Vol. IX, 1958.

Kearney, H., 'Christianity and the Study of History', *Downside Review,* Winter 1948/49.

Klenk, G. Friedrich, 'Gott in der Geschichte', *Stimmen der Zeit,* Heft 10, Band 152, 78 Jahrgang, 1952/1953.

Knowles, M. D., 'Academic History', *History,* Vol. XLVII, 1962.

——, 'The Bollandists', *Transactions of the Royal Historical Society,* 5th Series, Vol. VII, 1958.

——, 'The Maurists', *Transactions of the Royal Historical Society,* Vol. IX, 1959.

——, 'C. W. Privité-Orton 1877–1947', *Proceedings of the British Academy,* Vol. XXXIII, N. D.

Kracauer, Siegfried, 'Time and History', *Zeugnisse,* 1963.

Lee, N. E., 'History and Educational Reform', *Historical Studies, Australia and New Zealand,* N. D.

Lezcano, Victor Morales, 'La Historia de las Religiones en la Epoca de la Ilustración', Teses Doctoral 29, Facultad de Filosofía y Letras, Madrid, 1964.

Liebeschütz, Hans, 'Jewish Thought and its German Background', *Leo Baeck Institute Yearbook,* Vol. 1, 1956.

——, 'Judaism and History of Religion in Leo Baeck's Work', *Leo Baeck Institute Yearbook,* Vol. II, 1957.

——, 'Das Judentum im Geschichtsbild Jacob Burckhardts', *Leo Baeck Institute Yearbook,* Vol. IV, 1959.

——, 'Wissenschaft des Judentums und Historismus bei Abraham Geiger', no source or date.

van der Loon, P., 'Die alten chinesischen Geschichtswerke und die Entstehung historischer Ideale', *Saeculum,* Vol. VIII, 1957.

Loubère, Leo A., 'Louis Blanc et la Philosophie de l'Histoire', *Le Contrat Social,* Vol. II, No. 1, Jan. 1958.

Löwith, Karl, 'Christentum und Geschichte', *Numen,* Vol. II, Fasc. 3, Sept. 1955.

McCullagh, C. B., 'On Deciding the Present Significance of Biblical History', no source or date.

Macdonald, George, 'F. Haverfield 1860–1919', *Proceedings of the British Academy,* Vol. IX, N. D.

Mandelbaum, Maurice, 'A Note on "Universality" in Philosophies of History', text of a contribution to a symposium entitled 'Historia y Universalidad', published in Spanish in *Revista de la Universidad de Madrid,* Vol. XII, num. 45, 1963.

Marrou, H-I., 'La Foi Historique', *Les Etudes Philosophiques,* No. 2, Avril-Juin 1959.

——, 'L'Histoire et les Historiens', *Revue Historique,* N. D.

Martin, Father F. X., O. S. A., 'The Problem of Giles of Viterbo: A Historiographical Survey', Augustinian Historical Institute, Louvain, 1960.

Mayne, Ellen, 'The Christian Philosophy of Vladimir Solovyov', New Atlantis Foundation, Fourth Foundation Lecture, 1957.

Meldin, A. L., 'Historical Objectivity: a Noble Dream', *Journal of General Education.* Vol. VII, No. 1, Oct. 1952.

Momigliano, Arnaldo, 'L'Eredità della Filologia Antica e il Metodo Storico', *Rivista Storica Italiana,* Anno LXX, Fascicolo III, 1958.

——, 'Introduzione alla *Griechische Kulturgeschichte* di Jacob Burckhardt', Estratto da *Storia della civiltà greca,* di Jacob Burckhardt, 1955.

——, 'Il Linguaggio e la Tecnica dello Storico', *Rivista Storica Italiana,* Anno LXVII, Fascicolo III, N. D.

——, 'Pagan and Christian Historiography in the Fourth Century A.D.', in *Paganism and Christianity in the Fourth Century,* ed. by A. Momigliano, no publisher or date.

——, 'The Place of Herodotus in the History of Historiography', *History,* Vol. XLIII, 1958.

del Monte, A., 'La storiografia fiorentina dei secoli XII e XIII', *Bulletino dell'Instituto Storico Italiano per il Medioevo e Archivio Muratoriano,* No. 62, 1650.

Mullet, Charles F., 'New Historians for Old: English Historiography in the Early Nineteenth Century', *Midwest Journal,* Vol. 3, No. 2, Summer 1951.

Ong, Prof. Walter J., 'Religion, Scholarship and the Resituation of Man', *Daedalus, Journal of the American Academy of Arts and Sciences,* Vol. 91, No. 2, Spring 1962.

Parker, Dr. Harold T., 'What has happened in the 20th Century?', no source or date.

Peterson, Erling Ladewig, 'Stat og Historieskrivning i Islams Klassiske Periode, 7.–10. Aarh.', *Historisk Tidsskrift,* 11 Raekka, 5 Binds, 4 Hefte, 1958.

Plekhanov, G. V., 'The Role of the Individual in History', London, 1940.

Poole, Reginald L., 'The Beginning of the Year in the Middle Ages', *Proceedings of the British Academy,* Vol. X, 1921?.

Potter, G. R., 'Universal- und Weltgeschichte', no source or date.

Powicke, F. M., 'Sir Henry Spelman and the "Concilia" ', Raleigh Lecture on History, 1930, *Proceedings of the British Academy,* Vol. XVI, N. D.

Pringle-Pattison, A. S., 'The Philosophy of History', *Proceedings of the British Academy,* Vol. XI, N. D.

Rama, Carlos M., 'El problema metodológico en los actuales historiadores y sociólogos italianos', *La Revista de la Facultad de Humanidades y Ciencias,* No. 12, 1954.

Ritter, Gerhard, 'Bethmann Hollweg im Schlagicht des deutschen Geschichts-Revisionismus', *Schweizer Monatshefte,* 42 Jahr, Heft 8, Nov. 1962.

Robbins, Caroline, 'The Teaching of European History in the United States', *Quarterly Bulletin of the Polish Institute of Arts and Sciences in America,* July 1944.

Romein, Jan, 'Theoretical History', *Journal of the History of Ideas,* Vol. IX, No. 1, Jan. 1948.

Rossi, Pietro, 'Lo Storicismo nel Pensiero Contemporaneo', *Rivista Storica Italiana,* Anno LXXIII Fascicolo 1, N. D.

Rothfels, Hans, 'Friedrich Meinicke', lecture delivered in Berlin 27 Feb. 1954.

Ryan, Rev. Thomas, 'Orestes A. Brownson and Historiography', *Irish Ecclesiastical Record,* Jan.-Feb. 1956.

Sandford, Eva M., 'The Study of Ancient History in the Middle Ages', *Journal of the History of Ideas,* Vol. V, 1944.

Saunders, J. J., 'Review of Syed Abdul Vahid's *Iqbal, His Art and Thought. The Message of Milarepa,* (trans. by Sir Humphrey Clarke), and *Buddhist Scriptures,* (trans. by Ed. Conze), *Aumla,* No. 12, Nov. 1959.

Sayles, Prof. G. O., 'The Changed Concept of History: Stubbs and Renan', *Aberdeen University Review*, Vol. XXXV, No. 110, Spring 1954.

Schafer, Boyd C., 'History, not Art, not Science, but History: Meanings and use of History', *Pacific Historical Review*, May 1960.

Schieder, Theodor, 'Die Entstehung von Rankes "Epochen der Neueren Geschichte" ', *Historische Zeitschrift*, Heft 199/1, August 1964.

von Schlenke, Manfred, 'Das absolutistische Preussen in der englischen Geschichtsschreibung von 1945 bis 1955', *Archiv für Kulturgeschichte*, Band XXXIX, Heft 1, 1957.

——, 'Das friederizianische Preussen im Urteil der englischen öffentlichen Meinung 1740 bis 1763', *Geschichte in Wissenschaft und Unterricht*, Heft 4, 1963.

——, 'Aus der Frühzeit des englischen Historismus', *Saeculum*, Vol. 1, 1956.

——, 'Zur gegenwärtigen Situation der englischen Geschichtsschreibung', *Geschichte in Wissenschaft und Unterricht*, Heft 6, 1956.

——, 'Kulturgeschichte oder politische Geschichte in der Geschichtsschreibung des 18 Jahrhunderts – William Robertson als Historiker des europäischen Staatensystems', *Archiv für Kulturgeschichte*, Band XXXVII, Heft 1, 1955.

Schmidt, H. D., 'Jewish Philosophy of History and its Contemporary Opponents', *Judaism*, Spring 1960.

Schramm, P. E., 'Bürgerutm: Geschichte und Aufgabe', *Göttinger Jahrbuch*, 1954.

——, 'Die neuere und neueste Geschichte als Forschungsproblem', *Prisma der Georgia Augusta*, Nr. 4, Juni 1956.

Schwarzenberger, G., 'The Study of International Relations', *The Year Book of World Affairs*, Vol. 8, 1949.

Singer, Charles, 'Technology and History', L. T. Hobhouse Memorial Trust Lecture, No. 21, delivered at London School of Economics, Oct. 1951, Oxford, 1952.

Skalweit, Stephen, 'Ranke und Bismarck', *Historische Zeitschrift*, Heft 176/2, Oktober, 1953.

Southern, R. W., 'The Shape and Substance of Academic History', Inaugural Lecture, Oxford, Nov. 1961.

Spangenberg, H., 'Die Perioden der Weltgeschichte', *Historische Zeitschrift*, Vol. CXXVII, 1923.

Strand, Kenneth A., Foreword to 'Dawn of Modern Civilisation' produced in Honour of Prof. Hyma, 1962.

Strange, Hans O. H., 'Chinesische abendländische Philosophie. Ihr Unterschied und seine geschichtlichen Ursachen, *Saeculum*, Vol. 1, 1950.

Styles, Philip, 'Sir Simon Archer 1581–1662', *Dugdale Society Occasional Papers*, No. 6, 1946.

Sykes, Norman, 'Some Current Conceptions of Historiography and their significance for Christian Apologetic', *Journal of Theological Studies,* Vol. L, No. 197–8, Jan.-April 1949.

Sypher, G. W., 'La Popelinière's *Histoire de France', Journal of the History of Ideas,* Vol. XXIV, No. 1, Jan.-March 1963.

Talmon, J. L., 'The Nature of Jewish History – its Universal Significance', Inaugural Hillel Foundation Lecture, 1957.

Tate, R. B., 'Nebrija the Historian', *Bulletin of Hispanic Studies,* Vol. XXXIV, No. 3, July 1957.

Taylor, A. J. P., 'Pieter Geyl: Historian, Patriot, European', *Delta,* Autumn 1958.

Temperley, H., Research and Modern History', Inaugural Lecture, Cambridge, 1930.

Tout, T. F., 'Sir Adolphus William Ward 1837–1924', *Proceedings of the British Academy,* no volume or date.

Tout, T. F., 'Sir James Henry Ramsay 1832–1925', *Proceedings of the British Acadamy,* no volume or date.

Trevor-Roper, H. R., 'History Professional and Lay', Inaugural Lecture, Oxford, 1957.

Ullman, B. L., 'Leonardo Bruni and Humanistic Historiography', *Medievalia et Humanistica,* Fasc. IV, 1946.

Urban, C. Stanley, 'An Analysis of History and Historical Writing', Faculty Lecture Series, Park College, Parkville, Mo., Nov. 1954.

Vogt, Joseph, 'Geschichte des Altertums und Universalgeschichte', Institut für Europäische Geschichte Mainz Vorträge, Nr. 24., N. D.

Ward, Sir A. W., 'Presidential Address', British Academy, 1 July 1913.

Wendon, John, 'Christianity, History, and Mr. Toynbee', *The Journal of Religion,* Vol. XXXVI, No. 3, July 1956.

Wood, Prof. F. L., 'The Historian in the Modern Community', George Arnold Wood Memorial Lecture, University of Sydney, 1950.

Woodward, Sir E. Llewellyn, 'Some Considerations on the Present State of Historical Studies', Raleigh Lecture on History, 1950, *Proceedings of the British Academy,* Vol. XXXVI, N. D.

——, 'The Influence of History', Margaret Wallace Notestein Memorial Lecture, No. 3, at the College of Wooster, Ohio, Nov. 1956.

——, 'The Study of International Relations at a University', Inaugural Lecture, Oxford, 1945.

Yang, Lien-Sheng, 'Die Organisation der chinesischen offiziellen Geschichtsschreibung', *Saeculum,* Vol. VIII, 1957.

Index

Index